A Little Smalltalk

A Little Smalltalk

Timothy Budd
Oregon State University

Addison-Wesley Publishing Company
Reading, Massachusetts • Menlo Park, California
Don Mills, Ontario • Wokingham, England • Amsterdam • Sydney
Singapore • Tokyo • Madrid • Bogotá • Santiago • San Juan

Library of Congress Cataloging-in-Publication Data

Budd, Timothy.
    A Little Smalltalk.

    Includes index.
      1. Electronic digital computers—Programming.
2. Little Smalltalk (Computer system)   I. Title.
QA76.6.B835   1987   005.26   86-25904
ISBN 0-201-10698-1

Reprinted with corrections April, 1987

BCDEFGHIJ-DO-8987

Preface

The Little Smalltalk System: Some History

In the spring of 1984 I taught a course in programming languages at the University of Arizona. While preparing lectures for that course, I became interested in the concept of object-oriented programming and, in particular, the way in which the object-oriented paradigm changed the programmers approach to problem solving. During that term and the following summer I gathered as much material as I could about object-oriented programming, especially items relating to the Smalltalk-80 programming system[1] developed at the Xerox Palo Alto Research Center (Xerox PARC). However, I continued to be frustrated by my inability to gain experience in writing and using Smalltalk programs.

At that time the only Smalltalk system I was aware of was the original system running on the Dorado, an expensive machine not available (at that time) outside of Xerox PARC. The facilities available to me consisted of a VAX-780 running Unix[2] and conventional ASCII terminals. Thus, it appeared that my chances of running the Xerox Smalltalk-80 system, in the near term, were quite slim; therefore, a number of students and I decided in the summer of 1984 to create our own Smalltalk system.

In the fall of 1984 a dozen students and I created the Little Smalltalk system as part of a graduate level seminar on programming language implementation. From the outset, our goals were much less ambitious than those of the original developers of the Smalltalk-80 system. While we appreciated the importance of the innovative concepts in programming environments and graphics pioneered by the Xerox group, we were painfully aware of our own limitations, both in manpower and in facilities. Our goals, in order of importance, were:

☐ The new system should support a language that is as close as possible to the published Smalltalk-80 description (Goldberg and Robson 83).

☐ The system should run under Unix using only conventional terminals.

☐ The system should be written in C and be as portable as possible.

☐ The system should be small. In particular, it should work on 16-bit machines with separate instruction and data spaces, but preferably even on those machines without this feature.

---

1. Smalltalk-80 is a trademark of the Xerox Corporation.
2. Unix is a trademark of AT&T Bell Laboratories.

In hindsight, we seem to have fulfilled our goals rather well. The language accepted by the Little Smalltalk system is close enough to that of the Smalltalk-80 programming system that users seem to have little difficulty (at least with the language) in moving from one system to the other. The system has proved to be extremely portable: it has been transported to a dozen varieties of Unix running on many different machines. Over 200 sites now use the Little Smalltalk system.

About *A Little Smalltalk*

This book is divided into two parts. The first section describes the language of the Little Smalltalk system. Although most readers probably will have had some prior exposure to at least one other programming language before encountering Smalltalk, the text makes no assumptions about background. Most upper division undergraduate or graduate level students should be able to understand the material in this first section. This first part of the text can be used alone.

The second part of the book describes the actual implementation of the Little Smalltalk system. This section requires the reader to have a much greater background in computer science. Since Little Smalltalk is written in C, at least a rudimentary knowledge of that language is required. A good background in data structures is also valuable. The reader will find it desirable, although not strictly necessary, to have had some introduction to compiler construction for a conventional language, such as Pascal.

Acknowledgments

I am, of course, most grateful to the students in the graduate seminar at the University of Arizona where the Little Smalltalk system was developed. The many heated discussions and insightful ideas generated were most enjoyable and stimulating. Participants in that seminar were Mike Benhase, Nick Buchholz, Dave Burns, John Cabral, Clayton Curtis, Roger Hayes, Tom Hicks, Rob McConeghy, Kelvin Nilsen, May Lee Noah, Sean O'Malley, and Dennis Vadner. This text grew out of notes developed for that course, and includes many ideas contributed by the participants. In particular I wish to thank Dave Burns for the original versions of the simulation described in Chapter 7 and Mike Benhase and Dennis Vadner for their work on processes and the dining philosophers solution presented in Chapter 10.

Discussions with many people have yielded insights or examples that eventually found their way into this book. I wish to thank, in particular, Jane Cameron, Chris Fraser, Ralph Griswold, Paul Klint, Gary Levin, and Dave Robson.

Irv Elshoff provided valuable assistance by trying to learn Smalltalk from an early manuscript and by making many useful and detailed comments on the text.

J. A. Davis from Iowa State University, Paul Klint from the CWI, David Robson from Xerox Palo Alto Research Center, and Frances Van Scoy from West Virginia University provided careful and detailed comments on earlier drafts of the book.

Charlie Allen at Purdue, Jan Gray at Waterloo and Charles Hayden at AT&T were early non-Arizona users of Little Smalltalk and were extremely helpful in finding bugs in the earlier distributions.

I wish to thank Ralph Griswold, Dave Hanson, and Chris Fraser, all chairmen of the computer science department at the University of Arizona at various times in the last five years, for helping to make the department such a pleasant place to work. Finally I wish to thank Paul Vitanyi and Lambert Meertens for providing me with the chance to work at the Centrum voor Wiskunde en Informatica in Amsterdam for the year between my time in Arizona and my move to Oregon, and for permitting me to finish work on the book while there.

Obtaining the Little Smalltalk System

The Little Smalltalk system can be obtained directly from the author. The system is distributed on 9-track tapes in tar format (the standard unix distribution format). The distribution tape includes all sources and on-line documentation for the system. For further information on the distribution, including cost, write to the following address:

Smalltalk Distribution
Department of Computer Science
Oregon State University
Corvallis, Oregon
97331
USA

Table of Contents

P A R T
ONE

The Language

☰ C H A P T E R 1

This chapter introduces the basic concepts of the Smalltalk language; namely *object, method, class, inheritance* and *overriding.*

☰ C H A P T E R 2

This chapter introduces the syntax for literal objects (such as numbers) and the syntax for messages. It explains how to use the Little Smalltalk system to evaluate expressions typed in directly at the keyboard and how to use a few simple messages to discover information about different types of objects.

≡ C H A P T E R 3

Basic Classes 22

The basic classes included in the Little Smalltalk standard library are explained in this chapter.

≡ C H A P T E R 4

Class Definition 34

This chapter introduces the syntax used for defining classes. An example class definition is presented.

≡ C H A P T E R 5

A Simple Application 42

This chapter illustrates the development of a simple application in Smalltalk and describes how environments can be saved and restored.

≣ C H A P T E R 6

This chapter introduces the syntax for cascaded expressions and describes the notion of primitive expressions. It illustrates the use of primitives by showing how primitives are used to produce the correct results for mixed mode arithmetic operations.

≣ C H A P T E R 7

This chapter presents a simple simulation of an ice cream store, illustrating the ease with which simulations can be described in Smalltalk.

≣ C H A P T E R 8

This chapter introduces the concept of generators and shows how generators can be used in the solution of problems requiring goal-directed evaluation.

≣ C H A P T E R 9

Although graphics are not fundamental to Little Smalltalk in the same way that they are an intrinsic part of the Smalltalk-80 system, it is still possible to describe some graphics functions using the language. This chapter details three types of approaches to graphics.

CHAPTER 10

This chapter introduces the concepts of processes and semaphores. It illustrates these concepts using the dining philosophers problem.

P A R T
TWO

CHAPTER 11

This chapter describes the features that make an interpreter for the Smalltalk language different from, say, a Pascal compiler. Provides a high-level description of the major components in the Little Smalltalk system.

≣ C H A P T E R 12

The Representation of Objects 137

The internal representation of objects in the Little Smalltalk system is described in this chapter, which also overviews the memory management algorithms. The chapter ends with a discussion of several optimizations used to improve the speed of the Little Smalltalk system.

≣ C H A P T E R 13

Bytecodes 150

The techniques used to represent methods internally in the Little Smalltalk system are described in this chapter.

≣ C H A P T E R 14

The Process Manager 161

This chapter presents a more detailed view of the central component of the Little Smalltalk system, the process manager. It then goes on to describe the driver, the process that reads commands from the user terminal and schedules them for execution. The chapter ends by describing the class parser and the internal representation of classes.

≣ C H A P T E R 15

The Interpreter 176

This chapter describes the actions of the interpreter and the courier
in executing bytecodes and passing messages. It ends by describing
the primitive handler and the manipulation of special objects.

An annotated bibliography of references related to the Little Smalltalk
system.

Appendices

APPENDIX 1

Describes how to run the Little Smalltalk system. Lists the various
options available.

APPENDIX 2

Presents syntax charts describing the language accepted by the Little
Smalltalk system.

APPENDIX 3

Presents descriptions of the various messages to which the classes in
the standard library will respond.

P A R T
ONE

The Language

C H A P T E R

1

Basics

The traditional model describing the behavior of a computer executing a program is the process-state, or "pigeon-hole" model. In this view the computer is a data manager, following some pattern of instructions, wandering through memory, pulling values out of various slots (memory addresses), transforming them in some manner, and pushing the results back into other slots. By examining the values in the slots one can determine the state of the machine or the results produced by a computation. While this may be a more or less accurate picture of what takes place in a computer, it does little to help us understand how to solve problems using the computer, and it is certainly not the way most people (pigeons and postmen excepted) go about solving problems.

Let us examine a realistic situation and then ask how we might make a computer more closely model the methods people use for solving problems in everyday life. Suppose I wish to send some flowers to my grandmother for her birthday. She lives is a city many miles away. The task is easy enough to do; I merely go to a local florist, describe the kinds and number of flowers I want sent and I can be assured that they will be automatically delivered. If I investigate, I would probably discover that my florist sends a message describing my order to another florist in my grandmother's city. That florist then makes up the arrangement and delivers the flowers. I might inquire further to find out how the florist in my grandmother's city obtains the flowers and find, perhaps, that they are obtained in bulk in the morning from a flower wholesaler. If I persist, I might even be able to follow the chain all the way back to the farmer who grows the flowers, and discover what requests were made by each member of the chain in order to solicit the desired outcome from the next.

The important point, however, is that I do not *need*, indeed most of the time do not *want*, to know how my simple directive "send flowers to my grandmother" is going to be carried out. In real life we call this process "delegation of authority." In computer science it is called "abstraction" or "information hiding." At the heart, these terms amount to the same thing. There is a resource (a florist, a file server) that I wish to use. In order to communicate, I must know the commands to which the resource will respond (send flowers to my grandmother, return a copy of the file named "chapter1"). Most likely the steps the resource must take to respond to my request are much more complex than I realize, but there is no reason for me to know the details of how my directive is implemented as long as the response (the delivery of the flowers, receiving a copy of my file) is well defined and predictable.

The *object-oriented* model of problem solving views the computer in much the same fashion as just described. Indeed many people who have no training in computer science and no idea how a computer works find the object-oriented model of problem solving quite natural. Surprisingly, however, many people who have a traditional background in computer programming initially think there is something strange about the object-oriented view. The notion that "7" is an object and "+" is a request for an addition, may at first seem strange. But soon, the uniformity, power, and flexibility the object-message metaphor bring to problem solving makes this interpretation seem natural.

The Smalltalk universe is inhabited by *objects*. In my flower example, I am an object and the flower shop (or the florist in it) is another object. Actions are initiated by sending requests (or *messages*) between objects. I transmitted the request "send flowers to my grandmother" to the florist-object. The reaction of the *receiver* of my message is to execute some sequence of actions, or *method*, to satisfy my request. Maybe the receiver can immediately satisfy my request. On the other hand, in order to meet my needs, the receiver may have to transmit other messages to yet more objects (for example, the message my florist sends to the florist in my grandmother's city, or a command to a disk drive). In addition, there is an explicit *response* (a receipt, for example, or a result code) returned directly back to me. Dan Ingalls describes the Smalltalk philosophy (Byte 81):

> Instead of a bit-grinding processor raping and plundering data structures, we have a universe of well-behaved objects that courteously ask each other to carry out their various desires.

Such anthropomorphic viewpoints are common among Smalltalk programmers. In subsequent chapters we will see how the Smalltalk language embodies this object-oriented view of programming. By describing the solution of several problems in Smalltalk, we hope to show how the object-oriented model aids in the creation of large software systems and assists in the solution of many problems using the computer.

Objects, Classes, and Inheritance

In Smalltalk, everything is an *object*. There is no way to create, within the language, an entity that is not an object. Among major computer languages this uniformity in Smalltalk is rivaled perhaps only by LISP, and, as with LISP, the uniformity creates both the simplicity and power of the language.

An object possesses several characteristics (Figure 1.1). Every object contains a small amount of memory, accessible to only that object. That is, no object can read or modify memory values in another object. Of course, since everything in the system must be an object, an object's memory can contain only other objects. We will discuss this in more detail later.

Figure 1.1 ☐ *A typical object*

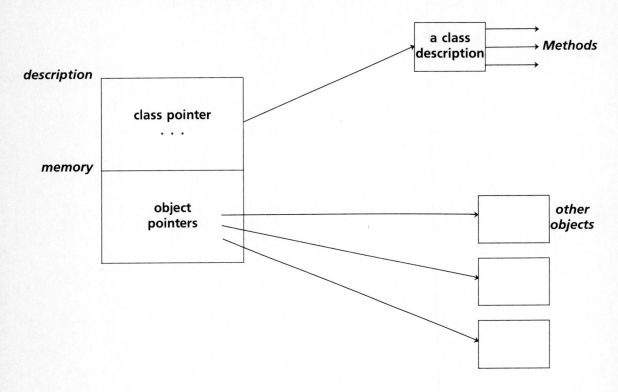

All actions in the Smalltalk system are produced by passing *messages*. A message is a request for an object to perform some operation, and it can contain certain argument values to be used in conjunction with the execution of the requested operation. There are two different ways to view this message passing operation. The first is simply that message passing corresponds to a subroutine call in a conventional procedural language, such as Pascal. This is true in that the actions of the sender are suspended while the receiver produces a result. The result is then returned to the sender, who continues execution from the point of call. Messages can be created dynamically at run-time, however, and the relationship between the sender and receiver of a message is typically much more fluid than the static relationship between a caller and the callee in a conventional programming language.

In the real world every object is individualistic; however, each also possesses common characteristics with other, similar, objects. In a bushel of apples, for example, each apple is distinct from all others. Yet certain statements can be made about all the apples; for example, they will all smell and taste a certain way, can all be used to bake pies in a similar manner, and so on. This process is called *classification*. That is, we can view an apple as an individual item or as an *instance* of a larger class (or category) of objects. let us denote the class of all apples by **Apple,** the capital letter and the boldface type serving to denote the fact that we are talking about a class, and not an individual.

Instances of class **Orange** are in many respects different from apples, and thus deserve their own category. But they also share many common characteristics with apples. Thus we can create a new class, **Fruit,** to be used when we wish to describe characteristics common to both apples and oranges. The Class **Fruit** encompasses both the classes **Apple** and **Orange.** Thus we say that **Fruit** is a *superclass* of **Apple** and **Orange,** and that **Apple** and **Orange** are in turn *subclasses* of **Fruit.**

Finally, we can take this analysis even one step further, making **Fruit** a subclass of a more universal category, which we can call **Object.** Thus we have a hierarchy of categories for objects, extending from the basic class **Object,** of which everything is a member, down through more and more specific classes until we reach the individual object itself.

The same situation holds regarding entities in Smalltalk. That is, every object is a member of some class. With the exception of class **Object,** that class will, in turn, be a subclass of some larger class, which in turn may be part of another class, up to one single class of which every object is a member. There is a natural tree structure (Figure 1.2) that illustrates this class-subclass hierarchy. As we have been doing, we will denote class names by capitalizing the first letter and denote object names without using the capital. So, for example, the number 7 is an instance of the class **Integer,** as is the number 8. Although 7 and 8 are distinct objects, they share some characteristics by virtue of their being instances of the same class. For example, both 7 and 8 will respond to the message "+" with an

Figure 1.2   □   *The tree structure of the class-subclass Hierarchy*

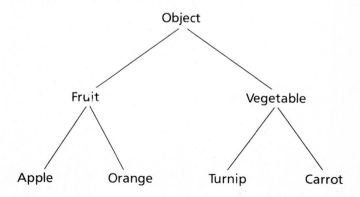

integer argument by performing integer addition. **Integer** is a subclass of a larger class, **Number.** There are other subclasses of **Number,** for example, **Float,** of which values such as 3.1415926 are instances. **Number** is a subclass of **Magnitude** (a class to be discussed later) which finally is a subclass of **Object.**

The behavior of an object in response to a specific message is dictated by that object's *class.* For example, 7 and 8 will respond to the message "+" in the same fashion, because they are both instances of class **Integer.** The list of statements that define how an instance of some class will respond to a message is called the *method* for that message. For example, in class **Integer** there is a method associated with the message "+." The entire set of messages associated with a class is called the *protocol* for that class. Class **Integer** contains in its protocol, for example, messages for +, −, *, and so on. In Smalltalk, a protocol is provided as part of a *class definition.* The syntax for class definitions will be described in a later section. It is not possible to provide a method for an individual object; rather every object must be associated with some class, and the behavior of the object in response to messages will be dictated by the methods associated with that class.

If an object is an instance of a particular class, it is clear how methods associated with that class will be used, but what about methods associated with superclasses? The answer is that any method associated with a superclass is *inherited* by a class. An example will help clarify this concept. When sent to a number, the message *exp* means "return the value of *e* (approximately 2.71828..) raised to your value." Thus 2 *exp* yields e^2, or approximately 7.38906. Now the class description for **Integer** does not provide a method for the message *exp,* so that when the Little Smalltalk system tries to find an associated method for the message *exp* in the class **Integer** protocol, it does not find one. So the Little Smalltalk system next examines the protocol associated with the immediate superclass of **Integer,** namely **Number.** There, in the protocol for **Number,** it finds a method and executes it. Thus, we say that the method for *exp* is *inherited* by the class **Integer** from the class **Number.**

In **Number,** the method associated with the message *exp* is as follows:

↑ self asFloat exp

We will explain the syntax in more detail later; for the moment we can translate this as "produce an instance of **Float** with your value (self *asFloat*) and send that object the message *exp* asking for *e* raised to its value. Return (the up arrow ↑ indicates returning a value) the response to that message." Thus the message *asFloat* is passed to the original integer, say, 2. The method associated with this message is executed, resulting in a floating point value, 2.0. The message *exp* is then passed to this value. This is the same message that was originally passed to the integer 2, only now the class of the receiver is **Float,** not **Integer.**

Figure 1.3 □ *The class structure of numbers*

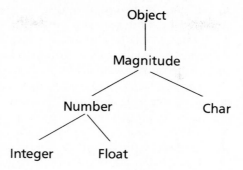

Figure 1.3 shows the hierarchy representing several classes, including numbers. As we have seen, a method for the message *exp* is defined in both the classes **Number** and **Float.** Search for a method begins with the class of an object and then proceeds through the various superclasses (along the *superclass chain*), as necessary. If a floating point value is given the message *exp* it will execute the method in class **Float,** not the method in class **Number.** Thus the method for *exp* in **Float** is said to *override* the method in class **Number.**

Classes such as **Number** and **Magnitude,** which usually do not have any explicit instances, are known as *abstract superclasses*. Abstract superclasses are important in insuring that instances of different classes, such as integers and floating point numbers, will respond in a similar manner in common situations. An addition, by eliminating the need to duplicate the methods for the messages in the superclass, they reduce the size of the descriptions needed to obtain a desired behavior.

History, Background Reading

The concepts relating to object-oriented programming found in Smalltalk are the products of a long process of language development and evolution. The fundamental notions of objects, messages, and classes came from the language Simula (Birtwistle 73). While Simula allowed users to create object-oriented systems, within a class the response to a message (the Simula equivalent of a method) was still expressed in the standard ALGOL data/procedure-oriented fashion.

Within the ALGOL family of languages, the concept of classes led to the development of the notion of modules and abstract data types (Shaw 80), the support for which was a fundamental goal in several languages such as Euclid, CLU, Modula, and Ada.

While the object-oriented philosophy was slowly gaining acceptance in the programming language world, similar ideas were gaining acceptance in the architecture community (Pinnow 82). Similarly, in operating systems design the notion of independent computations that interact with each other solely by exchanging messages was finding advocates (Wulf 74), (Almes 85). Such a view is natural and convenient when then the computations may physically be executing on distributed processors.

Direct ancestors of Smalltalk include the Flex system (Kay 69), Smalltalk-72 (Goldberg 76), and Smalltalk-76 (Ingalls 78). The Smalltalk languages were all produced as part of the Dynabook project initiated by Alan Kay in the Learning Research Group at the Xerox Palo Alto Research Center. The evolution of the language as traced in these documents shows the object-oriented model slowly being expanded to include more and more language concepts. For example, in Smalltalk-72, numbers and control structures are treated as objects, in contrast to Simula, but classes are still a special form. In Smalltalk-76, class descriptions are represented as objects, and the object-oriented point of view is extended to the programming interface. This interface becomes almost completely described in object-oriented form in the Smalltalk-80 programming environment (Goldberg 83).

The object-oriented view of programing has also influenced other computer languages, most notably in the notion of *actors* (Hewit 73) and *flavors* (Weinreb 80) in Lisp, and in the development of languages for animation and graphics (Reynolds 82). The development of actors in Lisp paralleled the development of Smalltalk, and the two languages had an influence on each other.

Koved and LaLonde present overviews describing the object-oriented viewpoint in various guises (Koved 84) (LaLonde 84). A number of papers describing various aspects of the Smalltalk-80 system were included in a special issue of the magazine *Byte (Byte* 81).

EXERCISES

1. Define the following terms:

object	subclass
message	superclass
receiver	inheritance
method	overriding
protocol	abstract superclass
class	

2. Give an example of a hierarchy from everyday life. List properties that can be found at each level, and distinguish those that are found in lower levels but not higher levels.

3. Read about the Simula *class* mechanism (Dahl 72) (Birtwistle 73). Compare and contrast this with the Smalltalk class mechanism.

4. In the real world, objects are often classified in orthogonal ways, rather than in the tree-like hierarchy of Smalltalk. For example, the bald eagle and the condor are both birds of prey, but one is a North American bird and the other a South American bird. The robin is also a North American bird but is not a bird of prey. These two distinguishing characteristics are orthogonal in that neither can logically be said to be a superset of the other. Thus, forcing the classification into a tree-like structure is either unnatural, inefficient, or both.

   How might Smalltalk objects be classified in orthogonal ways? What problems does this introduce for the inheritance mechanism? How might these problems be overcome?

	Bird of Prey	Not a Bird of Prey
North American	Bald Eagle	Robin
South American	Condor	?

C H A P T E R

2

Syntax

This chapter will describe the way in which objects are represented and manipulated in Little Smalltalk. As we noted in Chapter 1, everything in Smalltalk is an object. The discussion of syntax begins with a description of how objects are represented.

Literal Constants

Some objects, *literal* objects, are distinguished by the fact that their name uniquely identifies the object, independent of context, and by the fact that they do not have to be declared prior to being used. For example, the symbol 7, no matter where it appears, always denotes the same object. In Algol–like languages a symbol such as 7 conventionally denotes a "value" rather than an identifier. In Smalltalk this distinction is much less distinct. All entities, including numbers, are objects, and objects are characterized by the messages they accept and their response to them. Thus 7 denotes an object in the same way that an identifier, such as x (in the proper context), might denote an object.

Numbers are perhaps the most common literal objects. There are two classes of numbers that can be written as literal objects, namely integer and floating point values. Numbers respond to a variety of arithmetic messages (inherited from class **Number**) and relational messages (inherited from class **Magnitude**). An instance of class **Integer** consists of an optional sign followed by any number of digits. A **Float** consists of an integer followed by a period (the radix point) and another unsigned integer (the fractional part) and/or the letter e and a signed integer (the exponent part). Any number can be preceded by a *base*, which is a positive integer followed by the letter r. For bases greater than 10 the letters A through Z are interpreted as digit characters. Examples of numbers are:

```
7
16rFF
 − 3.1415926
2e32
2.4e − 32
15rC.ABC
```

The use of a base is merely for the sake of convenience and appearance. The number 16rFF is the same as the number 10r255, or just 255.

The class **Char** provides capabilities for dealing with character values. Characters are distinct from numbers. Since characters possess an ordering, given by a collating sequence, they can be compared and hence are a subclass of class **Magnitude.** A character is written as a dollar sign followed by the character symbol. The following are example instances of this class:

```
$A
$7
$
$$
```

An instance of class **String** is represented by a sequence of characters between single quote marks. Embedding a quote mark within a string requires two adjacent quote marks. A string is similar to an array; in fact the class **String** is a subclass of **ArrayedCollection,** as is the class **Array.** Both strings and arrays can be catenated together to form larger strings by using the comma (,) operator. Examples of strings are:

```
'a String'
'a String with an '' embedded quote mark'
```

An **Array** is written as a pound sign (#) followed by a list of array elements in parentheses. The elements in the array list are literal objects (numbers or symbols), strings, or other arrays. Within the array list the leading pound sign on symbols and arrays can be eliminated. Examples of Arrays are:

```
#(this is an array of symbols)
#(12 'abc' (another array))
```

Arrays and strings use the messages *at:* and *at:put:* to select and modify particular elements in their collection.

The class **Symbol** is another literal class. A symbol is written as a pound sign (#) followed by any sequence of characters. Spaces between characters are not allowed. Unlike a string (which is also a sequence of characters) a symbol cannot be broken into smaller parts. Furthermore the same sequence of letters will always denote the same object. Unlike numbers, characters, or strings, symbols do not possess an ordering and cannot be compared (except for, of course, object equality). Example symbols are:

```
#aSymbol
#AndAnother
# + + +
#very.long.symbol.with.periods
```

≡ Identifiers

Identifiers in Little Smalltalk can be divided into three categories: instance variables, class names, and pseudo-variables. An identifier beginning with a capital letter is always a class name, whereas an identifier beginning with a lowercase letter must represent either a pseudo variable or an instance variable.

At the command level, new instance variables can be defined merely by assigning a value to a name. The assignment arrow is formed as a two-character sequence consisting of a less than sign and a minus sign:[1]

    newname < - 17

Instance variables defined at the command level are known only at the command level and cannot be used within a method for any class. As we will see in a later chapter, instance variables within a class must all be declared.

Class identifiers respond to a variety of messages that can be used to discover information concerning the class the object represents. For example, the message *respondTo*, when passed to an object representing a class, will cause the class to print a list of the messages to which instances of the class will respond.

Pseudo variables look like normal identifiers (that is, they are named by a sequence of letters beginning with a lower case letter), but unlike identifiers they need not be declared. There are several pseudo variables: **self, super, selfProcess**[2], **true, false, nil,** and **smalltalk.** Arguments for a method (to be discussed shortly) are also considered to be pseudo-variables. Of the seven, **self, super,** and **selfProcess** are farthest from being literal objects because their meaning depends entirely upon context. We will discuss these in more detail when we describe class methods and processes. The next three, **true, false,** and **nil,** are defined to be instances (usually the only instances) of the classes **True, False,** and **UndefinedObject,** respectively. We will discuss these three in more detail when we outline the behavior of different classes. The final pseudo variable, **smalltalk,** is an instance of class **Smalltalk** and is used to centralize several pieces of information concerning the currently executing environment.

Other types of objects in the Little Smalltalk system, such as blocks and instances of user defined classes, will be discussed in later sections.

Messages

As noted in Chapter 1, all actions in Smalltalk are produced by sending *messages* to objects. This section begins by describing the syntax used to produce messages.

---

1. From now on the text will use the symbol ← to represent this two-character sequence.

2. The pseudo-variables selfProcess and smalltalk are unique to Little Smalltalk and are not part of the Smalltalk-80 system, where different techniques are used to obtain the currently executing process or to obtain information about the current environment. See Appendix 5 for an overview of the differences between Little Smalltalk and the Smalltalk-80 programming environment.

Any message can be divided into three parts; a *receiver*, a message *selector*, and zero or more *arguments*. The receiver and argument portions of a message can be specified by other message expressions, or they may be specified by a single token, such as an identifier or a literal.

The first type of message selector requires no arguments and is called a *unary* message. A unary message selector consists of an identifier, the first letter of which must be lowercase. For example:

7 sign

illustrates the message *sign* being passed to the number 7. Unary messages, like all messages, elicit a *response*, which is simply another object. The response to *sign* is an integer, either −1, 0, or 1, depending upon the sign of the object the message was sent to (the receiver). Unary messages parse left to right, so, for example:

7 factorial sqrt

returns $\sqrt{7!}$, or approximately 70.993.

The second form of message, called a *binary* message, takes one argument. A binary message is formed from one or two adjacent nonalphabetic characters.[3] Binary messages tend to be used for arithmetic operations, although this is not enforced by the system and there are notable exceptions. An example of a binary message is arithmetic addition:

7 + 4

At first the fact that this is interpreted as "send the message + with argument 4 to the object 7" may seem strange; however, soon the uniform treatment of objects and message passing in Smalltalk makes this seem natural.

Binary messages, like unary messages, parse left to right. Thus

7 + 4 * 3

results in 33, not 19. Unary messages have a higher precedence than binary messages, thus

7 + 17 sqrt

evaluates as 7 + (17sqrt), not (7 + 17) sqrt.

The most general type of message is a *keyword* message. The selector for a keyword message consists of one or more keywords. Each keyword is followed by an argument. A keyword is simply an identifier (again, the first character must be lower case) followed by a colon. The argument can be any expression, although if the expression is formed using a keyword

---

3. Some characters, such as braces, parenthesis or periods, cannot be used to form binary messages. See the description in Appendix 2 for a more complete description of the restrictions.

message, it must be placed in parentheses to avoid ambiguity. Example keyword expressions are:

    7 max: 14
    7 between: 2 and: 24

When we wish to express the name of the message being requested by a keyword message, we catenate the keyword tokens. Thus we say the message selector being expressed in the second example above is *between:and:*. There can be any number of keywords in a keyword message, although in practice few messages have more than three.

Keyword messages have lower precedence than either binary or unary messages. Thus

    7 between: 2 sqrt and: 4 + 2

is the same as

    7 between: (2 sqrt) and: (4 + 2)

Getting Started

You now have enough information to try getting some hands-on experience using the Little Smalltalk system. After logging on, type the command *st*. After a moment, the message "Little Smalltalk" should appear, and the cursor should be indented by a small amount on the next line. If, at this point, you type in a Smalltalk expression and hit the return key, the expression will be evaluated and the result printed. Try typing "3 + 4" and see what happens. The result should be a 7, produced at the left margin. The cursor then should advance to the next line and once more tab over several spaces. Try typing "5 + 4 sqrt." Can you explain the outcome? Try "(5 + 4) sqrt."

Try typing

    i <- 3

Notice that, since assignment expressions do not have a value, no value was printed. However, if you now type

    i

the most recent object assigned to the name will be produced.

The name *last* always contains the value of the last expression computed. Try typing

    27 + 3 sqrt

followed by

    last

Finding Out About Objects

There are various messages that can be used to discover facts about an object. The message *class*, for example, will tell you the class of an object. Try typing

    7 class

The message *superClass*, when passed to an instance of **Class,** will return the immediate superclass of that class. Try typing

    Integer superClass
    7 class superClass

What is the superclass of **Object?**

The keyword message *respondsTo:* can be used to discover if an object will respond to a particular message. The argument must be a symbol, representing the message. Try typing

    7respondsTo: # +
    $A respondsTo: #between:and:
    $A respondsTo: #sqrt

When passed to a class, the message *respondTo:* inquires whether instances of the class respond to the given message. For example,

    Integer respondsTo: # +

You can discover if two objects are the same using the binary message ==. The message~~is the logical inverse of ==. Try typing

    i ← 17
    i == 17
    17~~17

One way to tell if an object is an instance of a particular class is to connect the unary message *class* and the binary message ==. Try typing

    i class == Integer

A simple abbreviation for this is the message *isMemberOf:*. For example, the last expression given is equivalent to

    i isMemberOf: Integer

Suppose we want to tell if an object is a Number, but we don't care if it is any particular kind of number **(Integer** or **Float).** We could use the boolean OR bar (|), which is recognized by the boolean values **true** and **false:**

    (i isMemberOf: Integer)|(i isMemberOf: Float)

A simpler method is to use the message *isKindOf:*. This message asks whether the class of the object, or any of superclasses, is the same as the argument. Try typing

    i isKindOf: Number

Blocks

An interesting feature of Smalltalk is the ability to encapsulate a sequence of actions and then to perform those actions at a later time, perhaps even in a different context. This feature is called a *block* (an instance of class **Block)** and is formed by surrounding a sequence of Smalltalk statements with square braces, as in:

    [i←i + 1. i print]

Within a block (and, as we will see in the next chapter, in general within a method) a period is used as a statement separator. Since a block is an object, it can be assigned to an identifier or passed as an argument with a message or used in any other manner in which objects may be used. In response to the unary message *value*, a block will execute *in the context in which it was defined,* regardless of whether this is the current context or not. That is, when the block given above is evaluated, the identifier i will refer to the binding of the identifier i that was known at the time the block was defined. Even if the block is passed as an argument into a class in which there is a different instance variable i and then evaluated, the i in the block will refer to the i in the context in which the block was defined. Thus a block when used as a parameter is similar to the Algol-60 call-by-name notion of a *thunk*.

The value returned by a block is the value of the last expression inside that block. Frequently a block will contain a single expression, and the value resulting from that block will be the value of the expression.

One way to think about blocks is as a type of in-line procedure declaration. Like procedures, a block can also take a number of arguments. Parameters are denoted by colon-variables at the beginning of the block, followed by a vertical bar and then the statements composing the block. For example,

    [:x :y | (x + y) print]

is known as a two-parameter block (sometimes two-argument block). The message *value:* is used to evaluate a block with parameters the number of *value:* keywords given matches the number of arguments in the block. So, for the example given above, the evaluating message would be *value:value:*.

Comments and Continuations

A pair of double quote marks (") are used to enclose a comment. One must be careful not to confuse the double quote mark with two adjacent single quote marks (''), which look very similar. The text of the comment can be arbitrary and is ignored by the Little Smalltalk system.

The Little Smalltalk system assumes that each line typed at the terminal is a complete Smalltalk expression. Should it be necessary to continue a long expression on two or more lines, a special indication must be given to the Little Smalltalk system to prevent it from misinterpreting the partial expression on the first line and generating an unintentional error message. This special indication is a backwards slash (\) as the last character on all intermediate lines, for example:

```
    2+      \
    3*7     \
    +5
40
```

EXERCISES

1. Show the order of evaluation for the subexpressions in the following expression:

   7 / 2 between: 7 + 17 sqrt and: 3 * 5

2. Type the following expressions:

   ```
   7 = = 7
   'abc' = = 'abc'
   #abc = = #abc
   ```

   How do you explain this behavior?

3. What values will be printed in place of the question marks in the following sequence:

   ```
              i <- 17
              j <- [ i < - i + 1 ]
              i print
   ??
              j print
   ??
              i < - 23
              i print
   ```

Program Continued

??
        j value print
??
        i print
??
        j value print
??
        i print
??

CHAPTER

3

Basic Classes

The classes included in the Little Smalltalk system can be roughly divided into four overlapping groups. These groups are Basic Objects (**Object, UndefinedObject, Symbol, Boolean, True, False, Magnitude, Number, Char, Integer, Float, Radian, Point**), Collections (**Collection, Bag, Set, SequenceableCollection, KeyedCollection, Dictionary, Interval, List, ArrayedCollection, Array, String, File, Random, ByteArray**), Control Structures (**Boolean, True, False, Interval, Block**), and System Management (**Object, Class, Smalltalk, Process**). The following sections will briefly describe each of these categories. Appendix 3 provides detailed descriptions for each of the standard classes.

Basic Objects

The class **Object** is a superclass of all classes in the system and is used to provide a consistent basic functionality and default behavior. For example, the message = = is defined in class **Object** and is thus accepted by all objects in the Little Smalltalk system. This message tests to see if the expressions for the receiver and the argument represent the same object. Another message defined in class **Object** is the message *class,* which returns the object representing the class of the receiver.

The last chapter introduced the classes associated with literal objects. other types of objects are also basic to many applications. For example, instances of the class **Radian** are used to represent *radians.* A radian is a unit of measurement, independent of other numbers. Only radians will respond to trigonometric functions such as *sin* and *cos.* Numbers can be converted into radians by passing them the message *radians.* Similarly, radians can be converted into numbers by sending them the message *asFloat.* Only a limited range of arithmetic operations on Radians, such as scaling by a numeric quantity or taking the difference of two radians, are permitted. Radians are normalized by adding or subtracting multiples of 2π from their value.

The class **Point** is used to represent ordered pairs of quantities. Ordered pairs are useful in the solution of many problems, such as storing coordinate pairs in graphics applications. In fact, the class **Number** provides a convenient method for constructing points. All instances of class **Number** will respond to the message @ by producing a point consisting of the receiver and the argument. Thus 10 @ 12 generates a point representing the ordered pair (10,12). The first value is known as the x-value and will be returned in response to the message *x*. The second value is the y-value and is returned in response to the message *y*.

The class **String** provides messages useful in manipulating arrays of characters. One important property of this class is that its instances are the only objects in the Little Smalltalk system that can be displayed on an output device such as a terminal or printer. Any object to be displayed must first be converted into an instance of class **String.** The behavior defined in class **Object** for the message *print* is to convert the object into a string (using the message *printString*) and then to print that string (by passing the message *print* to it).

The message *printString* is uniformly interpreted throughout the Little Smalltalk system as "produce a string representation of your value." Classes for which this makes sense (such as **Integer**) must define a method for this message that will produce the appropriate string. By default (that is, by a method in class **Object** that will be invoked unless overridden), a string containing the name of the class of the object is produced. In subsequent chapters we will see several examples of how different classes respond to the message *printString*.

Collections

The different subclasses and varieties of **Collection** provide the means for managing and manipulating groups of objects in Smalltalk. The different forms of collections are distinguished by several characteristics, whether the size of the collection is fixed or unbounded, the presence or absence of an ordering, and their insertion or access method. For example, an array is a collection with a fixed size and ordering, indexed by integer keys. A dictionary, on the other hand, has no fixed size or ordering and can be indexed by arbitrary elements. Nevertheless, arrays and dictionaries share many features, such as their access method (*at:* and *at:put:*) and their ability to respond to *collect:, select:,* and many other messages.

The table below lists some of the characteristics of several forms of collections.

Collections of one type can frequently be converted into collections of different type by sending an appropriate message, for example, *asBag* (to convert a collection into a **Bag**), *asSet* or *asArray*.

We can group the operations into several categories, independent of the type of collection involved. The first basic action is adding an element to a collection. Here collections divide into two groups. Those collections that are indexed (**Dictionary, Array**) must be given an explicit key and value, and, thus, the insertion method is the two-argument message *at:put:*. Those collections that are not indexed store only the value and thus use the one argument message *add:*. A special case of this is the class **List,** which maintains elements in a linear ordering. Here, values can be added to the beginning or end of the collection by using the messages *addFirst:* and *addLast:*.

Protocols for adding an element to a collection are similar to those for removing an element from a collection. In collections that do not require

Name	Creation Method	Size Fixed?	Ordered?	Insertion Method	Access Method	Removal Method
Bag/Set	new	no	no	add:	includes:	remove:
Dictionary	new	no	no	at:put:	at:	removeKey:
Interval	n to: m	yes	yes	none	at:	none
List	new	no	yes	addFirst: addLast:	first last	removeFirst removeLast
Array	new:	yes	yes	at:put:	at:	none
String	new:	yes	yes	at:put:	at:	none

a key, an element can be removed with the message *remove:*, the argument being the object to be removed. In keyed collections, the removal message uses the key (*removeKey:*), and not the value. In collections with fixed sizes (**Array** and **String**), elements cannot be removed. In a **List,** an element can be removed from either the beginning of the list (*removeFirst*) or the end of the list (*removeLast*).

Once an element has been placed into a collection, the next step is to access the element. Those collections using keys require a key for access and use the message *at:*. For those that do not require a key, the only question (since one already has the value) is whether the value is in the collection. Thus the appropriate message is *includes:* (which also works for keyed collections). A special case is **List** where one can access either the beginning or the end of the list by using the messages *first* and *last*.

The access methods *at:* and *includes:* access a value by position. Frequently, however, one needs to access an element by value without knowing a position. For example, one may want to find the first positive element in an array of integers. To facilitate this search there is a message named *detect:*. The message *detect:* takes as an argument a one-parameter block.

It evaluates the block on each element in the collection and returns the value of the first element for which the block evaluates true. For example, if x is an array containing numeric values, the message *detect:* could be used to discover the first positive value.

```
x ← # ( −2 −3 4 5)
x detect: [ :y | y > 0 ]
```
4

An error message is produced and **nil** returned if no value satisfies the condition. This can be changed using the message *detect:ifAbsent:*

```
      x detect: [ :y | y > 10 ]
error: no element satisfies condition
nil
      x detect: [ :y | y > 10] ifAbsent: [ 23 ]
23
```

In ordered collections, the search is performed in order, whereas in unordered collections, the search is implementation dependent, and no specific order is guaranteed.

If, instead of finding the first element that satisfies some condition, you want to find all elements of a collection that satisfy some condition, then the appropriate message is *select:*. Like *detect:*, *select:* takes as an argument a one-parameter block. What it returns is another collection, of the same type as the receiver, containing those values for which the argument block evaluated true. A similar message, *reject:*, returns the complementary set.

```
      x select: [ :y | y > 0 ]
#( 4 5 )
      x reject: [ :y | y > 0 ]
#( −2 −3 )
```

The message *do:* can be used to perform some computation on every element in a collection. Like *select:* and *reject:*, this message takes a one-argument block. The action performed is to evaluate the block on each element of the collection.

```
      x do: [ :y | ( y + 1 ) print]
− 1
− 2
5
6
```

The message *do:* returns **nil** as its result. If, instead of performing a computation on each element, you want to produce a new collection containing the results, the message *collect:* can be used. Again like *select:* and *reject:*, this message takes as argument a one-parameter block and returns a collection of the same variety as the receiver. The elements of the new collection, however, are the results of the argument block on each element of the receiver collection.

```
      x collect: [ :y | y sign ]
#( −1 −1 1 1 )
```

Frequently the solution to a problem will involve processing all the values of a collection and returning a single result. An example would be taking the sum of the elements in a numerical array. In Little Smalltalk, the message used to accomplish this is *inject:into:* The message *inject:into:* takes two arguments: a value and a two-parameter block. The action performed in response to this message is to loop over each element in the collection, passing the element and either the initial value or the result of the last iteration as arguments to the block. For example, the sum of the array x could be produced using *inject:*

```
        x inject: 0 into: [ :a :b | a + b ]
    4
```

The following command returns the number of times the value 4 occurs in x:

```
        x inject: 0 into: [ :a :b | (a = = 4) ifTrue: [ b + 1 ] ifFalse: [ b ]]
    1
```

We have described the broad categories of messages used by collections. There are many other messages specific to certain classes; they are described in detail in Appendix 3. We next will provide a brief overview of the most common types of collections.

The classes **Bag** and **Set** represent unordered groups of elements. An element may appear any number of times in a bag but only once in a set. Elements are added and removed by value.

A **Dictionary** is also an unordered collection of elements; however, unlike a bag, insertions and removal of elements from a dictionary requires an explicit key. Both the key and value portions of a dictionary entry can be any object, although commonly the keys are instances of **String, Symbol** or **Number.**

The class **Interval** represents a sequence of numbers in an arithmetic progression, either ascending or descending. Instances of **Interval** are created by numbers in response to the message *to:* or *to:by:.* In conjunction with the message *do:*, an **Interval** creates a control structure similar to **do** or **for** loops in Algol-like languages.

```
        (1 to: 10 by: 2) do: [ :x | x print ]
    1
    3
    5
    7
    9
```

Although instances of class **Interval** can be considered to be a collection, they cannot have additional elements added to them. They can, however, be accessed randomly using the message *at:*.

```
        (2 to: 7 by: 3) at: 2
    5
```

A **List** is a group of objects having a specific linear ordering. Insertion and removal is from either the beginning or the end of the collection. Thus a list can be used to implement both a stack and queue.

A **File** is a type of collection in which the elements of the collection are stored on an external medium, typically a disk. A file can be opened in one of three *modes*. In *character* mode every access or read returns a single character from the file. In *Integer* mode every read returns a single word as an integer value. In *string* mode every read returns a single line as an instance of class String. Elements cannot be removed from a file, although they may be overwritten. Because access to external devices is typically slower than access to memory, many of the operations on files may be quite slow.

An **Array** is perhaps the most commonly used data structure in Little Smalltalk programs. Arrays have fixed sizes, and, while elements cannot be inserted or removed from an array, the elements can be overwritten. Literal arrays can be represented by a pound sign preceding a list of array elements, for example:

#(2 $a 'joe' 3.1415)

A **String** can be considered to be a special form of array, where the elements must be characters. In addition, as we have been illustrating in many examples, a literal string can be written by surrounding the text with quote marks.

The class **ByteArray** represents a special form of array where each element must be a number in the range 0 through 255. Byte arrays are used extensively in the internal representations of objects in the Little Smalltalk system. Byte arrays can be written as a pound sign preceding a list of elements enclosed in square braces, for example:

#[0 127 32 115]

There are two other classes that are commonly used to represent groups of data, although they are not subclasses of **Collection**. The class **Point**, already discussed, can be considered to be a small collection of two items. The class **Random** can be thought of as providing protocol for an infinite collection of pseudo-random numbers. This "list," of course, is never actually created in its entirety; rather each number is generated as required in response to the message *next*. The values produced by instances of class **Random** are floating values in the range 0.0 to 1.0. Other messages can be used to convert this into either an integer or a floating value in any range.

Control Structures

One of the more surprising aspects of Smalltalk is the fact that control structures are not provided as part of the basic syntax but rather are defined using the message passing paradigm. The basic control structure in Smalltalk, as in most computer languages, is the conditional test: **IF** some condition is satisfied **THEN** perform some actions **ELSE** perform some other actions. In Smalltalk this is accomplished by passing messages to instances of class **Boolean.** The class **True** (a subclass of **Boolean**) defines methods for the messages *ifTrue:* and *ifFalse:* (similar methods are defined for class **False**). The arguments used with these messages are blocks. If the condition is satisfied (i.e., the receiver is **true** and the message is *ifTrue:*, or the receiver is **false** and the message is *ifFalse:)*, the argument block is evaluated, and the result it produces is returned. If the condition is not satisfied, the value **nil** is returned.

```
    (3 < 5) ifTrue: [ 17 ]
17
    (3 < 5) ifFalse: [ 17 ]
nil
```

The combined forms *ifTrue:ifFalse:* and *ifFalse:ifTrue:* are also recognized:

```
    (3 < 5) ifTrue: [ 17 ] ifFalse: [ 23 ]
17
    (3 > 5) ifTrue: [ 17 ] ifFalse: [ 23 ]
23
```

The message *and:* and *or:* are similar to *ifTrue:* and *ifFalse:*. They are also used with booleans and passed as arguments objects of class **Block.** *And: i* and *or:* provide "short circuit" evaluation of booleans; that is, the argument block is evaluated only if necessary to determine the result of the boolean expression.

```
    ((i < 10) and: [ (b at: i) = 4] ifTrue: [ i print ]
```

In this example, the expression "(b at:i) = 4" will be evaluated only if the expression "(i<10)" is true. If the first expression returns false, the argument block used with the *and:* message is not evaluated.[1] Notice that the relational < returns either **true** (an instance of class **True**) or **false** (an instance of class **False**) and that the message *and:* is implemented in class **Boolean,** a superclass of both **True** and **False.** Various other boolean operations, such as *not* are also defined in this class.

Next to conditional tests, the most common control structure is a loop. A loop is produced by passing the *timesRepeat:* message with a parameterless bock as an argument to an integer. The value of the integer is the number of times to execute the loop. For example;

```
    5 timesRepeat:[ 8 print ]
8
8
```

---

1. In actual fact the Little Smalltalk parser will, for efficiency, often optimize conditions to remove the message passing overhead. Nevertheless, the underlying paradigm holds true and will, in fact, be used under some conditions (for example, when the arguments are not a block).

```
8
8
8
```

will print the number 8 five times.

A more general loop is used to produce numbers in arithmetic progression. The messages *to:* and *to:by:*, when passed to a number, produce an instance of class **Interval.** As we noted in the last section, an interval is a collection of values in arithmetic progression. We can then use the message *do:* to enumerate the elements in the progression. For example:

```
(2 to: 9 by: 3) do: [ :x | x print ]
2
5
8
```

A more general form of loop is the *while* loop. A while loop is formed using blocks as both receiver and argument. The result of the receiver block must be a boolean. The actions performed by the block are to evaluate the receiver block and, as long as it returns true, to evaluate the argument block. For example, by using an additional variable the previous loop could have been written:

```
i ← 2.
[ i < = 9 ] whileTrue: [ i print . i ← i + 3 ]
2
5
8
```

Since both the receiver and the argument block can contain any number of expressions (the value of a block is always the value of the last expression, regardless of how many expressions the block contains), sometimes no argument block is necessary. The unary message **whileTrue** (or **whileFalse)** can then be used. For example:

```
i ← 2.
[i print . i ← i + 3 . i < = 9] whileTrue.
2
5
8
```

Class Management

The class **Class** is used to provide protocol for manipulating classes. Thus, for example, the methods *new* and *new:* are implemented in class **Class** to allow instance creation. Classes themselves cannot be created by *new* but must be generated by compilation (which is the topic of the next chapter).

The messages *new* and *new:* are treated differently in one respect by the Little Smalltalk system: if a class defines a method for these messages, then, each time a new instance of the class is created (by sending the message *new* or *new:* to the class object), the newly created object is immediately initialized by sending it the same message, and the resulting object is returned to the user. This happens at all levels of the class hierarchy, even if the message is defined multiple times. (That is, later definitions of *new* are in addition to, and do not override, definitions higher in the class hierarchy). One should be careful to distinguish the message *new* passed to the class object used to create the object from the same message passed to the newly created object used for initialization. Since the second message is produced internally, and not by the user, it is easy to overlook.

```
    Array new: 3
#( nil nil nil )
    UndefinedObject new
nil
```

The argument used with *new:* is not used by the object creation protocol but only by the object initialization method. In later chapters we will see how this feature can be used to automatically initialize objects.

The class **Smalltalk** provides protocol for the pseudo variable **smalltalk.** By passing messages to **smalltalk,** the user can discover and set many attributes of the currently executing environment.

```
    smalltalk date
Fri May 24 14:03:16 1985
```

Another message, *time:*, requires a block as argument. The integer value it returns represents the number of seconds elapsed in evaluating the block.

```
    smalltalk time:[ ( 1 to: 10000 ) do: [:x | ] ]
104
```

Smalltalk is a subclass of **Dictionary** and thus responds to the messages *at:* and *at:put:*. Since **smalltalk** is accessible anywhere in any object, it can be used to pass information from one object to another or to provide global information used by a number of objects. Of course, it is the user's responsibility to insure that two objects do not try to store different information using the same key. With the exception of message passing, this pseudo variable is the only means of communication between separate objects. Although permitted, the use of the pseudo-variable in this manner is at odds with the pure object-oriented philosophy of Little Smalltalk and should be discouraged. The necessity for global variables is often the mark of a poorly developed solution to a problem.

The pseudo variable **smalltalk** also provides a means to construct and evaluate messages at run time by using the message *perform:with Arguments:*. The first argument to this message must be a symbol indicating the message to be processed. The second argument must be an array representing the receiver and arguments to be processed. The second argument must be an array representing the receiver and arguments to be used in evaluating the message. The response is the value returned by the first argument of this array in response to the message, with the remainder of the arguments in the second array as the argument values for the message. For example:

```
smalltalk perform: #between:and: withArguments: #(3 1.0 3.14 )
True
```

An instance of class **Process** is used to represent a sequence of Smalltalk statements in execution. Processes cannot be created directly by the user but are created by the system or by passing the message *new-Process* or *fork* to a block. Processes will be discussed in more detail in Chapter 10.

Abstract Superclasses

We did not discuss the classes **Collection, KeyedCollection, SequenceableCollection,** or **ArrayedCollection** in the last section, even though they were listed as forms of "collection" in the beginning of this chapter. These classes, along with such classes as **Boolean, Magnitude,** or **Number,** are what are known as *abstract superclasses*. Instances of abstract superclasses are seldom useful by themselves, but the classes are important in providing methods that can be inherited by subclasses. For example, while it is legal in Smalltalk to say:

```
x ← Collection new
```

and the resulting variable x will indeed be an instance of class **Collection,** the object is not particularly useful. It has no insertion or deletion protocol, for example. An instance of class **Set,** however, is very useful, and the messages defined in class **Collection** are important in providing functionality to objects of this class and to other subclasses of class **Collection.**

The selection and design of abstract superclasses is one of the more important arts in Smalltalk programming. For example, if one were designing a system to manipulate banking accounts, a class **Account** might be a useful abstract superclass for classes **CheckingAccount** and **SavingsAccount.** The actions specific to the individual types of accounts would be in the subclasses, whereas any common behavior, such as the actions necessary for opening and closing an account or querying the balance, might be implemented in the superclass.

EXERCISES

1. Suppose you created a new instance of the class UndefinedObject, as follows:

   i←UndefinedObject new

   How does i respond to *print?* To *isNil* or *notNil?* To the object comparison message = = with **nil** ? Is *i* nil? List facts to support your answer.

2. Note that the messages *arcSin* and *arcCos* produce an object of type **Radian** and not of type **Float.** Furthermore, only objects of type **Radian** respond to *sin* and *cos.* An alternative would have been to eliminate the class **Radian** and to permit all objects of class **Float** to respond to the messages *sin* and *cos.* Discuss the advantages and disadvantages of these two different arrangements.

3. Suppose you have a **Bag** containing numbers. How would you go about producing an instance of the class **List** containing the numbers listed in sorted order?

4. What is the class of **Class?** what is the superclasss of **Class?**

5. Many times, two or more different sequences of messages to collections will have the same effect. In each of the following, describe a sequence of messages that will have the same effect as the indicated message.

   a) implement reject: in terms of select:
   b) implement size in terms of inject:into:
   c) implement includes: in terms of inject:into:.

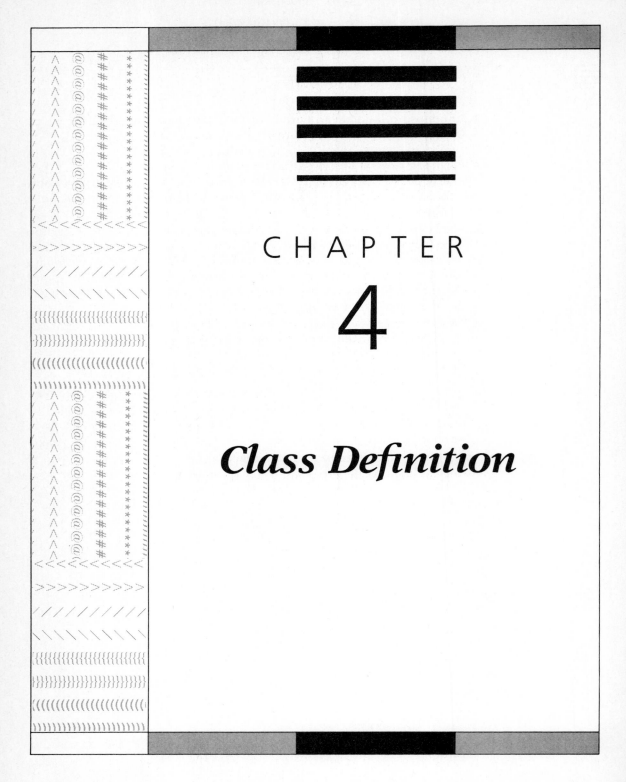

C H A P T E R

4

Class Definition

The last chapter introduced some of the standard classes in the Little Smalltalk system. This chapter will show how the user can define new classes to provide additional functionality for the Smalltalk language.

Class descriptions cannot be entered directly at the keyboard during a Little Smalltalk session. Instead, class descriptions must be prepared beforehand in a file, using a standard editor. There can be any number of class descriptions in a file, although it is convenient to keep each class description in a separate file for ease in program development. The textual representation of a class description consists of two main parts, the class **Heading,** followed by a sequence of one or more *method descriptions.* We will discuss each portion in turn. The syntax for class descriptions is given in detail in Appendix 2.

Figure 4.1 shows a prototypical class description, in this case the description for the class **Set.** The initial part of the description, the class *header,* consists of the keyword **Class** (the first letter capitalized) followed by a class name (also capitalized). Following the class name, the superclass name preceded by a colon, is given. The superclass name is optional and, if not given, the class **Object** will be assumed.

After the class and superclass names, the class description lists instance variable names. Instance variables provide the local memory for instances of the class. Each class instance is given its own set of instance variables, and no other object can modify or change an instance variable in another object. The list of instance variable names is surrounded by a pair of vertical bars. Note that Smalltalk has no notion of variables being declared to be of a specific *type,* thus any instance variable can contain any accessible object or expression. Although the syntax is free form, it is conventional to place the instance variables on a line separate from the class name. Instance variables are initially given the value **nil.** If a class does not contain any instance variables, the entire list, including the vertical bars, can be omitted. Following the heading, a pair of square braces surround the methods that comprise the protocol for the class.

Each *method* in the class protocol defines how instances of the class

Figure 4.1 □ *Class description for class* **Set**

```
Class Set:Collection
| list |
[
        first message pattern
            first message method
    |
        second message pattern
            second message method
]
```

will respond to a single message. The particular message being defined by the method is given by the message *pattern*. The pattern is the first of the three major portions of a method; the other two portions are a list of temporary variables and the message body.

A message pattern defines both the name of the message for which the method is providing protocol and the names to be used when referring to parameters associated with the message. There are three forms of message pattern, corresponding to the three forms of messages (unary, binary, and keyword). Example methods using two of those forms are given in Figure 4.2. These methods are from class **Collection.** Note that method descriptions are separated by vertical bars. The one exception to the free form notation for class descriptions is that this vertical bar *must* appear in the first column.

An optional list of temporary identifier names can appear following a message pattern. For example, the message description for the message *do:* in Figure 4.2 lists a temporary identifier named *item*. Temporary identifiers are created when the method is initiated in response to a message, and they exist as long as the message body is being executed or there is a block in existence that can refer to the temporary value. Like instance variables, temporary variables are initially given the value **nil.**

A *method body* consists of a sequence of one or more Smalltalk expressions separated by periods. Note that the period is an expression separator, not an expression terminator, and does not follow the final expression in the method body. The final expression in a method body, or the final expression in any block created within the method body, can be preceded by an up arrow to indicate that the following expression is to be returned as the response to the message. (On some terminals the up arrow looks like a "caret" or ^.) If no explicit value is returned, the default action at the end of a method is to return the receiver as the response to the message.

Figure 4.2 □ *Method descriptions from class **Collection***

```
        do: aBlock            | item |
            item ← self first.
            [ item notNil ] whileTrue:
                [ aBlock value: item. item ← self next ].
            ↑ nil
    |
        isEmpty
            ↑ (self size = 0)

    |
        remove: oldObject
        self remove: oldObject ifAbsent:
        [ ↑ self error: 'attempt to remove object not found in collection' ].
        ↑ oldObject
```

Note that the up arrow indicates an immediate return from the current method description even if the arrow occurs within a block. This is different from a block returning a value, which, as we saw in Chapter 2, is implicitly the value of the last expression in the block.

Within a method body there are four types of variables that can be accessed, namely instance variables, argument variables, temporary variables, and pseudo variables. In addition to the pseudo variables discussed in the last chapter **(true, false, nil** and **smalltalk),** the pseudo variables **self, super,** and **selfProcess** can be used. Both the variables **self** and **super** refer to the receiver of the current message. When a message is passed to **self,** the search for a method begins with the class description associated with the class of the receiver. On the other hand, when a message is passed to **super,** the search begins with the class description of the superclass of the class in which the current message is defined. For example, if an expression in class **Set** (Figure 4.1) passed a message to **super,** the search for a matching method would begin in class **Collection,** the superclass of class **Set.** A message passed to **self** would initiate a search for an associated method in class **Set.**

To illustrate the actions of **self,** suppose variable "x" is an instance of class **Set.** The methods shown in Figure 4.2 are from class **Collection,** a superclass of class **Set.** In response to the message "x *isEmpty,*" the method *isEmpty* shown in Figure 4.2 is initiated. This method, in turn, passes the message *size* to the pseudo variable **self,** which in this case represents x. Thus the search for a method matching the message *size* would begin in class **Set,** the class of x. If, on the other hand, the method for *isEmpty* had passed the message *size* to the pseudo variable **super,** the search for a corresponding method would have begun in the class **Object,** the super class of **Collection.**

Two messages are singled out for special treatment. If either of the messages *new* or *new:* is defined in a class protocol, then, when an instance of that class is created, the associated message (either *new* or *new:*) will automatically be passed to the new instance before any further processing. Thus, these messages can be used to provide automatic initialization of instance variables. The next section describes in detail one class, the class **Set,** and illustrates the use of this feature.

An Illustrative Example

Figure 4.3 gives the complete class description of the class **Set.** A set is a collection of objects; each object occurs no more than once in the collection. (See Exercise 2.) The data structure used to implement the set will be a list. Recall that a list is also a collection but one that maintains values in order.

Figure 4.3 □ *Class description for Set*

```
Class Set :Collection
| list |
[
    new
        list←List new

    | add: newElement
        (list includes: newElement)
            ifFalse:[list add: newElement]

    | remove: oldElement ifAbsent: exception Block
        list remove: oldElement ifAbsent: exceptionBlock

    | size
        ↑ list size

    | occurrencesOf: anElement
        ↑ (list includes: anElement) ifTrue: [ 1 ] ifFalse: [ 0 ]

    | first
        ↑ list first

    | next
        ↑ list next
]
```

As we have already seen, the class **Set** maintains one instance variable, *list*. Each instance of class **Set** will have a separate instance variable that cannot be accessed by any other object. The method for message *new* will automatically create an instance of class **List** in the variable *list* whenever an instance of class **Set** is created.

When an element is added to a set, a test is first performed to see if the element is already in the set. If so, no further processing is done; if not, the element is added to the underlying list. Similarly, to remove an element, the actions in the method in **Set** merely pass the removal message on to the underlying list. Note that the long form of the *remove:* message is defined; it includes a second argument, indicating what actions should be taken if the given item is not found. As we saw in Figure 4.2, the class **Collection** defines the short message (*remove:*) in terms of this longer message. Thus either form of the message can be used on a **Set.**

The messages *first* and *next* are used to produce *generators*. Generators will be the topic of a later chapter; it is sufficient to say here that *first* and *next* provide a means to enumerate all elements in a collection. The message *first* can be interpreted informally as "initialize the enumeration of items in the collection and return the first item, or **nil** if there are no items in the collection." Similarly, *next* can be defined as "return the next item in the collection, or **nil** if there are no remaining items." The protocol for *do:* (Figure 4.2) illustrates how these messages can be used to construct a loop to access every item in a collection. In Class **Set,** the generation of items in response to these messages is provided by passing the same messages to the underlying list.

Processing a Class Definition

Once you have created a class description, the next step is to add the class to the collection of standard classes provided by the Little Smalltalk system. Suppose, for example, you have defined a class **Test** in the file *test.st;* to add this class definition to a running Little Smalltalk execution you would type the following command in place of a Smalltalk expression:

>)i test.st

The i can be thought of as mnemonic for "include." At this point the class description will be parsed, and, if there are syntax errors, a number of descriptive error messages will be produced. If there are no syntax errors, the class definition will be added to the collection of classes known to the Little Smalltalk system. Whether there are syntax errors or not, the cursor should advance by one tab stop when the system is ready to accept the next command.

If there are syntax errors, the class description can be edited without leaving the Little Smalltalk system. To do this, type the following command:

>)e test.st

The)e command will place the user in an editor mode to view the designated file.[1] When the user exits the editor, another attempt will be made to include the file, as if the)i command were typed.

Once a class definition has been successfully included, the defined class can be used the same as any other class in the Little Smalltalk system. For example, a new instance can be created using the command *new.*

> i←**Test** new

There are other system commands, similar to)i and)e, described in

---

1. On UNIX Systems the editor selected can be changed by modifying the **EDITOR** environment variable.

Appendix 1. These commands are provided with an alternative syntax, rather than as messages passed to **smalltalk,** because they are used during the bootstrapping process before any objects have been defined. The bootstrapping of the Little Smalltalk system will be discussed in the second section of this book.

EXERCISES

1. A **Bag** is similar to a **Set;** however, each entry may occur any number of times. One way to implement the class **Bag** would be to use a dictionary, similar to the way a **List** was used to implement the class **Set** in Figure 4.3. The value contained in the dictionary for a given entry would represent the number of times the entry occurs in the bag. The framework for such an implementation is shown below. Change the name of the class from **Bag** to **MyBag,** and complete the implementation of class **Bag.**

    ```
    Class Bag :Collection
    | dict count |
    [
        new
            dict←Dictionary new
    |   several missing methods
        ...

    |   first
            (count ← dict first) isNil ifTrue: [ ↑ nil ].
            count ← count − 1.
            ↑ dict currentKey

    |   next
            [count notNil]whileTrue:
                [(count>0)
                    ifTrue:[count←count − 1. ↑ dict currentKey]
                    ifFalse:[count←dict next]].
            ↑ nil
    ]
    ```

    Keep in mind that instances of **Dictionary** respond to *first* and *next* with values and not keys. However, the current key is accessible if you use the message *currentKey*.

2. The collections described in Chapter 3 were all *linear,* meaning they could all be represented by a linearly written list. A common nonlinear data structure in computer science is the binary tree. Implement the

class **BinaryTree.** Instances of **BinaryTree** contain a left subtree (or **nil**), a right subtree (or **nil),** and a value. Instances of the class should respond to the following messages:

left   Return the left subtree, usually either **nil** or other instances of **BinaryTree.**

left: Set the left subtree to the argument value.

right   Return the right subtree.

right: Set the right subtree to the argument value.

value   Return the value of the current node.

value: Set the value of the current node to the argument.

How should instances of **BinaryTree** respond to the enumeration messages *first* and *next?* How about *print* or *printString?* What should be the superclass of **BinaryTree?**

≡

CHAPTER

5

A Simple Application

This chapter depicts the development of a simple Smalltalk application. The application chosen, a tool to help keep track of employee information in a small business, is considerably less important than the design techniques being illustrated.

The first, and probably one of the most important steps, is deciding exactly what you want to do. This involves not only stating the desired functionality, but also describing the intended user interface (the set of messages to which the application should respond).

Because programming in Smalltalk is so easy compared to many other programming languages, a particularly attractive technique of developing an application is *rapid-prototyping*. Using this technique, you first define a minimal system that will still exhibit the important aspects of the desired functionality. That is, you strive to find the core of the functions you want at the expense of enhancements or features you might think ultimately desirable. You then design the simplest, most straightforward implementation of this bare system, ignoring for the moment such features as user friendliness and efficiency.

Once you have an executable system, you experiment with it. There is a great psychological benefit to having an executing system, even one that is very simple. High level logical mistakes are most easily exposed with the aid of an executing system, and thus a working version helps considerably in getting more complex versions running. An important aspect of software is its *feel*, a notion nearly impossible to define and almost as difficult to predict before you have a working system.

The necessity for devoting time to a complete and thorough job of specification and design cannot be understated. However, it is likely that there will be many changes in the design stage of any realistic piece of software. It is also likely (perhaps unfortunately) that the user's concept of the problem at hand and the correct solution also will change as the user's experience with the initial versions increases. Users often discover that the set of enhancements they thought were important before a project was implemented are not the same as those they want after experimenting with the initial version. Thus time spent creating a complete system, beyond a minimal system for experimentation purposes may not be productive. (Even with the best planning it may be necessary to throw away at least one version, and oftentimes more, and start anew. This is not a sign of poor programming practice. It is far better to throw away the first attempt at a program, after learning from the mistakes, and to rewrite it than to take a poorly designed and less than adequate program and try to fix it by "patching.")

What is the minimal functionality we could desire for our employee database? At the simplest, we must be able to add and delete information from the records. But what information? Let us start with four fields:

name   a string giving the name of the employee
idNumber   a unique internal identification number

position   a symbol representing the employee job classification
salary   a number giving the salary of the employee

In a realistic situation there would probably be many more fields one would want to maintain (length of employment, social security number, department, and so on) but the four fields listed are sufficient for our examples. For a first approximation, we need not create any new classes at all. We can merely use an instance of class **Dictionary** as our database and an **Array** for each employee. The key for each dictionary entry can be the employee number (since they must be distinct, and names may not be) and the value field can be the rest of the information.

```
employeeDatabase ← Dictionary new
employeeDatabase at: 14737 put: # ( 'David Smith' # clerk 14000 )
employeeDatabase at: 16432 put: # ( 'Roger Jones' # clerk 13500)
employeeDatabase at: 2431 put: #( 'Fred Brown' # president 68020 )
```

Information on a particular employee can be extracted using *at:*

```
employeeDatabase at: 16432
# ( 'Roger Jones' # clerk 13500 )
```

Searches of various sorts can be performed by using *select:*

```
    employeeDatabase select: [:x | (x at: 2) = = # president ]
Dictionary ( 2431 @ #( 'Fred Brown' president 68020 ) )
    employeeDatabase select: [:x | (x at: 3) < 20000 ]
Dictionary ( 14737 @ #( 'David Smith' #clerk 14000 )
    16432 @ # ( 'Roger Jones' # clerk 13500 ) )
```

Output which looks slightly better can be obtained by using *do:*

```
    employeeDatabase do: [:x | ((x at: 3) < 20000) ifTrue: [ x print ] ]
#( 'David Smith' #clerk 14000)
#( 'Roger Jones' #clerk 13500)
```

A record can be updated by combinations of *at:* and *at:put:*

```
    (employeeDatabase at: 16432) at: 3 put: 13750
    employeeDatabase at: 16432
# ( 'Roger Jones' # clerk 13750)
```

While it required almost no work to produce this first approximation, it is obvious that this scheme has some deficiences. One of the most serious deficiencies is that the user of the database must know the position of each field in the employee record in order to understand or update the information. One mistake in updating (using the wrong field number, for example) can damage the record badly. Therefore our first improvement will be to replace each employee record with an instance of a new class, **EmployeeRecord.** Instances of **EmployeeRecord** will themselves contain instance variables for each field of interest. A pair of messages is defined for each field: one to set the value and one to return it. The following class description shows one of these pairs.

```
Class EmployeeRecord
| name idNumber position salary |
[
    name: aString
        name ← aString
|
    name
        ↑ name
...
]
```

We still use a **Dictionary** for the entire database but replace the entries in the dictionary by instances of **EmployeeRecord.** In a certain sense we have complicated matters since it is now necessary to initialize each field separately. Also it is now possible to retrieve only a single field, not the entire structure, of the employee record.

```
        employeeDatabase ← Dictionary new
        employeeDatabase at: 2431 put: EmployeeDatabase new
        (employeeDatabase at: 2431) name: 'Fred Brown'
        (employeeDatabase at: 2431) position: #president
        (employeeDatabase at: 2431) salary: 68020
        employeeDatabase at: 2431
EmployeeRecord
        (employeeDatabase at: 2431) position
#president
```

Let us deal first with the problem of the difficulty in retrieving all information at once. The message *printString* is used uniformly throughout the Little Smalltalk system to produce a printable representation of an object. If no method is provided for this message, the default method (in class **Object**) produces the class name, as illustrated above. We can produce a more meaningful output, however, by concatenating the various fields with strings showing the field names.

```
    printString
        ↑ 'name: ', name,
            ' position: ', position,
            'salary: ' , salary
```

Now when we try to print an individual record, the result is more helpful.

```
        employeeDatabase at: 2431
name: Fred Brown position: president salary: 68020
```

The solution to the problem of initialization is slightly more complicated. As a first step, we can create a new message *initialize* and use the message *getString* with the pseudo variable **smalltalk** to return a string in response to a prompt. In order for the prompt and the response to appear on the same line, we use the printing command *printNoReturn*.

```
initialize
      'name: ' printNoReturn.
      name ← smalltalk getString.
      'position: ' printNoReturn.
      position ← smalltalk getString asSymbol.
      'salary: ' printNoReturn
      salary ← smalltalk getString asInteger
```

Thus we can initialize all the fields at the same time with one command:

```
      employeeDatabase ← Dictionary new
      employeeDatabase at: 2431 put: EmployeeRecord new
      (employeeDatabase at: 2431) initialize
name: Fred Brown
position: president
salary: 68020
      employeeDatabase at: 2431
name: Fred Brown position: president salary: 68020
```

There is a shortcut in Smalltalk to make the initialization of newly created objects easier. If the class of an object defines a method for the message *new*, then this message is passed to each new instance of that class as it is created, before the new object is returned to the user. Thus, we can define the following message in class **EmployeeRecord:**

```
new
      self initialize
```

The message *initialize* will then be sent automatically to each new instance of **EmployeeRecord.**

```
      employeeDatabase ← Dictionary new
      employeeDatabase at: 2431 put: EmployeeRecord new
name: Fred Brown
position: president
salary: 68020
      employeeDatabase at: 2431
name: Fred Brown position: president salary: 68020
```

One can update a record in the same manner as initialization. That is, to update a record on a specific individual, you merely pass the message *initialize* to the record for that individual and retype the information, making changes where appropriate. We still can use the messages we defined at the start to update single fields individually. Both of these alternatives may be error prone. A better scheme would be to display each field as it is currently contained in the database, then making any changes desired. As with *initialize,* the system would prompt for each field, giving the current value of the field. If the user merely typed return, the current value would be retained.

```
        (employeeDatabase at: 2431) upDate
name (Fred Brown):
position (president):
salary (68020): 72000
        employeeDatabase at: 2431
name: Fred Brown position: president salary: 72000
```

Here only the salary field was changed.

Note that we are performing the same actions for each field. Thus it is easier to abstract the desired behavior into a lower level message, passing messages to **self** for each individual field. For that lower level message, it is necessary to print the prompt, including the current value; retrieve the user's response, and, if blank, return the current value, or, if not blank, return the user's response. Thus there are two essential pieces of information that must be passed as arguments; namely, the string with which to prompt and the current value for the field. We can write *upDate* as follows:

```
upDate
    name ← self promptString: 'name' currentValue: name
    position ← (self promptString: 'position' currentValue: position) asSymbol
    salary ← (self promptString: 'salary' currentValue: salary) asInteger
|
promptString: aString currentValue: aValue      | reply |
    ( promptString, ' ( ', currentValue, ' ):' ) printNoReturn.
    reply ← smalltalk getString.
    (reply size = 0)
        ifTrue: [ ↑ currentValue ]
        ifFalse: [ ↑ reply ]
```

Now let us return once more to the representation of the database as a whole. We have up to this point merely been using an instance of class **Dictionary** and the insertion and deletion messages *at:* and *at:put:.* Thus the abstract actions, namely creating, updating, and listing employee entries, must be phrased (sometimes awkwardly) in terms of messages **Dictionary** understands. (Recall the messages required to list all employees with salaries less than 20,000, for example.) A better scheme would be to create a new class, like **EmployeeDatabase,** that would respond to messages more appropriate for our application. A set of messages might be the following:

```
newEmployee
```

create a new employee record.

upDate: aNumber

update the fields for the employee with the given number.

list: aBlock

print out information on all employees that satisfy the condition given by the argument block.

A typical session using this class might appear as follows:

```
    employeeDatabase ← EmployeeDatabase new
    employeeDatabase newEmployee
id: 2431
name: Fred Brown
position: president
salary: 68020
    employeeDatabase update: 2431
name (Fred Brown):
position (president):
salary (68020): 72000
    employeeDatabase list: [:x | x position = #president ]
name: Fred Brown position: president salary: 7200
```

The new database must still retain the information somewhere. One way is to maintain an internal dictionary. This can be established at the time an instance of the database class is created, using the special semantics of the *new* message.

```
Class EmployeeDatabase
| records |
[
    new
        records ← Dictionary new
    ...
]
```

The messages *upDate:* and *list:* merely pass appropriate commands to the dictionary.

```
    upDate: idNumber
        (records at: idNumber) upDate
|
    list: condition
        records do: [:x | (condition value: x) ifTrue: [ x print ] ]
```

The message *new Employee* requires an additional prompt to return the employee number.

```
newEmployee          | newNumber |
    'id: ' printNoReturn.
    newNumber ← smalltalk getString asInteger.
    records at: newNumber put: EmployeeRecord new
```

The exercises propose various further extensions that could be made to this application.

Saving Environments

Updating an employee database is not something you do once and then never again; rather it must be done periodically, as new employees are hired or retire. One way to update an employee database is to record the final values for the database on a slip of paper. Before the start of the next session you initialize the database by initializing each entry. This may be somewhat unsatisfactory; slips of paper tend to get lost. Since computers usually have a much better memory for such things, a good alternative is to use the Little Smalltalk system to save and restore *environments*. We use the term *environment* to denote the set of all objects accessible at any one time. The command

)s *filename*

saves a representation of the current environment in the indicated file.[1] In response to this command, a message indicating the number of bytes written to the file will be printed. These files tend to be rather large; too many of them can clutter your directory.

After saving an environment, you can then continue execution or exit the Little Smalltalk system by typing control-D. A saved environment can later be restored by typing the command

)l *filename*

This command loads the environment saved in the indicated file. Notice that in doing so, it totally erases the environment that existed before the)l command was issued, replacing it with the restored environment. In response to this command, a message indicating the number of bytes read in will be produced. This figure should match the figure written after the)s command. All names that denoted accessible objects before the)s com-

---

1. The)s and)l commands do not work on all machines on which the other portions of the Little Smalltalk system will operate. Check with your system manager, or experiment yourself, to see if they work on your system.

mand are now valid, and the user can continue as if neither the)s nor the
)l commands had been issued.

Note that the same environment can be loaded many times. A common
use for this feature is for users to save an environment containing their
favorite classes and objects that they have created. This environment can
then be quickly loaded, and the classes will be available without having to
issue)i commands for each one.

EXERCISES

1. Add messages to delete employees from the database.

2. Is it necessary to have both the messages *initialize* and *upDate* in **EmployeeRecord** ? Can one be replaced with the other? What changes would the user notice?

3. As it stands, the application is rather lax about error checking. Add checks to make sure a new employee record does not override an older one and that a request to update specifies a valid employee identification number.

4. In the scheme described in this chapter, identification numbers are different from the other fields in the employee record. They are kept only as keys in the database and not as part of the record, for example. Change the class **EmployeeRecord** so that it maintains the identification number as part of the record. What changes are then required in **EmployeeDatabase** ?

5. Instead of maintaining an instance of **Dictionary** in **EmployeeDatabase,** one could make it a subclass of **Dictionary.** How would this change the methods for this class? What are the advantages and disadvantages of both schemes?

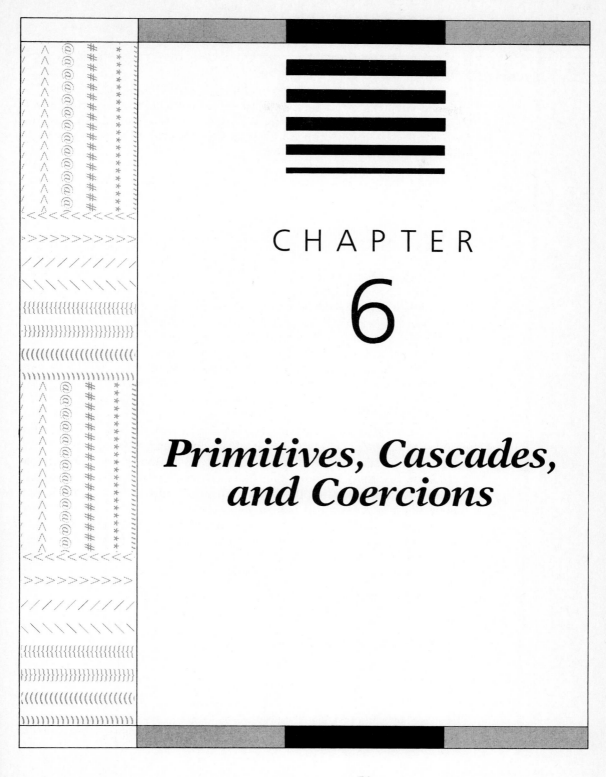

C H A P T E R

6

Primitives, Cascades,
and Coercions

Cascades

Suppose you wanted to send a number of messages to the same object. For example, suppose you wanted to create a new instance of class **Bag** and to initialize it with the values 0 and 1. One way to do this would be to use a temporary variable as in:

```
i←Bag new
i add: 0
i add: 1
```

Another way is to use a *cascade*. A cascade is a type of Smalltalk expression.[1] It is written as an expression followed by a semicolon followed by another expression *without* a *receiver*. When a cascade is evaluated, the first expression is computed, and then used as the receiver for the second expression. The result of a cascade is not the result of the second expression but the result of the first expression. In other words, the result of the second expression is ignored and discarded. Since a cascade is an expression, it can be used to form another cascade, and so on, to any desired level. The result of a cascade of any depth is always the result of the first expression. Thus, for example, you can create a new **Bag** and initialize it all with one expression, as in:

```
Bag new ; add: 0 ; add: 1
```

The receiver for both the messages *add: 0* and *add: 1* is the result of the expression *Bag new*, as is the result of the entire expression.

There are several advantages to using cascaded expressions. Since there is no necessity to name the intermediate object, a cascade obviates the need for a great many temporary variables. Also, since the entire sequence is an expression, it can be used anywhere expressions are legal, for example, as an argument. Finally a cascade can often be used in place of parentheses to separate two keyword messages or to apply one message to another of lower precedence. For example, to print the result yielded by a keyword message you could write:

```
Integer respondsTo: #+ ; print
```

in place of

```
(Integer respondsTo: #+)print
```

---

1. Note that although similar concepts appear in both the Little Smalltalk system and the Xerox Smalltalk-80 programming environment, the syntax and meaning of cascades and primitives are different in the two systems. Appendix 5 describes how cascades and primitives are handled in the Xerox system.

≣ Primitives

At this point you may be wondering how anything ever gets accomplished in Smalltalk. As described so far, actions are produced by one object sending a message to another object. In response to this message, the second object may in turn send still other messages to more objects. If this were all there were to the language, there would seem to be a sort of infinite regress preventing any substantial action from taking place.

The solution to this problem is yet another form of expression, called a *primitive*. A primitive can be thought of as a system call, permitting access to the underlying virtual machine. Syntactically, a primitive is denoted by an angle bracket followed by a name followed by a list of objects followed by a closing angle bracket, for example:

```
<IntegerAddition i j >
```

Alternatively, every primitive is also assigned a number. The primitive name can be replaced by the keyword "primitive" and this number. Thus, since the integer addition primitive is number 10, the above expression could also be written as:

```
<primitive 10 i j >
```

However, the second form is less representative of the operation being performed. Primitives are chiefly used in class descriptions and should almost never by typed directly at the command level. In any case, only the second form (expressing the desired primitive by number) is recognized at the command level.

Note that a primitive call is not the same as a message passing, although the differences are largely hidden from the user. There is no notion of a "receiver" in a primitive expression, and a primitive cannot send further messages in producing its response. For this reason most primitive operations, as the name suggests, are very simple. A table of primitives is given in Appendix 4. In general the value **nil** is returned, and an error message produced, if arguments to a primitive are not correct or the primitive cannot produce the desired result.

A portion of the class description for the class **Radian** is given in Figure 6.1. This class uses the primitives **Sin** and **Cos** to compute the value of the trigonometric functions on radian inputs. Notice how the class **Radian** responds to the message *printString* by concatenating the string representation of its value with the literal string "radians." Thus the message "x print," if x is a radian with value 0.85, will produce the message "0.85 radians." This technique is used in many classes to provide more informative printed representations of objects.

There is a temptation on the part of many novice Little Smalltalk users to use primitives in place of Smalltalk expressions in the name of "effi-

---

Figure 6.1 □ *The class **Radian***

```
ClassRadian :Magnitude
| value |
[
    new: x
        value ← x asFloat
|   < arg
        ↑ value < arg asFloat
|   = arg
        ↑ value = arg asFloat
|   sin
        ↑ <Sin value>
|   cos
        ↑ <Cos value>
|   tan
        ↑ self sin / self cos
|   asFloat
        ↑ value
|   printString
        ↑ value asString, ' radians'
]
```

ciency." This should be avoided. Such gains in efficiency are usually negligible, if they exist at all. More importantly, the notion of primitive is really just a pragmatic device permitting some operations to be specified that could not otherwise be given in Smalltalk. The syntax is a bit obscure, and the notion does not fit quite smoothly into the object-oriented framework of the rest of Smalltalk. Thus primitives should be used only as a last resort, only after a great deal of thought as to the alternatives, and only in extremely simple methods that put a more "Smalltalk-like" cloak over the primitive call.

Numbers

The class hierarchy for numbers could be described as follows:

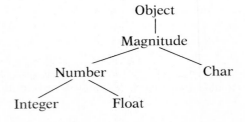

Each of the classes **Integer, Float,** and **Number** implements methods for the arithmetic operations. The classes **Integer** and **Float** perform operations only for arguments of their own type. If an argument is not of the correct type, the message is then passed to the superclass, **Number.** For example the method for + in the class **Integer** looks something like the following:

```
+ aNumber
    ↑ <SameTypeOfObject self aNumber>
      ifTrue: [ <IntegerAddition self aNumber> ]
      ifFalse: [ super + aNumber ]
```

The primitive **SameTypeOfObject** tests whether the two objects given as arguments are instances of the same class. Since the pseudo variable **self** is an instance of the class **Integer,** in this context the use of this primitive can be thought of as equivalent to:

```
aNumber isKindOf: Integer
```

although the primitive expression, since it does not require any further message passing, is somewhat more efficient.[2] If the argument is of the correct class, primitive **IntegerAddition** produces the integer sum of the two arguments. If the argument is not an instance of class **Integer,** the message "+" is passed to the superclass, namely **Number.** In the class **Number** the following methods appear:

```
maxtype: aNumber
    ↑ <GeneralityTest self aNumber>
      ifTrue: [self]
      ifFalse: [aNumber coerce: self]
|

+ aNumber
    ↑ (self maxtype: aNumber) + (aNumber maxtype: self)
```

To understand these methods, consider that a hierarchy of number classes can be defined, consisting of **Integer** at the lowest level, followed by **Float,** then followed by any others (including user-defined classes). When presented with two objects of different levels in the hierarchy, the class **Number** chooses the object with the more general class and passes to it the message *coerce:* with the other object as an argument. For example typing **2 + 3.5** results in the message *coerce: 2* being passed to the object 3.5. The class **Float,** and any user-defined classes, must implement a method for this message.

---

2. The use of the primitive here is justified on the grounds that arithmetic operations are used much more frequently than other messages. Even so, some regard this as a weak argument and would advocate the more direct and obvious Smalltalk expression over the less clear primitive call.

To find the most general form for the operation you use the message *maxtype:*. The method for this message uses the primitive **GeneralityTest,** which returns true if the first argument is of a more general class than the second, and false otherwise.[3] The method for *maxtype:* therefore either returns its first argument or coerces the argument into being of the class represented by the second argument:

coerce: aNumber
    ↑ aNumber asFloat

When **Number** has coerced both arguments into being the same type, the original message is then passed back to the modified objects. Assuming the response to *coerce:* was as expected, the objects should now be able to respond correctly to this message, and the expected result is finally produced.

☰ EXERCISES

1. One advantage cited for cascaded expressions was that several Smalltalk statements could be combined together into one expression. For example the initialized **Bag** discussed in the text could be used as an argument to another object as follows:

   anObject foo: (Bag new; add: 0; add 1)

   How else might this be done in a single expression without using cascading? You can use temporary variables, if you wish.

2. What will the result of typing the following expression be? Explain why.

   2 + (3 print) ; + 4

3. Examine the class descriptions for the classes **Object, Magnitude, Number, Integer,** and **Float.** Explain in detail how radians respond to the messages <= and >=.

4. Rewrite the methods for = and < in class **Radian** so that radians can be compared only to other radians.

5. Does the class **Integer** need to provide a method for *coerce:?* Why or why not? How about the class **Number?**

---

3. There is a problem here in determining the relative generality of two user-defined classes, or even the generality of user-defined classes and known classes, such as **Float.** One of the projects described at the end of the book invites the student to examine this problem and produce more general solutions.

6. An alternative to having instances of class **Radian** maintain their value in an instance variable would be to make the class a subclass of class **Float**. Discuss the advantages and disadvantages of this approach.

7. Recall that in the hierarchy of number classes all other classes have a higher ranking then any of **Integer** or **Float**. Assume that the class **Number** contains the following method

   i

   $\uparrow$ Complex new ; imagpart: self

   That is, in response to the message i, a number will create a new instance of the type **Complex** and initialize it with the current object.

   Using this method, define the class **Complex** used to manipulate complex numbers. Your class should implement methods for the following messages:

   new — Set both the imaginary and real portions of the complex number to zero.

   realpart: — Define the real part of the current number to be the argument.

   imagpart: — Define the imaginary part of the current number to be the argument.

   coerce: — Coerce a non-complex, returning an equivalent complex number with zero imaginary part.

   + — Complex addition.

   * — Complex multiplication.

   printString — produce a printable representation of the number.

   Test your class description by typing several example expressions involving complex numbers.

8. A useful control structure in many programming languages is a multiway switch statement, which permits the selection of one out of several possibilities based on the value of some selection key. Using cascades and blocks we can implement a multiway switch in Smalltalk. The class **Switch** will use the message *new:* both as a creation message and to assign the switch selection key. The message *case:do:* will compare the first argument to the selection key, and, if equal, the second argument (a block) will be evaluated. The message *test:do:* uses blocks for both arguments. The first argument, a one parameter block, is evaluated using the selection key; if it returns true, the second argument is evaluated. A flag is maintained by each instance of **Switch** indicating whether any condition has been satisfied. The message *default:* executes the argument, a block, if no previous condition has been met.

For example, the following statement uses a variable *suit* representing the suit of a card from a deck of cards. It places into *color* a string representing the color of the card.

```
Switch new: suit ;
      case: #spade do: [ color←'black'] ;
      case: #club do: [ color←'black' ] ;
      test: [:x | (x = #diamond) or: [ x = #heart] ] do: [ color←'red'] ;
      default: [ self error: 'unknown suit ' , suit ]
```

Provide a class description for **Switch.**

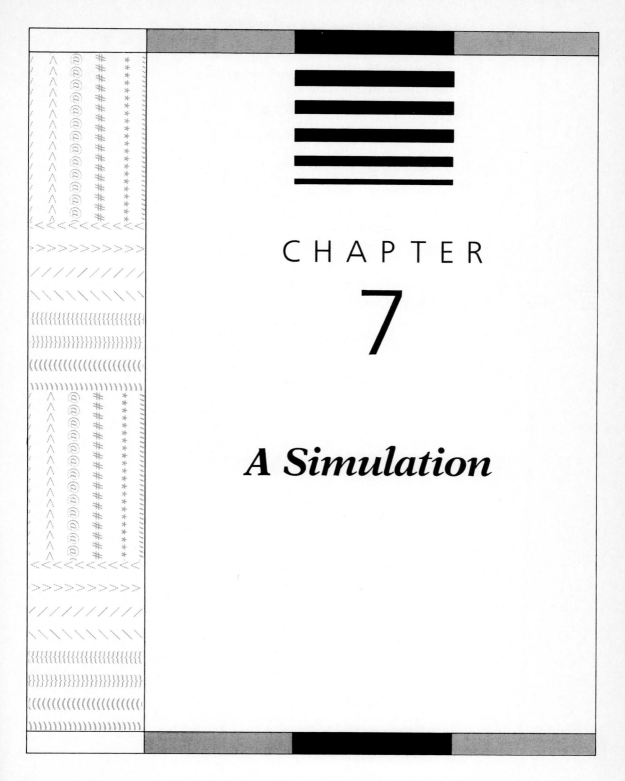

C H A P T E R

7

A Simulation

The programming paradigm employed in Smalltalk, that of a large number of independent objects communicating via message passing, is particularly suitable for constructing simulations of processes that can be described as the interaction of a finite number of events. Each object can represent some object in the simulation model, with the local memory of the object maintaining information about the state of the model object. Messages correspond to interaction between the simulation objects. Indeed, the language was developed largely with just such applications in mind. This chapter will illustrate the construction of a simple simulation describing the operation of an ice cream store. The reader interested in more extensive simulation techniques can consult some of the references listed at the end of this chapter.

The Ice Cream Store Simulation

In writing a simulation, such as our simulation of an ice cream store, the first question to ask is what the different objects in the simulation should represent and what functionality they should possess. At its simplest, our simulation must involve at least two classes of objects: a class representing the actions of the various customers that come to the store and a class representing the actions of the store itself in response to the requests of the customers.

The application we will describe is known as a discrete, event-driven simulation. This means that the actions of the simulation will revolve around the recording and processing of a finite number of individual *events*. An event is simply the occurrence of some action that is important in the context of the simulation. Each event is marked with a time at which the event should take place. A "clock" records the current "time," which need not be related in any way to conventional time; a simple counter will suffice. As time progresses, the occurrence of each event controls the sequence of further actions in the simulation.

Our first, and very simple, attempt at simulating an ice cream store will illustrate these concepts. A *pending event* is defined as any event that has not yet taken place. Assume, first, that there is never more than one pending event. At the moment we need not concern ourselves with how each event is to be encoded, but only that it can be represented by an object. We can isolate the actions of the simulation that are independent of any particular application in an abstract superclass called **Simulation.** Particular simulations, such as in the ice cream store, will then be subclasses of **Simulation.**

The first version of the class **Simulation** is shown in Figure 7.1. The class maintains the current "time" in the variable currentTime. The message *proceed* will indicate that the next action should take place. Since the

Figure 7.1 □ *The class **Simulation** (version 1)*

```
Class Simulation
| currentTime nextEvent nextEventTime |
[
    new
        currentTime ← 0
    |
    time
        ↑ currentTime
    |
    addEvent: event at: eventTime
        nextEvent ← event.
        nextEventTime ← eventTime
    |
    proceed
        currentTime ← nextEventTime.
        self processEvent: nextEvent
]
```

actual interpretation of an event will differ from one simulation to the next, *proceed* leaves the task of interpreting the event to a subclass by passing the message *processEvent:* to the pseudo variable **self.** The message *processEvent:* must therefore be recognized in each subclass.

Having described the framework for keeping track of the simulation "bookkeeping," we can go on to describe the actions of our ice cream store. We start with a simple model in which customers arrive, order some number of scoops of ice cream, and leave. Each scoop of ice cream produces some amount of profit for the store. At the end of the simulation period we will want to know the profit.

It is, however, not sufficient to merely describe what actions take place in the store; we must also describe how often those events should take place. For example, how often do customers arrive, how many scoops of ice cream will each customer order, and so on. We could make a simple assumption, such as a new customer will arrive every two minutes and order three scoops of ice cream. Such a deterministic assumption, however, defeats the necessity for the simulation at all since we can easily predict the outcome: in 15 minutes seven customers will arrive and order 21 scoops of ice cream. Instead, it is more interesting (to say nothing of being more realistic) to define the outcome of an event in terms of a random value chosen from a selected distribution.

For example, let us suppose that at each instance the next customer will appear at a time uniformly chosen from the numbers 1 to 5. The phrase "uniformly chosen" means that each outcome (or each time) is equally likely, and thus we can use a random number generator to select

---

Figure 7.2 □ *A portion of the class **IceCreamStore** (version 1)*

```
Class IceCreamStore :Simulation
| profit rand |
[
    new
        profit ← 0.
        rand ← Random new.
        rand randomize.
        self scheduleArrival
    |
    scheduleArrival
        self addEvent: Customer new
            at: (self time + (rand randInteger: 5))
    |
    ...
    |
    reportProfits
        ('profits are ', profit) print
]
```

a value in this range to represent the time for the next arrival. Letting **IceCreamStore** be the class representing our simulation of the store, this could be computed as shown in the method for the message *scheduleArrival* in Figure 7.2. Note that the instance variable rand is initialized to be an instance of the random number generator, and that during initialization the first customer is scheduled. The message *randomize* is used to insure that a new random sequence is generated each time we invoke the simulation.

Notice we have chosen to represent events by an instance of class **Customer.** In our first simulation very little functionality is required of the customer. Each customer must arrive and upon arrival decide the number of scoops of ice cream he or she will order. Thus the class shown in Figure 7.3 suffices for customers.

The only remaining part of our simulation is deciding how the class **IceCreamStore** should respond to the message *processEvent:*. Since the event is an instance of class **Customer,** all that is required is determining the amount of ice cream to be dispensed (and thus the profit to be made) and scheduling the next customer. The latter requirement may not be obvious, but is important. For our simulation to work, each event must generate some number of other events. The decision about where and when each event should schedule the next is not always obvious, but must be made someplace.

Figure 7.3 ☐ *The class **Customer** (version 1)*

```
Class Customer
| rand |
[
    new
        rand ← Random new.
        rand randomize
    |
    numberOfScoops      | number |
        number ← rand randInteger: 3.
        ('customer has ', number , ' scoops ') print.
        ↑ number
]
```

Let us assume that each scoop of ice cream generates seventeen cents profit for the store. The response to the message *processEvent:* can then be represented as follows:

```
processEvent: event
    ('customer received at ', self time ) print.
    profit ← profit + ( event numberOfScoops * 0.17 ).
    self scheduleArrival
```

To determine how much profit might be produced in 15 minutes, we could then run our simulation as follows:

```
store ← IceCreamStore new

[store time < 15] whileTrue: [store proceed]
customer received at 1
customer has 1 scoops
customer received at 2
customer has 3 scoops
customer received at 5
customer has 1 scoops
customer received at 8
customer has 1 scoops
customer received at 11
customer has 1 scoops
customer received at 16
customer has 2 scoops

    store reportProfits
profits are 1.53
```

Now, having produced our first simulation, let us go back and examine some of the assumptions we made to decide if they are really accurate. Do customers really arrive with a uniform distribution? Do they always arrive individually? Do they really order some number of scoops with a uniform probability?

Let us tackle the last question first. Suppose we observe a real ice cream store for some period of time and note that 65% of the time customers will order one scoop, 25% of the time they order two scoops, and only 10% of the time do they order three scoops. This is certainly a far different distribution from the one given by our assumption that all three outcomes are equally likely. In order to simulate this behavior, we must generate a random integer that returns one 65% of the time, two 25% of the time, and three 10% of the time. A distribution of values such as we have described is known as a *weighted discrete probability*. One way to generate a random value satisfying our requirements is to generate a uniform random number between 1 and 100. If this uniform value is less than or equal to 65, we return 1; if less than or equal to 90, we return 2; otherwise, we return 3. We can generalize this to work for any weighted distribution we like, producing the class **DiscreteProbability** shown in Figure 7.4. In response to the message *next*, an instance of this class will return a value between 1 and the size of the weights array, distributed according to the weights given.

Figure 7.4 □ *The class DiscreteProbability*

```
Class DiscreteProbability
| weights rand max |
[
        defineWeights: anArray

                weights ← anArray.
                rand ← Random new.
                rand randomize.
                max ← anArray inject: 0 into [:x :y | x + y]
        |
        next | index value |

                value ← rand randInteger: max.
                index ← 1.
                [ value > (weights at: index) ]
                    whileTrue: [ value ← value − (weights at: index).
                        index ← index + 1 ].
                ↑ index
]
```

The distribution of ice cream orders was obtained by observing a large body of customers. So we can argue whether the number of scoops an individual will order should be part of the protocol for the **Customer** class (since the customer is issuing the order) or for the **IceCreamStore** class (since the distribution is taken from observations of ice cream store customers as a group). The last simulation illustrated the first variation. The following simulation will illustrate the second variation.

Let us alter the assumption that customers arrive one by one; since it is a social process, people tend to eat ice cream in groups. Each instance of class **Customer** will be changed, therefore, to represent a group of individuals. Upon creation, each instance will determine its group size, which will thereafter be returned in response to a request via the message *groupSize*. Given these changes, our second simulation can be given as shown in Figure 7.5.

Suppose we complicate things now by adding an inside dining area to our ice cream store. There are several more factors to consider. Whereas formerly we assumed we could accommodate as many customers as would arrive in any particular time period, now we can only accommodate those customers who can find chairs. In this new situation, the sequence of events affecting a single customer or a group of customers is now more complicated than the previous case, where the only event of importance from the customer's point of view was the receipt of the ice cream. Now the following sequence will take place:

1. Some group of customers will arrive. If there are not enough chairs, they will immediately leave. Otherwise, they will take seats and start to look at the menu.

2. Later the group of customers will place an order and receive their ice cream.

3. Still later, the group will have finished their ice cream and will leave.

Furthermore, we can now have several events happening simultaneously. One group of customers can be eating their ice cream, while another is ordering, and a third is just arriving. Thus, the basic assumption that there is always just one pending event is no longer valid. Now the class **Simulation** must be altered to keep a queue of pending events. In response to the message *proceed*, the event with the next smallest time marker is removed from the queue and initiated. One convenient data structure to maintain both the pending events and their time for initiation is a dictionary using the time as a key and the event as the value. However, two events can happen at the same time (for instance, one group can order while another arrives). Therefore the value of the dictionary cannot be simply a single event, but must be a set of events. Our revised class **Simulation** is shown in Figure 7.6.

Events are now more complicated. We must remember not only a group of customers but also what state they are in: whether they have just arrived, are about to order, or are about to leave. One way to do this is to store as an event a block which when evaluated will move the customer to the next state. Recall that a block evaluates in the context in which it is defined and not until passed the message *value*. Thus, for example, the protocol for *scheduleArrival* might be given as follows:

```
scheduleArrival          | newCustomer |

    newCustomer ← Customer new.
    self addEvent: [self customerArrival: newCustomer]
        at: (self time + (rand randInteger: 5))
```

Figure 7.5 □ *Ice cream store simulation (version 2)*

```
Class IceCreamStore :Simulation
| profit rand scoopDistribution |
[
    new
        profit ← 0.
        rand ← Random new.
        scoopDistribution ← DiscreteProbability new
        scoopDistribution defineWeights: #(65 25 10).
        self scheduleArrival
    |
    scheduleArrival

        self addEvent: Customer new
            at: (self time + (rand randInteger: 5))
    |
    processEvent: event

        ('customer received at ', self time ) print.
        profit ← profit + ((self scoopsFor: event groupSize) * 0.17).
        self scheduleArrival
    |
    scoopsFor: group          | number |

        number ← 0.
        group timesRepeat:
            [number ← number + scoopDistribution next].
        ('group of ', group , ' have ' , number , ' scoops ') print.
        ↑ number
```

Program Continued

```
|

reportProfits

    ('profits are ', profit ) print
]

Class Customer
| groupSize |
[

    new
        groupSize ← (Random new randomize) randInteger: 8
|
    groupSize
        ↑ groupSize
]
```

A new customer is created and placed in the temporary variable **new Customer.** A block is then installed in the event queue. Since this block references the temporary variable **newCustomer,** the temporary will be retained (i.e., the storage it uses will not be reclaimed) as long as the block exists. However, each time the message *scheduleArrival* is received, a new instance of **Customer** will be created. The processing indicated by the block will not take place until the block is evaluated using the message *value*. This takes place when the event is processed:

processEvent: event

    event value.
    self scheduleArrival

Figure 7.6 □ *The class Simulation (version 2)*

```
Class Simulation
| currentTime eventQueue |
[

    new
        eventQueue ← Dictionary new.
        currentTime ← 0
|
    time
        ↑ currentTime
|
    addEvent: event at: eventTime
```

Program Continued

```
        (eventQueue includesKey: eventTime)
            ifTrue: [(eventQueue at: eventTime) add: event]
            ifFalse: [eventQueue at: eventTime
                put: (Set new ; add: event)]

    addEvent: event next: timeIncrement

        self addEvent: event at: currentTime + timeIncrement

    proceed          | minTime eventset event |

        minTime ←99999.
        eventQueue keysDo:
            [:x | (x < minTime) ifTrue: [minTime ← x]].
        currentTime ← minTime.
        eventset ← eventQueue at: minTime ifAbsent: [ ↑ nil].
        event ← eventset first.
        eventset remove: event.
        (eventset isEmpty) ifTrue: [eventQueue removeKey: minTime].
        self processEvent: event
```

When the block created in scheduleArrival is evaluated, it will send
the message *customerArrival:* to the pseudo variable self, that is, to the
simulation object. Upon arrival, if there are a sufficient number of chairs,
the customers sit down and order, otherwise they leave. Let us use an
instance variable *remainingChairs* to represent the number of free chairs
at any point. The time between arriving and ordering will be a random
value from one to three. The protocol for *customerArrival:* can then be
given as follows:

customerArrival: customer | size |

```
        size ← customer groupSize.
        ('group of size ', size , ' arrives') print.
        (size < remainingChairs)
            ifTrue: [remainingChairs ← remainingChairs — size.
                'take chairs, schedules order' print.
                self addEvent: [self customerOrder: customer]
                    next: (rand randInteger: 3).
                ]
        ifFalse: ['finds no chairs, leaves' print]
```

Notice that again a block has been used to represent the next event.
When evaluated, this block will pass the message *customerOrder:*. The
protocol for this message is as follows:

```
customerOrder: customer          | size numScoops |
    size ← customer groupSize.
    numScoops ← 0.
    size timesRepeat:
        [numScoops ← numScoops + scoopDistribution next].
    ('group of size ', size , ' orders ' , numScoops , ' scoops') print.
    profit ← profit + (numScoops * 0.17).
    self addEvent:
        [self customerLeave: customer]
        next: (rand randInteger: 5)
```

Once more the time between a group of customers ordering and leaving is determined by a random value chosen between 1 and 5. When the customers finally do leave, they relinquish their chairs.

```
customerLeave: customer          | size |
    size ← customer groupSize.
    ('group of size ', size , ' leaves') print.
    remainingChairs ← remainingChairs + customer groupSize
```

We will make one final change to illustrate how our simulation can be made even more realistic. In practice, few random events ever occur with uniform probability. More often, other distributions, such as a Bernoulli distribution or a Poisson distribution, are observed to model a process. One very common form is the Normal distribution, which is characterized by values clustering around a mean, with the chances of a value decreasing exponentially the farther they move from the mean. Figure 7.7 shows one class that can be used for generating random values with a normal distribution. No attempt is made to motivate the algorithm used in the method for the message *next;* an interested reader can refer to the end of this chapter for additional literature.

Given the ability to produce random values from a normal distribution, we can change our assumption about customers arrivals to be more realistic. For example, we could assume customers arrive in a normal distribution with a mean of 3 minutes and a standard deviation of 1 minute. Figure 7.8 shows the class header and the protocol for the initialization message *new* and the message *scheduleArrival* incorporating these changes. In the method for *scheduleArrival* we have also incorporated a "closing time" by adding events corresponding only to customers who arrive before some fixed limit. After closing time, no new customers will arrive, but the customers waiting to order and waiting to leave will still be processed. This is so that the event queue can be flushed out and the simulation terminate in a clean fashion.

Other random values used in the simulation could be modified to use a different distribution by making changes such as the ones we have illustrated for the arrival time distribution.

We end with an example session of our final simulation:

Figure 7.7 □ *The class Normal*

```
Class Normal :Random
| mean deviation |
[
    new
        self setMean: 1.0 deviation: 0.5
|
    setmean: m deviation: s
        mean ← m.
        deviation ← s
|
    next    | v1 v2 s u |
        s ← 1.
    [s > = l] whileTrue:
            [v1 ← (2 * super next) − 1.
            v2 ← (2 * super next) − 1.
            s ← v1 squared + v2 squared ].
        u ← ( − 2.0 * s ln / s) sqrt.
        ↑ mean + (deviation * v1 * u)
]
```

Figure 7.8 □ *The class IceCreamStore (version 3)*

```
Class IceCreamStore :Simulation
| profit arrivalDistribution rand scoopDistribution remainingChairs |
[
    new
        profit ← 0.
        remainingChairs ← 15.
        rand ← Random new.
        ←arrivalDistribution ← Normal new:
            setMean: 3.0 deviation: 1.0.
        scoopDistribution ← DiscreteProbability new:
            defineWeights: #(65 26 10).
        self scheduleArrival
|
    scheduleArrival                    | newCustomer time |
        newCustomer ← Customer new.
        time ← self time + (arrivalDistribution next).
```

Program Continued

```
(time < 15) ifTrue: [ self addEvent: [ self customerArrival: newCustomer ]
                       at: time]
...
]
```

```
    store ← IceCreamStore new
    [store time < 60] whileTrue: [store proceed]
event received at 3.46877
group of size 8 arrives
takes chairs, schedules order
event received at 5.81336
group of size 8 arrives
finds no chairs, leaves
event received at 6.46877
group of size 8 orders 11 scoops
event received at 7.46877
group of size 8 leaves
event received at 8.91228
group of size 1 arrives
takes chairs, schedules order
event received at 10.9123
group of size 1 orders 1 scoops
event received at 10.9499
group of size 7 arrives
takes chairs, schedules order
event received at 11.8463
group of size 5 arrives
takes chairs, schedules order
event received at 12.0194
group of size 2 arrives
finds no chairs, leaves
event received at 12.8463
group of size 5 orders 6 scoops
event received at 12.9123
group of size 1 leaves
event received at 12.9499
group of size 7 orders 13 scoops
event received at 13.8077
group of size 7 arrives
finds no chairs, leaves
event received at 14.6301
group of size 5 arrives
finds no chairs, leaves
```

Program Continued

event received at 16.9499
group of size 7 leaves
event received at 17.8463
group of size 5 leaves
    store reportProfits
profits are 5.27

Since Smalltalk objects can be created, removed, and in general placed in a one-to-one correspondence with objects in the abstract model being simulated (the objects representing the customer groups, for example). It is relatively easy to take any model expressed in the discrete event-driven form and enunciate it in Smalltalk. Similarly the development of new simulations is simplified by the inheritance of common behavior from class **Simulation.** Finally, once a simulation has been developed, it is easy to modify, for example, replacing a value generated with a normal distribution with one generated according to a Bernoulli distribution.

≡ **Further Reading**

A good introduction to the concepts of simulation can be found in (Maryanski 80). A more theoretical treatment is given in (Zeigler 76). The definitive description of the Smalltalk-80 language (Goldberg 83) illustrates many more extensive simulations in Smalltalk. Other programming languages designed for simulation include Simula (Birtwistle 73), Demos (Birtwistle 79), and GPSS (Greenberg 72). The algorithm for computing the normal distribution is taken from Knuth (Knuth 81, Vol. 2). A large collection of references to computer games and simulation exercises is found in (Gibbs 74).

≡ **EXERCISES**

1. Deciding when to use subclassing and when to use an instance variable is not always easy. An argument can be made that **DiscreteProbability** should really be a subclass of **Random,** such as the following:

Class **DiscreteProbability** :Random
| weights max |
[

Program Continued

```
defineWeights: anArray
      weights ← anArray.
      max ← anArray inject: 0 into: [:x :y | x + y]
|
   next | index value |
        value ← super randInteger: max.
        index ← 1.
        [value > (weights at: index)]
          whileTrue: [value ← value - (weights at: index).
              index ← index + 1].
        ↑ index
]
```

Look at the class description for **Random,** in particular the response to the message *randInteger:,* and then describe why this class description will not produce the desired result.

2. An alternative method of defining a discrete probability is to provide the actual sample space in a collection. For example, suppose a group of boys are observed to have heights represented by the array #(60 54 60 62 50). We can then ask for the height of a randomly selected boy. The following shows how a class **SampleSpace** might be used for this purpose:

```
sample ← SampleSpace new ; define: #(60 54 60 62 50)
sample first
60
```

Produce a class description for **SampleSpace.**

3. If written in a manner analogous to **DiscreteProbability,** the class **SampleSpace** defined in the last exercise is said to provide "random selection with replacement." The alternative, random selection without replacement, is frequently more useful. For example, a sample space might represent a deck of cards, and a random selection, the choosing of a card. This card should then be thought of as being removed from the deck and not available for return in subsequent selections.
Describe how to modify the class **SampleSpace** to provide random selection without replacement.

CHAPTER

8

Generators

In Little Smalltalk, the term *generator* describes any object that represents a collection of other objects and that responds to the following two messages:

first   The response should be an element of the collection, or the special value **nil** if there are no elements in the collection.

next   The response should be another element in the collection, or **nil** if there are no more elements in the collection.

For example, instances of the standard data structures, such as **Array, String,** or **Bag,** can all be considered to be generators. Instances of **Array** or **String** return the element stored in their first subscript position (if they have at least one subscript position) in response to the message *first.* On subsequent *next* messages they respond with the remaining elements in order. This functionality is provided by class **ArrayedCollection,** using an instance variable *current* (Figure 8.1.)

Some data structures, such as instances of the class **Bag,** do not possess a "natural" ordering, and thus the order in which elements are produced in response to *first* and *next* messages is not defined, other than that all elements are eventually produced and no element is produced more than once.

Notice that nothing is said about *how* a generator produces the object to be yielded in response to one of these messages. Some objects, such as instances of **Bag** or **Array,** maintain their collections in memory, and thus the response to *first* and *next* is merely to enumerate their elements. Instances of **File** are similar, only the values are retrieved from an external disk as required. Other generators, such as instances of **Interval,** maintain only the information necessary for generating each new element as required, and that recompute each new element on demand (Figure 8.2). Indeed, the list of elements represented by instances of class **Random** can

Figure 8.1 □ *A portion of the class ArrayedCollection*

```
| current |
[

    ...
|
    first
        current ← 1.
        ↑ (current < = self size) ifTrue: [ self at: current]
|
    next
        current ← current + 1.
        ↑ (current < = self size) ifTrue: [ self at: current]
]
```

Figure 8.2 □ *A portion of the class* Interval

```
Class Interval :SequenceableCollection
| lower upper step current |
[
    ...
|
    inRange: value
        ↑ (step strictlyPositive)
            ifTrue: [ value between: lower and: upper ]
            ifFalse: [ value between: upper and: lower ]
|
    first
        current ← lower.
        ↑ (self inRange: current) ifTrue: [ current ]
|
    next
        current ← current + step.
        ↑ (self inRange: current) ifTrue: [ current ]
]
```

be considered to be infinite in length, and thus cannot be stored entirely in memory.

From the point of view of the message passing interface, there is no distinction between classes that iterate over their elements in memory and classes that produce new elements on demand. Even in cases where the sequence to be produced in response to *first* and *next* is finite, there may be advantages to computing elements as needed rather than all at once when the object is defined.

An example will illustrate how generators assist problem solving in Smalltalk. Consider the problem of producing prime numbers. By definition, a prime number is a value having only two divisors, itself and 1. A generator for prime numbers will produce the first prime value (namely 2) when offered the message *first*, and successive prime numbers in response to each *next* message.

If a number *n* divides a number *m*, then the prime factors of *n* must also divide *m*. Thus, to tell if a number *m* is a prime, we need not test all values less than *m*, only those values that are prime. Therefore a simple generator for primes can be constructed by merely retaining the previously generated primes in a **Set.** As each new value is requested, an object representing the last prime produced is incremented and tested until a value having no factors is found. The new value is then inserted into the set and returned.

```
Class Primes
| prevPrimes lastPrime |
[
    first
        prevPrimes ← Set new.
        prevPrimes add: (lastPrime ← 2).
        ↑ lastPrime
|
    next
        [ lastPrime ← lastPrime + 1.
          self testNumber: lastPrime ] whileFalse.
        prevPrimes add: lastPrime.
        ↑ lastPrime
|
    testNumber: n
        prevPrimes do: [:x | (n \ \ x = 0) ifTrue: [ ↑ false ] ].
        ↑ true
]
```

A few simple observations will improve the efficiency of this algorithm and will also illustrate the proper choice of data structures. The loop in the method for *testNumber:* halts and returns as soon as a previous prime is shown to be a factor of the number under consideration. Two is a factor of exactly one half of all numbers. Similarly three is a factor of one third of all numbers, and so on. If we could arrange to test previous primes in numeric order (that is, in the order in which they were generated) we would on average remove nonprimes much more quickly than the more or less random order given to us by a **Set.** The appropriate data structure for an ordered collection without keys is a **List.** Thus we rewrite the algorithm to use a **List** and the insertion method *addLast:,* which adds elements to the end of the list, rather than *add:,* which would add to the front of the list. In fact, keeping the previous primes in order allows yet another improvement in the algorithm since we can terminate the search of previous primes as soon as a value larger than $\sqrt{n}$ is reached where n is the value being tested.

```
Class Primes
| prevPrimes lastPrime |
[
        first
        prevPrimes ← List new.
        prevPrimes add: (lastPrime ← 2).
          ↑ lastPrime
|
    next
        [ lastPrime ← lastPrime + 1.
```

```
            self testNumber: lastPrime ] whileFalse.
        prevPrimes addLast: lastPrime.
        ↑ lastPrime
|

testNumber: n .
    prevPrimes do: [:x |
        (x squared > n) ifTrue: [ ↑ true ].
        (n \ \ x = 0) ifTrue: [ ↑ false ] ]
]
```

An obvious problem with both of these prime number generators is that they require an ever-increasing amount of storage to maintain the list of previous prime numbers. If you were constructing a long list of prime values, the size of this storage could easily become a problem. An alternative, which trades slightly longer computation time for reduced storage, is a *recursive* generator. This is analogous to a recursive procedure in programming languages such as Pascal. The following program does not maintain the list of previous primes but instead regenerates the list each time a new number is to be tested.

```
Class Primes
| lastPrime |
[
    first
        ↑ lastPrime ← 2
|

    next
        [ lastPrime ← lastPrime + 1.
          self testNumber: lastPrime ] whileFalse.
        ↑ lastPrime
|

    testNumber: n
        (Primes new) do: [:x |
            (x squared > n) ifTrue: [ ↑ true ].
            (n \ \ x = 0) ifTrue: [ ↑ false ] ]
]
```

You may have noted that the message *do:* is being passed to an instance of class **Primes,** which does not contain a method for this message. The method for *do:* is inherited from class **Object** and is defined in terms of *first* and *next.*

```
do: aBlock          | item |
    item ← self first.
    [ item notNil ] whileTrue:
        [ aBlock value: item. item ← self next ].
    ↑ nil
```

The fact that *do:* is in class **Object** and therefore provides functionality for all objects illustrates the pervasive nature of generators in Little Smalltalk. Any object can be manipulated as a generator merely by providing methods for the messages *first* and *next*.

Filters

An entirely different program can solve the same task as the prime number generators described in the last section. It uses another programing technique, *filters,* that is frequently useful in conjunction with generators. Externally (that is, examining only the messages to which an object responds) a filter looks just like a generator. Unlike a "true" generator, however, a filter does not produce new values in response to *first* or *next* but takes values produced by a previously defined generator and modifies them or filters out values.

The class **FactorFilter** exemplifies some of the essential features of a filter. Instances of **FactorFilter** are initialized by giving them a generator and a specific nonnegative value. In response to *next* (the message *first* is in this case replaced by the initialization protocol), values from the underlying generator are requested and returned, except values for which the given number is a factor are repressed. Thus the sequence returned by an instance of **FactorFilter** is exactly the same as that given by the underlying generator, with the exception that values for which the given number is a factor are filtered out.

```
Class FactorFilter
| myFactor generator |
[
    remove: factorValue from: generatorValue
        myFactor ← factorValue.
        generator ← generatorValue
|
    next    | possible |
        [ (possible ← generator next) notNil ]
            whileTrue:
                [ (possible \ \ myFactor ~ = 0)
                    ifTrue: [ ↑ possible ] ].
        ↑ nil
]
```

Using **FactorFilter,** you can construct a simple generator for prime numbers. First an instance of **Interval** that will generate all numbers from 2 to some fixed limit is constructed. As each value is removed, a filter is inserted in front of the generator to insure that all subsequent multiples of the value will be eliminated. A new value is then requested from the updated generator.

```
Class Primes
| primeGenerator lastFactor |
[
    first
        primeGenerator ← 2 to: 100.
        lastFactor ← primeGenerator first.
        ↑ lastFactor

    |

    next
        primeGenerator ← (FactorFilter new ;
                            remove: lastFactor
                            from: primeGenerator ).
        ↑ lastFactor ← primeGenerator next
]
```

Pictorially, the underlying generator constructed by the first occurrence of the message *next* can be viewed as follows:

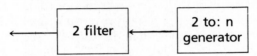

When asked for the next prime, the generator is modified by adding a filter, this time for the last prime value returned, the number 3.

The program continues. Each time a new prime is requested, a filter is constructed to remove all factors of the previous prime. in this fashion, all the primes are eventually generated.

Of course, like the first two programs in the last section, the storage required for the chain of filters is proportional to the number of primes generated so far. Despite this, timings of actual programs show that the filter program is the fastest of the prime number generating programs described in this chapter.

Goal-Directed Evaluation

A useful programming technique when used in conjunction with generators is *goal-directed evaluation*. By this technique, a generator is repeatedly queried for values until some condition is satisfied. In a certain sense the notion of filters we have just described represents a simple form of goal-directed evaluation. The goal of instances of **FactorFilter,** for example, is to find a value from the underlying generator for which the given number is not a factor. In the more general case of goal directed evaluation, the condition frequently involves the outcome of several generators acting together. An example will illustrate this method.

Consider the problem of placing eight queens on a chess board in such a way that no queen can attack any other queen (Figure 8.3). In this section we will describe how such a problem can be formulated and solved using generators, filters, and goal directed evaluation.

We first observe that in any solution, no two queens can occupy the same column, and that no column can be empty. We can therefore assign a specific column to each queen at the start, and reduce the problem to finding a correct row assignment for each of the eight queens.

In general terms, our approach will be to place queens from left to right (the order in which we assign numbers to columns). An *acceptable solution for column n* is one in which no queen in columns 1 through n can attack any other queen in those columns. Once we have found an acceptable solution in column 8 we are finished. Before that, however, we can formulate the problem of finding an acceptable solution in column n recursively, as follows:

1. Find an acceptable solution for column $n - 1$. If there is none, return **nil,** there is no acceptable solution. Otherwise, place the queen for column n in row 1. Go to step 2.

Figure 8.3 □ *A solution to the eight queens problem*

	1	2	3	4	5	6	7	8
1	Q							
2				Q				
3								Q
4					Q			
5		Q						
6				Q				
7		Q						
8			Q					

2. Test to see if any queen in columns 1 through $n - 1$ can attack the queen in column n. If not, then an acceptable solution has been found. If the queen can be attacked, then go to step 3.

3. If the queen for column n is in row 8, go to step 4, otherwise advance the queen by one row and go back to step 2.

4. Find the next acceptable solution for column $n - 1$. If there is none, return **nil,** otherwise, place the queen for column n in row 1 and go to step 2.

Of course, all positions are acceptable in column 1. Responding to *first* corresponds to starting in step 1, whereas responding to *next* corresponds to starting in step 3. We represent each queen by a separate object, an instance of class **Queen.** Each queen maintains its own position in a pair of variables and also a pointer to the immediate neighbor on the left. A skeleton for the class **Queen** is shown in Figure 8.4. With this skeleton, our eight queens can be initialized as follows:

```
lastQueen ← nil
(1 to: 8) do: [:i | lastQueen ← Queen new ; setColumn: i neighbor:
lastQueen ]
```

Following the execution of this code the variable **lastQueen** points to the last (rightmost) queen.

We have already described our algorithm in terms of finding the first acceptable position and finding the next acceptable position. It is therefore easy to apply our generator paradigm (using the messages *first* and *next)* to this situation. Step 1, for example, corresponds to the following method:

```
first
    (neighbor notNil)
        ifTrue: [ neighbor first ].
    row ← 1.
    ↑ self testPosition
```

Figure 8.4 □ *The class Queen*

```
Class Queen
| row column neighbor |
[
        setColumn: aNumber neighbor: aQueen
            column ← aNumber.
            neighbor ← aQueen
    |
        ...
]
```

Rather than falling directly into step 2 as we did in the informal description of the algorithm, an explicit message *(testPosition)* is used to perform step 2. Before describing the method for this message, we describe the method used to find the *next* acceptable position, which is a combination of steps 3 and 4 in our description.

```
next
    (row = 8)
        ifTrue: [ ((neighbor isNil) or: [ neighbor next isNil ])
                ifTrue: [ ↑ nil ].
            row ← 0 ].
    row ← row + 1.
    ↑ self testPosition
```

All that remains is to test a position to see if any queen to the left can attack. As we have already noted, any position is acceptable to the leftmost queen. Otherwise, we will pass a new message to the neighbor queen asking if it can attack the position of the current queen. If the neighbor queen can attack, it will return true; otherwise, it will pass the message on to its neighbor, and so on, until the leftmost queen is reached. If the leftmost queen cannot attack, it will return false. Notice the recursive use of the message *next* to find the next acceptable position.

```
testPosition
    (neighbor isNil) ifTrue: [ ↑ self ].
    (neighbor checkRow: row column: column)
        ifTrue: [ ↑ self next ]
        ifFalse: [ ↑ self ]
```

We have reduced the problem to the much simpler one of each queen taking a pair of coordinates for a queen positioned to the right and responding whether it or any queen to the left can attack that position. Since we know the current queen is in a column different from the queen under test, it can be attacked only if it is in the same row or if the differences in the columns is equal to the differences in the rows (i.e., a diagonal).

```
checkRow: testRow column: testColumn          | column Difference |
    columnDifference ← testColumn − column.
    (((row = testRow) or:
    [ row + columnDifference = testRow ] ) or:
    [ row − columnDifference = testRow ])
        ifTrue: [ ↑ true ].
    (neighbor notNil)
        ifTrue: [ ↑ neighbor checkRow: testRow column: testColumn ]
        ifFalse: [ ↑ false ]
```

A final method is useful for producing the answer in a visual form:

printBoard
    (neighbor notNil)
        ifTrue: [neighbor printBoard].
    ('column ', column, ' row ', row) print

Putting all the methods for class **Queen** together, we could type the following example script:

```
lastQueen ← nil.
(1 to: 8) do: [:i | lastQueen ← Queen new ; setColumn: i neighbor: lastQueen ]
lastQueen first
lastQueen printBoard
column 1 row 1
column 2 row 5
column 3 row 8
column 4 row 6
column 5 row 3
column 6 row 7
column 7 row 2
column 8 row 4
    lastQueen next
    lastQueen printBoard
column 1 row 1
column 2 row 6
column 3 row 8
column 4 row 3
column 5 row 7
column 6 row 4
column 7 row 2
column 8 row 5
```

Operations on Generators

Chapter 3 discussed several messages that could be used in conjunction with subclasses of **Collection** to form new collections in various ways. The message *select:*, for example, constructed a new collection consisting of only those elements from the original collection that satisfied some property. Thus

(1 to: 10) select: [:x | x \\ 2 = 0]

produced the collection consisting of the even numbers less than 10.

As noted in chapter 3, if all we consider is the message passing interface there is no way to determine whether an object in response to *first* and *next* is merely looping over values contained in memory, the way most subclasses of **Collection** will, or whether it produces values on demand, such as instances of **Interval** and the generators described earlier in this chapter. We can consider both as representing collections (in the case of the first primes program described, even an infinite collection) of values. Just as *collect: select:* and *reject:* operate on collections to produce new collections, we would like some method for operating on existing generators to produce new generators.

Unfortunately, merely making our generator a subclass of class **Collection** will not suffice. The method used in class **Collection** and similar subclasses to respond to these messages is to form a new collection, iterate over the receiving collection gathering the new elements, finally coercing the new collection, if necessary, into being one of the appropriate class. Clearly this will not work for infinite generators, such as the prime number generator. Consider the problem of producing the sequence of values that are one greater than the prime numbers. We would like to be able to do something like the following:

```
primePlusOne ← (Primes new) collect: [:x | x + 1]
primePlusOne first
3
    primePlusOne next
4
```

In order to do this, it is necessary that the response to messages such as *collect:* and *select:* is to construct a new generator which will, when called upon, produce the appropriate elements, but will not produce any values until demanded.

For the purposes of exposition we will divide the operators into two categories: *selection* operators, such as *select:* and *reject:*, which return some subset of the values of the original underlying generator; and *transformation* operators, such as *collect:*, which modify the values of the underlying generator. Of course, combinations and variations on these ideas are possible and are explored further in the exercises. In addition, we can consider ways of combining the sequences from two generators to form a generator for a new sequence. There are three paradigms we will consider. A *dot-product* produces a new sequence by combining the values item-wise from two sequences; the resulting sequence will be the same length as the shorter of the two original sequences. A *shuffle* is an intermixing of the values from the two sequences; the resulting sequence will be the same length as the sum of the lengths of the two original sequences. Finally a *cross-product* is produced by considering all pairs of values from the two sequences; the resulting sequence will have a length equal to the product of the two original lengths. This list is not intended to be comprehensive but merely to illustrate some of the possibilities.

In order to provide a common functionality to the various forms of generators we define methods for these messages in a new class, **Gener-**

ator. We will make **Generator** a subclass of **Collection.** Like **Collection,** instances of **Generator** will not by themselves be useful. However, when classes such as the **Primes** class of an earlier section are made into subclasses of **Generator,** the full functionality of generators can be obtained through inheritance. To simplify the production of examples in this section, assume also that the class **Interval** has been redefined so as to make it a subclass of **Generator.**

In response to each of these messages we will produce an object, which must necessarily be of some class. Let us call the class **AbstractGenerator.** Because instances of **AbstractGenerator** are generators, they must respond to *first* and *next*. Their behavior in response to these messages, however, will vary in different circumstances. One general way of providing a wide degree of flexibility in behavior is to have the actions of **AbstractGenerator** be given by a pair of blocks. Thus the class and methods for **AbstractGenerator** can be simple (Figure 8.5), but, as we shall see, extremely flexible.

Consider first the problem of transforming the values returned by a given generator. A prose description of the operation of *collect:* might be "Produce a value from the underlying generator. If the value is **nil,** return **nil;** otherwise, return the value transformed as indicated by the argument block." This can be rendered into Smalltalk almost directly:

```
collect: collectBlock          | testBlock |
    testBlock ← [:x | (x notNil) ifTrue: [ collectBlock value: x ] ].

    ↑ AbstractGenerator new ;
        firstBlock: [ testBlock value: self first ]
        nextBlock: [ testBlock value: self next ]
```

Figure 8.5   □   *The class AbstractGenerator*

```
Class AbstractGenerator:Generator
| firstBlock nextBlock |
[
    firstBlock: blockOne nextBlock: blockTwo
        firstBlock ← blockOne.
        nextBlock ← blockTwo
    |
    first
        ↑ firstBlock value

    |
    next
        ↑ nextBlock value
]
```

The temporary variable **testBlock** is in this case used to factor out the commonality between the actions taken in response to *first* and those taken in response to *next*. Used in this manner, the block is in many ways similar to an in-line procedure, with the ability to take parameters (the argument list) and the ability to be invoked from several locations. Notice that because blocks must be evaluated in the context in which they are defined, the "temporary" variable **testBlock** is not released when the method terminates but must exist for as long as the abstract generator created in the method exists.

To illustrate the creation of a generator that produces a subset of the elements from the underlying generator, we present the method for *reject:*. The protocol for other methods is similar, and some are explored in more detail in the exercises at the end of this chapter. In general terms, the method for *reject:* must loop over values produced by the underlying generator until either the base generator becomes exhausted or until a value failing to satisfy the rejection criteria is encountered. Again, as in the case of *collect:*, a block is used to factor out the common behavior in the two messages. Note that the value of a block is always the value of the last expression computed in the block; thus the solitary variable **result** in **testBlock** serves to indicate the value to be returned by the block.

```
reject: selectBlock          | testBlock result |

    testBlock ← [:x | result ← x.
        [ (result notNil) and: [ (select Block value: result) ] ]
            whileTrue: [ result ← self next ].
        result ].

    ↑ AbstractGenerator new ;
        firstBlock: [ testBlock value: self first ]
        nextBlock: [ testBlock value: self next ]
```

Using *reject:*, we can form the set of values from one sequence that are *not* elements in a second sequence as follows:

```
        a ← 1 to: 10
        b ← 3 to: 15 by: 2
        c ← a reject: [:x | b includes: x ]
        c print
AbstractGenerator ( 1 2 4 6 8 10)
```

Using the companion message, *select:*, we can generate the intersection of two sequences:

```
        d ← a select: [:x | b includes: x ]
        d print
AbstractGenerator ( 3 5 7 9 )
```

Now consider the problem of combining two generated sequences to form a new generator. The simplest form is the dot product, which takes a pair of values, one from each generator, and produces a new value depending upon this pair. The new generator halts when one or both of the underlying generators becomes exhausted. The method is very similar to that used for *collect:*.

```
dot: buildBlock with: secondGenerator          | y testBlock |

    testBlock ← [:x :y | ((x notNil) and: [ y notNil ])
        ifTrue: [ buildBlock value: x value: y ] ].

    ↑ AbstractGenerator new ;
        firstBlock: [ testBlock value: self first
            value: secondGenerator first ]
        nextBlock: [ testBlock value: self next
            value: secondGenerator next ]
```

For example the dot product can be used to produce a generator which represents the maximum values of two sequences.

```
a ← 1 to: 9 by: 4
b ← 2 to: 8 by: 2
a dot: [:x :y | x max: y ] with: b
AbstractGenerator ( 2 5 9 )
```

The problem of producing a shuffle is considerably more difficult, although intuitively the concept is simple. Consider a message of the following form:

```
first-generator shuffle: [:x :y | some expression ] with: second-generator
```

At each step a pair of values, one from each of the generators, is evaluated using the shuffle block. If the block returns a false value, the value returned is that of the first generator, which is then advanced. If the result of the shuffle block is true the value returned is that of the second generator. When either generator becomes exhausted, the remaining values from the other generator are returned.

For example, a shuffle placing values into numerical order could be written as follows:

```
a ← 1 to: 9 by: 4
b ← 2 to: 6 by: 2
a shuffle: [:x :y | x > y] with: b
AbstractGenerator (1 2 4 5 6 9 )
```

A perfect shuffle can be formed by using a counter.

```
        a ← 1 to: 3
        b ← 10 to: 12
        i ← 0.
        a shuffle: [:x :y | (i ← i + 1) \ \ 2 = 0] with: b
AbstractGenerator (1 10 2 11 3 12 )
```

Placing a constant in the shuffle block will result in a *catenation*.

```
        a shuffle: [:x :y | true ] with: b
AbstractGenerator ( 10 11 12 1 2 3 )
        a shuffle: [:x :y | false ] with: b
AbstractGenerator ( 1 2 3 10 11 12 )
```

Since at each step a comparison must be made between the next values from each of the underlying generators, it is clear that the method for shuffle must buffer at least one value from each. Let the variables *nextx* and *nexty* be the next values from the first and second generators, respectively; then the major portion of the shuffle algorithm can be given as follows:

```
if nextx is nil
    then if nexty is nil
        then return nil
    else return nexty and advance the second generator
else if nexty is not nil and the comparison is false
    then return nexty and advance the second generator
else return nextx and advance the first generator
```

Adding the code to initialize the buffer variables, this is rendered in Smalltalk as follows:

```
shuffle: shuffleBlock with: secondGenerator      | nextx nexty result testBlock|

    testBlock ← [(nextx isNil)
                ifTrue: [(nexty isNil)
                    ifTrue: [ result ← nil ]
                    ifFalse: [ result ← nexty. nexty ← secondGenerator next ] ]
                ifFalse: [((nexty notNil) and:
                    [ shuffleBlock value: nextx value: nexty ] )
                    ifTrue: [ result ← nexty. nexty ← secondGenerator next ]
                    ifFalse: [ result ← nextx. nextx ← self next ] ].
                result ].
    ↑ AbstractGenerator new ;
        firstBlock: [ nextx ← self first.
            nexty ← secondGenerator first.
            testBlock value ]
        nextBlock: testBlock
```

The catenate form of shuffle occurs often enough to deserve a method of its own.

```
, secondGenerator
    ↑ self shuffle: [:x :y | false ] with: secondGenerator
```

We earlier saw how to produce a partial difference of two sequences. By combining this with a catenation, we can form a nonrepeating union of two generators.

```
a ← 1 to: 10
b ← 3 to: 15 by: 2
c ← a , ( a reject: [:x | b includes: x ])
c print
AbstractGenerator ( 1 2 3 4 5 6 7 8 9 10 11 13 15 )
```

Preliminary to a method for forming the cross-product of two generators, consider a slightly simpler problem: using each value from an underlying generator as a base, construct a new intermediate generator; the desired sequence is formed by the catenation of the values produced by the intermediate generators. Here is an example:

```
a ← 10 to: 30 by: 10
b ← a atEachGenerate: [:x | (x + 1) to: (x + 3) ]
b print
AbstractGenerator ( 11 12 13 21 22 23 31 32 33 )
```

The generator *a* by itself produces the three-element sequence 10 20 30. Each of these values is passed in turn to the argument block, which responds with a new three element generator. By catenating together the values from each of these generators, a resulting nine element sequence is produced.

The method for *atEachGenerate:* incorporates by far the most general and flexible use of blocks shown in this chapter and illustrates once more the procedure-like nature of blocks. Two recursive blocks are used to construct each new value. The block *buildGen* takes a value from the underlying sequence and constructs an intermediate generator from it, returning the first value from this generator. The block *testBlock* examines a value from an intermediate generator and either returns it (if it is not **nil)** or produces the next intermediate generator. Note the difference between the block used in the **AbstractGenerator** to construct the first element and that used to construct each successive element.

```
atEachGenerate: genBlock | generator buildGen testBlock |

    buildGen ← [:x | (x notNil)
        ifTrue: [ generator ← genBlock value: x.
            testBlock value: generator first ] ].
```

```
testBlock ← [ :x | (x notNil) ifTrue: [ x ]
        ifFalse: [ buildGen value: self next ] ].

↑ AbstractGenerator new ;
        firstBlock: [ buildGen value: self first ]
        nextBlock: [ testBlock value: generator next ]
```

Once the method for *atEachGenerate:* is defined, it is a simple matter to combine this with a *collect:* to produce the cross product.

cross: crossBlock **with:** secondGenerator

```
↑ self atEachGenerate:
    [:x | secondGenerate collect:
        [:y | crossBlock value: x value: y ] ]
```

The following illustrates the type of sequence produced by the method for *cross:with:*.

```
a ← 1 to: 4
b ← 10 to: 12
a cross: [:x :y | x @ y ] with: b
AbstractGenerator ( 1@10 1@11 1@12 2@10 2@11 2@12 3@10 3@11
3@12 4@10 4@11 4@12 )
```

≡ Further Reading

In the basic form of an expression that can be repeatedly activated to provide a succession of different values, the concept of generators appears in a number of different languages, notably Alphard (Shaw 81), CLU (Liskov 81), MLISP (Smith 80), and Icon (Griswold 83). In most of these languages, however, the use of generators is very restricted. For example, in Alphard and CLU, generators can be used to iterate over the elements of a programmer-defined data structure but are accessible only in the context of a particular type of **for** statement. The use of backtracking and goal directed evaluation in conjunction with generators was introduced by the language Icon, a descendent of SNOBOL4 (Griswold 71) and SL5 (Hanson 78). The language Cg (Budd 82) was an attempt to add Icon style generators to the programming language C. However in Cg, and partially in Icon, generators are still restricted to a specific expression in a specific location. The notion of associating the sequence of values produced by a generator with a named variable or an object, and not with a specific occurrence of an expression, is achieved in Icon by a related type of object called a co-expression. Like generators in Smalltalk, co-expressions are not limited to a single specific expression in a program but carry with them memory of which values have been already produced and can return portions of their sequence in different places in a program.

It is, of course, possible to view generators both as objects producing a succession of values and as an embodiment of an actual (perhaps even infinite) sequence. The experimental language Seque (Griswold 85) is an attempt to deal directly with sequences as abstract mathematical objects rather than as data structures.

In the Smalltalk-80 language (Goldberg 83), the concept of *streams* is in many ways similar to the idea of generators. For the most part, streams use a slightly different interface, namely the pair of messages *reset* (which initializes the generator but does not return any value) and *next* (which is used for both the first and all succeeding elements). The message *do:* is adapted from the streams of (Goldberg 83). An article by Deutsch (*Byte* 81) discusses in more detail many aspects of generators in the Smalltalk-80 system.

EXERCISES

1. Rewrite the primes program from the section on filters to use instances of **AbstractGenerator** in place of **FilterFactor**.

2. Consider the three variables formed in the following manner:

   a ← 1 to: 3
   b ← AbstractGenerator new ; firstBlock: [a] nextBlock: [nil]
   c ← AbstractGenerator new ; firstBlock: [a first] nextBlock: [a next]

   Discuss the similarities and differences among a, b and c. In particular how does each of them react to the messages *first, next* and *do:?*

3. Look at the method inherited for *select:* and *reject:* in class **Collection**. Explain why it is necessary to implement only one of these messages in class **Generator**.

4. An alternative to the *first next* paradigm described in this chapter is the following pair of messages:

   reset   Reset the generator to the start of the sequence, but do not produce a value.

   next   Return the next value from the sequence (which may be the first value if the last message sent to the receiver was *reset).*

   Similarly, instead of returning **nil** to indicate the end of sequence, a message *atEnd* could be implemented by each generator. This message would return true if no more elements could be returned by the generator, and false otherwise. Discuss the advantages and disadvantages of these techniques. Support your opinions by rewriting some of the generators described in this chapter so that they use these alternatives.

5. Explain why the following does not produce the expected result:

    ```
    a ← 1 to 9
    b ← a shuffle: [:x :y | true] with: a
    ```

    Is this a problem inherent with the generators technique described in this chapter? How might it be overcome?

6. Why does the following not succeed in producing a sequence of length 4?

    ```
    i ← (Primes new) select: [:x | x < 10 ]
    ```

    Show how to implement methods for the following messages:

    while: The argument must be a one-parameter block returning a boolean value. Return values from the underlying generator as long as the block evaluates to true. Terminate when the underlying generator is exhausted or when a value is found for which the block is not true.

    until: Like *while:* The argument must be one-parameter block returning a boolean value. Produce values from the underlying generator until the block returns true, or until the generator is exhausted.

    Is it necessary to implement both of these in terms of **Abstract-Generator?** Show how, if a method exists for either one, the other can be implemented in terms of it.

7. The following method in class **Generator** produces a sequence consisting of the first *n* elements of the underlying generator, where *n* is the integer argument.

    ```
    first: limit          | counter testBlock |

        testBlock ← [:x | counter ← counter + 1.
            (counter > limit)
                ifFalse: [ x ] ].
        ↑ AbstractGenerator new ;
            firstBlock: [ counter ← 0.
                testBlock value: self first ]
            nextBlock: [ testBlock value: self next ]
    ```

    Show how to implement a method for the message *from:to:*, that can be used to extract any contiguous set of values from the underlying generator, specified in terms of indices. Extend this to return any set of values for which the indices form an arithmetic progression.

8. Let us say a generated sequence is *enumerable* if every value in the

sequence will eventually be produced, assuming the generator is queried long enough. Consider the message *atEachGenerate:;* under which of the following conditions is the resulting sequence enumerable?

    a) The underlying generator is finite; each of the intermediate generators is finite.

    b) The underlying generator is finite; however, some of the intermediate generators are infinite.

    c) The underlying generator is infinite; however, all of the intermediate generators are finite.

    d) The underlying generator is infinite, and some of the intermediate generators are also infinite.

9. Consider the following scheme for assigning indices to the values produced as a result of the message *atEachGenerate:*. Let $(1,1)$ be the index of the first value produced by the first intermediate generator; $(1,2)$, the index of the second value produced by the first generator; $(2,1)$, the first value produced by the second generator, and so on. If the first intermediate generator produces n values and the second intermediate generator m values, then the sequence of indices produced can be represented as follows:

    (1,1) (1,2) ... (1,n) (2,1) (2,2) ... (2,m) (3,1) ...

Construct a method which produces the same values but in the following dovetailed sequence:

    (1,1) (1,2) (2,1) (1,3) (2,2) (3,1) (1,4) (2,3) (3,2) (4,1) ...

Note that this involves keeping a list of intermediate generators, rather than just the single intermediate generator required for *atEach-Generate:*. Under which of the conditions given in problem 6 is the resulting sequence enumerable?

C H A P T E R

9

Graphics

The Smalltalk language was originally conceived as part of an ambitious project to design a Dynabook. The Dynabook project grew out of ideas developed in the late 1960s by Alan Kay. A premise of Kay's work was that eventually it would be possible to place a computer with power equal to machines that occupied entire rooms into a portable box about the size of a notebook. In the early 1970s, Kay went to the Xerox Palo Alto Research Center (Xerox PARC) and there formed the Learning Research Group. As a first step toward the Dynabook, a goal of the LRG was to develop a programming environment that would be useful and accessible to nonspecialists, particularly children. (One experiment involved teaching the Smalltalk-72 language to a group of children ranging in ages from six to fifteen.[1]) That project eventually developed the Smalltalk-80 programming environment.

The Dynabook was conceived as incorporating a page-sized, high resolution, bit-mapped display and a pointing device that could be used to reference and manipulate images on the screen. In its original idealization, the screen itself was sensitive to the user's touch, and thus a portion of the screen could double as a keyboard. Actual "interim Dynabooks" developed at PARC kept the bit-mapped display but replaced the touch screen with a separate keyboard and a pointing device called a mouse. In the Smalltalk-80 system, the bit-mapped display and the mouse are represented as an intrinsic part of the programming environment.

Unfortunately, for many computer users, access to high resolution bit-mapped displays still represents an unfilled aspiration rather than an everyday experience. One of the first motives in developing the Little Smalltalk system was a desire to provide for a large number of people who might otherwise not be exposed to Smalltalk. To achieve this, it was necessary to design a system that could execute under a conventional operating system on conventional processors using nothing more than conventional character-oriented terminals. Thus the Little Smalltalk project represented a much less revolutionary and ambitious project than the Smalltalk-80 programming environment, but, because of its nature, a slightly more accessible one.

---

1. See "Microelectronics and the Personal Computer" (Kay 77) for a description of this project. The following quote is notable:

"After observing this project we came to realize that many of the problems involved in the design of the personal computer, particularly those having to do with expressive communication, were brought strongly into focus when children down to the age of six were seriously considered as users. We also realized that children require more computer power than an adult is willing to settle for in a time-sharing system. The best outputs that time-sharing can provide are crude green-tinted line drawings and square-wave musical tones. Children, however, are used to finger paints, color television and sterophonic records, and they usually find the things that can be accomplished with a low-capacity time-sharing system insufficiently stimulating to maintain their interest."

Despite the lack of emphasis on graphics in the Little Smalltalk system, it is still possible to produce some graphics functions using Little Smalltalk. The type of graphics capabilities attainable depends on the nature of the devices on which the Little Smalltalk system is executed. For this reason this chapter is divided into three parts. The first part describes routines for simple character graphics. Character graphics require nothing more than conventional terminals but are therefore severely constrained in the nature and quality of the results. The second part of this chapter, line graphics, discribes routines for devices such as the Tektronix 4014 terminal, which can display straight lines, circles, and other line forms. The final part, bit-mapped graphics, develops techniques that can be used with devices which permit the user to set the value of individual pixels (dots). It is assumed that most users will have access to devices for which the first forms are possible, many will find the second level accessible, and a few will be able to experiment with the third form of graphics.

Character Graphics

The primitive operation upon which all our character graphics will be constructed is moving the cursor to a specific location on the screen (usually expressed by a **Point** representing an x—y coordinate pair) and at that location, printing a string. Unfortunately, as with almost all attempts at device-independent graphics, even such a simple operation as this is thwarted by the great number and diversity of terminals in existence. Each terminal manufacturer seems to use a different protocol for screen operations.

One attempt to circumvent this problem is the termlib/curses facility.[2] The name *termlib* is used to describe a database of terminal descriptions. The *curses* terminal output package consults this database, finding the entry which matches the terminal the user is running on. From the description given there, it determines the correct sequence of operations necessary to perform simple terminal output, such as clearing the screen, backspacing, inserting characters, or moving the cursor to a specific location and printing a string.

_____

2. The curses screen package is described in ''Screen Updating and Cursor Movement Optimization: A Library Package'' by Kenneth C. R. C. Arnold. This document is usually distributed along with the Berkeley 4.2 (and subsequent) version of Unix. It is also available under many versions of Unix that advertise ''Berkeley enhancements.'' The curses package actually provides many more capabilities than are used here, such as the ability to do windowing. The interested reader may wish to investigate how these can be incorporated into the Little Smalltalk system. (See the section on windowing in the Projects chapter.)

The primitive operations necessary to support character graphics are implemented using calls on the curses output package. You can discover whether your system has been configured to use the package by sending the message *printAt:* to a string, for example

'hello world' printAt: 10 @ 10

If the result is printed at the specified location, the curses routines are operational on your system.

The primitive units with which character graphics are defined are *forms*, and in particular, so as to distinguish them from the forms we will discuss in subsequent sections, instances of the class **CharacterForm.** A form represents some printable image. We can categorize the operations we will provide for forms into four groups: *definition* operations which describe the basic nature of the form; *transformation* operations which metamorphose the form into a different, but related, form; *combination* operations which combine one form with another; and *display* operations which print a form on the output.

Internally, the class **CharacterForm** maintains an array of strings, representing the text for the form (Figure 9.1). The size of this array represents the height of the form and the maximum size of any string the width. Elements in the text array are defined row by row, using the message *row:put:*. For example, the following sequence:

```
plane ← CharacterForm new.
plane row: 1 put: '                           '.
plane row: 2 put: '     \                     '.
plane row: 3 put: '    |\          --------'.
plane row: 4 put: '    |\ _____/ /___|'.
plane row: 5 put: '    | --   *    //      0'.
plane row: 6 put: '    <--------/ /-----|'.
plane row: 7 put: '              --------    '.
```

would produce a form representing an airplane, which displays as follows:

Figure 9.1   □   *The class Character Form*

```
Class CharacterForm
| text |
[
    new
        text ← Array new: 0
    |
    columns
        ↑ text inject: 0 into: [ :x :y | x max: y size ]
    |
    extent
        ↑ self rows @ self columns
    |
    row: index
        ↑ text at: index ifAbsent: [ ' ' ]
    |
    row: index put: aString
        (index > text size)
            ifTrue: [ [ text size < index ] whileTrue:
                [ text ← text grow: ' ' ] ].
        text at: index put: aString
    |
    rows
        ↑ text size
]
```

Because of the ability to print a string at a specific location on the terminal, instances of **CharacterForm** can also be displayed at a specific location using the following method:

```
printAt: aPoint          | location |
    location ← aPoint copy.
    text do: [ :x | x printAt: location.
        location x: (location x + 1) ]
```

Note the spaces surrounding the characters in our plane example. By using the fact that these spaces will overprint earlier versions, we can use this example to produce a simple type of animation. For example the following will cause the plane to move to the right and down, starting in the upper left hand corner of the screen:

```
(1 to: 9) do: [ :i | plane printAt: i @ (3 * i) ]
```

Reversals, rotations and clipping are among the transformations to modify a form. A reversal is merely a mirror image of a form and can be constructed using the following method:

```
reversed                    | newForm columns NewRow |
    columns ← self columns.
    newForm ← CharacterForm new.
    (1 to: self rows) do: [ :i |
        newRow ← ( text at: i ) padTo: columns.
        newForm row: i put: newRow reversed ].
    ↑ newForm
```

Note that the original form can be "ragged," that is, the rows need not all be of the same width. To insure that columns line up correctly in the reversal each row must be padded with spaces to a uniform length. Unfortunately, only the strings, and not the individual characters are reversed. This can cause odd effects if a great number of asymmetric characters are used. For example, our plane becomes the following when reversed:

Rotations have a similar problem, since an image with an equal number of columns and rows does not display as square. Nevertheless, a rotation can be accomplished using the following method:

```
rotated          | newForm rows newRow |
    rows ← self rows.
    newForm ← CharacterForm new.
    (I to: self columns) do: [:i |
        newRow ← String new: rows.
        (I to: rows) do: [ :j |
            newRow at: ((rows − j) + 1)
                put: ((text at: j)
                        at: i ifAbsent: [ $ ] ) ].
        newForm row: i put: newRow ].
    ↑ newForm
```

A clipping represents a square subportion of a form, identified by a pair of points representing the upper left-hand and lower right-hand corners of the clipping. For example, the clipping from 2 @ 2 to 5 @ 9 of our plane example produces the following:

Clippings can be produced using the following method:

clipFrom: upperLeft **to:** lowerRight
  | newForm newRow rsize left top rText |

    left ← upperLeft y − l. " left hand side"
    top ← upperLeft x − l.
    rsize ← lowerRight y − left.
    newForm ← CharacterForm new.
    (upperLeft x to: lowerRight x) do: [:i |
        newRow ← String new: rsize.
        rText ← self row: i.
        (l to: rsize) do: [:j |
            newRow at: j
                put: (rText at: (left + j)
                        ifAbsent: [$])].
        newForm row: (i − top) put: newRow].
    ↑ newForm

A form can be placed into another form in one of two ways. An *opaque*
overlay completely obliterates whatever was originally found in the area
where the form is being placed. The more useful *transparent* overlay places
only the nonspace characters, allowing whatever was located in the original
to show through. A transparent overlay of one form on another can be
accomplished using the following method.

overLayForm: sourceForm **at:** startingPoint
  | newRowNumber rowText left rowSize |

    newRowNumber ← startingPoint x.
    left ← startingPoint y − l.
    sourceForm do: [:sourceRow |
        rowText ← self row: newRowNumber.
        rowSize ← sourceRow size.
        rowText ← rowText padTo: (left + rowSize).
        (l to: rowSize) do: [:i |
            ((sourceRow at: i) ~= $)
            ifTrue: [rowText at: (left + i)
                put: (sourceRow at: i)]].
        self row: newRowNumber put: rowText.
        newRowNumber ← newRowNumber + l]

Slightly better "animation" can be produced using transparent overlay. Suppose, for example we have defined a pair of forms, one our plane and the second a cloud. Each "frame" of the animation can be displayed by creating a new form, placing the cloud at the appropriate location and then transparently laying the plane over the cloud. With the transparent overlay, the plane will appear to be in front of the cloud, but the cloud will still appear through any blank spaces in the plane form. As each frame is constructed it is printed and work is begun on the next frame.

The exercises at the end of this chapter suggest several other uses for character graphics.

Line Graphics

Some terminals, such as the Tektronix 4014, can draw a limited range of figures, such as straight lines or circles. A Unix interface has been provided to these through the plot(3) routines.[3] In character graphics the fundamental unit was the **CharacterForm.** In line graphics the fundamental object is the **Pen.**[4] Conceptually, a **Pen** can be thought of as a writing instrument for the terminal screen. Four quantities describe the state of the Pen. The first two are a pair of coordinates, describing the current location of the pen. Using the message *extent:to:*, the user can control the range of legal values for pen coordinates. The third quantity is a direction, expressed as a value between 0 (straight up) and 2π (also straight up). The final quantity is a binary state which is either up, in which case pen motions do not produce any output, or down, in which case the pen produces a line as it is dragged across the terminal screen. The interface to the class **Pen** is shown in Figure 9.2.

By a sequence of simple directives, pens can be used to draw various shapes. For example, the following expression:

---

3. Note that unlike the curses routines, which determine the terminal type at run time, the plot routines use a different C library for each terminal type. Thus the terminal type is compiled as part of the executable file. For this reason there may be a different version of *st* created for each device supporting the plot(3) functions. Also note that some other terminal types, such as the HP 2048, may have a C interface permitting terminal manipulation that is different from the plot(3) interface. To use these terminals may require modifying the primitive handler. (See Chapters 11–15.)

4. The class **Pen** is adapted from the Smalltalk-80 graphics kernel, which in turn was inspired by "Turtle Geometry" in the language LOGO (Abelson 81).

Figure 9.2 ☐ *Interface to the classPen*

message	function
circleRadius:	Draw a circle centered at the current location with a radius given by the argument.
direction	Return the current direction of the pen (a number between 0 and 2π).
direction:	Set the pen to point in the direction given by the argument.
down	Set the pen state to down (movement will cause output).
erase	Erase the terminal screen.
extent:to:	Establish the coordinate range for the pen. The arguments represent the lower left-hand and upper right-hand corners, respectively.
go:	Move in the current direction by an amount given in the argument.
goTo:	Move to the location given by the argument, which must be a **Point**.
isUp	Return **true** if the pen is currently up, **false** otherwise.
location	Return the current location of the pen as a **Point**.
turn:	Turn the direction of the pen clockwise by the amount given in the argument.
up	Set the state of the pen to up. When up, movement will not cause output.

```
4 timesRepeat: [ aPen go: 10 ; turn: 0.5 pi ]
```
draws a box:

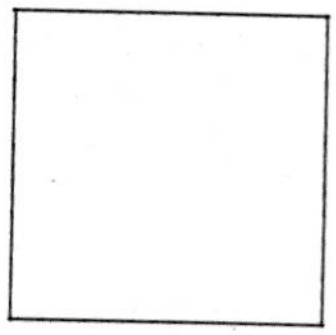

We can try this with various numbers of sides to draw a sequence of regular polygons:

(3 to: 6) do: [:nsides | nsides timesRepeat: [aPen go: 10 ; turn: (2 pi / nsides)]]

Producing the following picture:

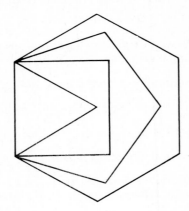

A pen permits one to draw directly on a screen. In order to preserve and manipulate images, it is necessary to store the information about a given image. A first step is to define a class representing an individual line. Instances of class **Line** (Figure 9.3) maintain a starting and ending point and can be instructed to display themselves using a specified pen. In addition, a new **Line** can be created offset from the original.

Figure 9.3   □   *The class Line*

```
Class Line
| startPoint endPoint |
[
    from: sPoint to: ePoint
        startPoint ← sPoint.
        endPoint ← ePoint
|
    + offset
        ↑ Line new ; from: (startPoint + offset)
            to: (endPoint + offset)
|
    drawWith: APen
        aPen up.
        aPen goTo: startPoint.
        aPen down.
        aPen goTo: endPoint
]
```

Figure 9.4 □ *The Class LineForm*

```
Class LineForm
| lines |
[
    new
        lines ← Bag new
    |
    add: startingPoint to: endingPoint
        lines add: ( Line new ; from: startingPoint to: endingPoint )
    |
    with: aPen displayAt: location
        lines do: [ :aLine |
            (aLine + location) drawWith: aPen ]
]
```

A **LineForm** (Figure 9.4) consists of a collection of **Lines.** New lines are added to the collection by means of the message *add:to:*. Like **CharacterForms,** instances of **LineForm,** can be instructed to, display themselves at a specific location on the terminal screen. Also, as with the character case, methods to produce various transformations (such as reversals, rotations by an arbitrary amount, or clipping) and combinations of line forms can be constructed.

The class **LineForm** is useful by itself if the starting and ending points are easy to compute. If a figure is produced as part of a computation using a Pen, however, it would be inconvenient to rewrite the computation merely to save the endpoints of the lines generated. A better solution is to use a subclass of **Pen,** called **Stencil** (Figure 9.5). A **Stencil** is like a **Pen,** but, instead of actually writing on the terminal screen, it saves the lines it would have generated in a form. Because of inheritance, it is necessary only to redefine the single message *goTo:*. Note carefully the use of **self** and **super** to insure the messages are matched to the correct methods.

Using stencils and forms, we could make three copies of our polygon picture as follows:

```
aForm ← LineForm new
aPen ← Stencil new; setForm: aForm
(3 to: 6) do: [ :nsides | nsides timesRepeat:
    [ go: 10 .aPen turn: (2 pi / nsides ) ] ]
penTwo ← Pen new
aForm with: penTwo displayAt: 0 @ 0
aForm with: penTwo displayAt: 10 @ 10
aForm with: penTwo displayAt: 0 @ 20
```

Producing the following picture:

Figure 9.5 ☐ *The Class Stencil*

```
Class Stencil: Pen
| saveForm |
[
    setForm: aForm
        saveForm ← aForm
|
goTo: APoint
        (self isUp)
            ifTrue: [ super goTo: aPoint ]
            ifFalse: [ saveForm add: self location to: aPoint.
                self up.
                super goTo: aPoint
                self down ]
]
```

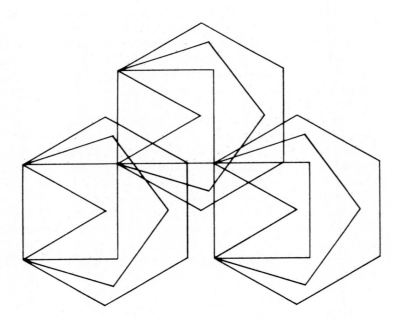

Bit-Mapped Graphics

The most general type of graphics requires the ability to turn on and off individual pixels (dots) on the terminal screen. A device that can do this is often called a "Bit-Mapped Display." Unfortunately, such devices are

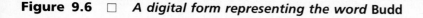

Figure 9.6 □ *A digital form representing the word* Budd

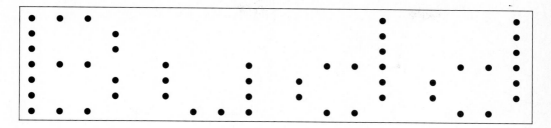

still relatively new and their interface completely unstandardized. There-fore the concepts of bit-mapped graphics can be discussed only in rough general terms, leaving the specific details for the user to work out.

Abstractly, a digital (bit-map) form can be thought of as a two-dimensional array of bits, representing either dots or spaces. Figure 9.6 illustrates a digital form representing the word "Budd." A two-Dimensional form possesses a height (7 in this case) and a width (19).

Internally, this form can be represented in a number of ways. For example, the height and width could be maintained by a **Point** (7 @ 19) and the bit values by a **ByteArray** (#[224 4 50 0 134 64 16 242 94 121 74 120 231 56], for example, if we group bits by eight and read from top to bottom, left to right). Primitive operations would have to be defined to turn on and off a specified set of pixels on the terminal from this representation.

Bit-mapped graphics are very powerful since they can be used to represent anything that can be displayed on the screen. For example, the class **Pen,** described in the last section, can be constructed out of bit operations.[5] The only message which would require changing to support pens is the drawing produced by the message goTo:. We here describe only a portion of the algorithm necessary to support this command. Assume the endpoints of a line have been already normalized, so we wish to draw a line from pixel (fx, fy) to (tx, ty). Assume furthermore that fx is to the left of tx. The following algorithm then draws a rough line one pixel wide.

```
yf ← fy asFloat.
ydiff ← (ty − fy) / (tx − fx).
(fx to: tx) do: [ :x |
    set point at x @ (yf rounded)
    yf ← yf + ydiff ]
```

---

5. The **Pen** described here is extremely crude. For a more detailed description of a better pen algorithm, see the description of the graphics kernel (Goldberg 83).

Depending upon the quality of the output device being used, it may be possible to achieve quite complex effects, such as shading and halftoning. Unlike the Smalltalk-80 system, these effects are only incidental to Little Smalltalk, so we will not discuss the possibilities here; however, an excellent description of the techniques used in the Smalltalk-80 graphics kernel can be found (Goldberg 83[6]).

≡

---

6. The Smalltalk-80 book gives a detailed description of the infamous BitBlt (for bit block transfer) operation, which is at the heart of the Smalltalk-80 graphics kernel. As an indication of the complexity these operations can involve, instances of BitBlt are initialized with the eight-argument message destForm:sourceForm:halftoneForm:combinationRule: distOrigin:sourceOrigin:extent:clipRect:

CHAPTER

10

Processes

The notion of *generator*, introduced in chapter 8, can be viewed in terms of a producer-consumer relationship. That is, the generator can abstractly be considered to be producing some commodity, and the calling routine considered to be a consumer processing instances of the commodity. In a system where either the producer or consumer must directly request action from the other via a message, there are basically two organizing schemes one could use: either the generator process is considered to be "in control" and it calls the consumer process for processing each element, or the consumer process is considered to be the dominant force, calling the generator for each new element produced. These two viewpoints are reflected in the two protocols described in Chapter 8 for dealing with generators.

In the first scenario (Figure 10.1), the consumer is "in control." When the consumer requires a value, it initiates the producer using *first*. Each time a subsequent value is requested, the producer is queried using *next*. Notice that the consumer can follow any desired control flow, but that the response of the producer is given by the same code and is executed repeatedly in response to *first* and *next*. Between calls to *next*, no execution takes place in the producer.

An alternative organization is shown in Figure 10.2. Here, once control is given to the producer via the message *do:*, the producer is "in control." The producer is free to interpret this message in whatever manner it desires, following whatever control flow is necessary. As each element in the generated sequence is produced, the block used as argument with the *do:* command is executed using the value as argument. Between these uses, no execution takes place in the consumer.

Which of these two viewpoints is the "correct" way to view the producer-consumer relationship will depend upon circumstances. They both have their advantages. In some instances, however, a third alternative is preferable. Rather than one process subordinate to the other, they can run

---

Figure 10.1   □   *The producer-consumer relationship, consumer controlling*

	Consumer
Producer	...
	consumer requires a value
	producer *next*
	consumer is suspended
producer produces a value	
↑ value	
	consumer resumes execution

Figure 10.2 ☐ *The producer-consumer relationship, producer controlling*

Producer   **Consumer**

producer started using do:

...

computes a new value
consumerBlock *value:* newValue

(producer is suspended)

                                                          consumer is started

                                                          consumer executes block

                                                          consumer returns

producer resumes execution

in parallel (Figure 10.3). As the producer generates each value, the values are placed into a common container called a *mailbox* or *port*.[1] Each time the consumer requires a value, it retrieves the object most recently placed into the mailbox. A class description for a simple form of mailbox is shown in Figure 10.4. Note that in this scheme neither process initiates the other, and each can execute independently. Because of the symmetry of this relationship, such processes are called coroutines. As long as the sequence of deposits and retrievals meshes correctly, the results will be correct.

If the coroutine technique is to be allowed in Smalltalk, two or more processes must be permitted to execute in parallel.[2] In Little Smalltalk the user can create a new process using the message *newProcess* and a block.

aProcess ← [*some actions*] newProcess

---

1. The term port in this context and many of the ideas used in this chapter are due to L. Peter Deutsch (Byte 81).

2. Of course, on a single processor machine very little ever actually happens physically in parallel, at least at the program level. The term here refers to logical, not physical, parallelism.

Figure 10.3 □ *The symmetric producer/consumer relationship*

Producer	Consumer
producer produces first element	
places element in mailbox	consumer picks first element from mailbox
producer starts producing second element	
	consumer processes first element
places second element in mailbox	
	consumer picks second element from mailbox
starts producing third element	

...

A newly created process does not immediately begin execution. Instead, it is said to be in a *suspended* state. There are four possible states in which a process can be. They are described as follows:

Active   An active process is one that is currently executing. An active process can be temporarily halted by passing it the message *suspend*. It can be permanently halted by passing it the message *terminate*.

Suspended   A suspended process is one that is ready for execution but is not currently executing. A suspended process can be made active by passing it the message *resume*.

Figure 10.4 □ *A simple version of class MailBox*

```
Class MailBox
| holder |
[
    place: anItem
        holder ← anItem
|
    retrieve
        ↑ holder
]
```

Blocked   A blocked process is one that is currently on some semaphore queue (described below). Blocked processes are unblocked by the associated semaphore.

Terminated   A terminated process is one that has either finished normally or been terminated explicitly by a *terminate* message.
A terminated process cannot be restarted, although the object representing it will continue to exist as long as there
are pointers to it.

A newly created process can be directed to commence execution by
passing it the message *resume*.

aProcess resume

The pseudo variable **selfProcess** always refers to the currently running
process. A process can commit suicide by passing the message *terminate*
to **selfProcess.**

The message *state* will return a symbol indicating the current state of
a process. The message *yield* is a no-op (it returns **nil)** but has the side
effect of passing control to the next process in the queue of active processes.
The process sending the message will be restarted again when it reaches
the front of the queue.

The message *fork* is a combination of *newProcess* and *resume* and can
be used to create unnamed processes. Executing processes run in parallel
with each other, and output from two separate processes may intermix in
arbitrary ways. For example:

```
[ 5 timesRepeat: [ 'process one' print ] ] fork
5 timesRepeat: [ 'process two' print ]
```
process one
process two
process two
process one
process one
process one
process two
process one
process two
process two

These are also versions of *fork:* and *newProcess:* which permit parameters to be passed to arguments in blocks.

```
[ :num | num timesRepeat: [ 'did it' print ] ] forkWith: #( 3 )
```
did it
did it
did it

Figure 10.5 □ *A problem with the simple mailbox*

Producer	Consumer
mailbox place: 'abc'	
...	
mailbox place: 'xyz'	
...	mailbox retrieve
	...
	mailbox retrieve

Semaphores

The fact that we cannot predict ahead of time the way in which two independent processes will interleave illustrates one of the pitfalls of concurrency. Consider the sequence of events shown in Figure 10.5. Here input 'abc' is placed into the box, and then overridden without being read. Furthermore, input 'xyz' is read twice. The first problem is easy to fix by maintaining in the mailbox a list of entries rather than just a single item. The second problem is more difficult.

In order to synchronize the actions of two or more executing processes, Little Smalltalk defines a new class of objects call **Semaphore.** A sema-

Figure 10.6 □ *An improved mailbox*

```
Class MailBox
| items counter |
[
    new
        items ← List new.
        counter ← Semaphore new: 0
    |
    place: anItem
        items addLast: anItem.
        counter signal.
    |
    retrieve
        counter wait.
        ↑ items removeFirst
]
```

phore responds to a pair of messages, *signal* and *wait,* and can abstractly be thought of as implementing a non-negative counter and a queue of pending processes. The message *wait* attempts to decrement the counter. If the counter is nonzero, its value is merely updated. If the counter is zero, the currently running process is suspended. The message *signal* either increments the counter, if it already has a nonzero value, or resumes the first process waiting for the semaphore. A semaphore can be created with any desired initial value for the counter by passing a number with the message *new:.*

In the producer/consumer example, one use for a semaphore is as a counter measuring the number of items placed in the mailbox. When the consumer attempts to remove an object from an empty mailbox, it will be suspended until the producer has had time to produce an entry. Such a solution is shown in figure 10.6

Monitors

There is one problem that is not solved by the use of semaphores in Figure 10.6. Suppose the producer and the consumer attempt to access the mailbox *at the same time.* Since both methods may attempt to modify the list containing the mailbox entries simultaneously, the results can be unexpected. Sections of code for which it is important that only one process be executing at any time are called *critical sections.*

The critical section problem can be solved using a binary semaphore. A binary semaphore is simply a semaphore that takes on the values zero and one. Such a semaphore can be thought of as encoding a permission to perform some task. A value of one means no process currently has this permission, and any process that asks for it will be granted. A value of zero means that some process currently is holding the permission, and any other process that requests it will be suspended until the process currently holding the permission relinquishes it. The class **Semaphore** provides the following method for implementing critical sections:

```
critical: aBlock
    self wait.
    aBlock value.
    self signal
```

If two or more processes attempt to execute blocks established as critical sections for the same semaphore, all but the first will be suspended, and each will be restarted in turn as the earlier processes are finished.

Using this facility, our mailbox example can be improved as shown in Figure 10.7. Here two semaphores are used. The first, as before, is a counter and is used to suspend the consumer if there are no elements in the items

Figure 10.7 ☐ ***The mailbox as a monitor***

```
Class MailBox
| items counter mutex |
[
    new
        items ← List new.
        counter ← Semaphore new: 0.
        mutex ← Semaphore new: 1
    |
    place: anItem
        mutex critical: [ items addLast: anItem ].
        counter signal.
    |
    retrieve          | result |
        counter wait.
        mutex critical: [ result ← items removeLast ].
        ↑ result
]
```

list. The second semaphore is used to implement a critical section around the insertion or removal of information from the list. The encapsulation of a data structure in an object which manages its own critical section behavior, such as the mailbox example provides for the items list, is known as a *monitor*.

Dining Philosophers Problem

To further illustrate the utility of semaphores, we will examine a solution to the "dining philosophers" problem. The dining philosophers is considered a classical problem in synchronization, not because of any practical importance, but because it can be considered a model for a large class of concurrency control problems.

The problem can be stated as follows (from J. L. Peterson and A. Silberschatz, *Operating System Concepts*, (Reading, Massachusetts: Addison-Wesley, 1985), pp. 347-348.):

"Five philosophers spend their lives thinking and eating. The philosophers share a common circular table surrounded by five chairs, each belonging to one philosopher. In the center of the table there is a bowl of rice, and the table is laid with five chopsticks (Figure 10.8). When a philosopher thinks, he does not interact with his colleagues. From time to time, a

Figure 10.8 □ *The table used by the dining philosophers*

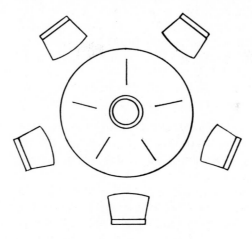

philosopher gets hungry and tries to pick up the two chopsticks that are closest to him (the chopsticks that are between him and his left and right neighbors). A philosopher may only pick up one chopstick at a time. Obviously, he cannot pick up a chopstick that is already in the hand of a neighbor. When a hungry philosopher has both his chopsticks at the same time, he eats without releasing his chopsticks. When he is finished eating, he puts down both of his chopsticks and starts thinking again."

The principal difficulties encountered in a solution to this problem are twofold. First, we must ensure that no two adjacent philosophers can pick up the same chopstick at the same time. This problem is easily solved by representing each chopstick by a (binary) semaphore. A philosopher endeavors to possess a chopstick by passing the *wait* message to the associated semaphore. Similarly, the chopstick is released by passing the *signal* message to the semaphore. Thus the life of a philosopher can be described as follows:

```
[true] whileTrue:
    [ "pick up chopsticks"
      leftChopStick wait.
      rightChopStick wait.
      self eat.
      " set down chopsticks "
      leftChopStick signal.
      rightChopStick signal.
      self think.
    ].
```

While the use of semaphores guarantees that no two philosophers can eat simultaneously, it does not overcome the second problem associated with this exercise, namely that of deadlock. Imagine that each of the five philosophers becomes hungry simultaneously. Each will grab his left chopstick. Since no philosopher will release either of his chopsticks until he has eaten, as each philosopher tries to grab his right chopstick he will be delayed. Thus our philosophers will sit forever, each holding one chopstick in his left hand waiting patiently for his neighbor to finish eating (although his neighbor is similarly waiting for *his* neighbor).

Several possible remedies to the problem of deadlock can be proposed. For example, Peterson and Silberschatz list the following:

☐ Allow at most four philosophers to be sitting simultaneously at the table (so there is always an empty place).

☐ Allow a philosopher to pick up his chopsticks only if both of them are available.

☐ Use an asymmetric solution. That is, an odd philosopher picks up first his left chopstick and then his right chopstick, while an even philosopher picks up his right chopstick and then his left chopstick.

We will use the third solution. Each philosopher is assigned a unique number, maintained in the variable *name*. We will also use this value to print out a message each time the philosopher changes state (for example going from thinking to eating). If the number is even, the philosopher picks up his left chopstick first; otherwise, he picks up his right chopstick first. The method *getChopSticks* describes the selection of both chopsticks, using the method *printState* to print out a record of the change of state.

```
GetChopSticks
    self printState: 'moving'.
    ((name \ \ 2) = = 0)
        ifTrue: [ leftChopStick wait. rightChopStick wait ]
        ifFalse: [ rightChopStick wait. leftChopStick wait ]
```

```
printState: state
    ( 'Philosopher ', name, ' is ', state) print
```

Similarly the method *releaseChopSticks* implements the transition from eating to non-eating.

```
releaseChopSticks
    self printState: 'finished'.
    leftChopStick signal.
    rightChopStick signal
```

In order to introduce a bit of nondeterminism into the solution, we include a random variable. Each philosopher eats or thinks for a period of time randomly determined, represented by the process yielding control to the next process a random number of iterations. Thus if *rand* is the random variable, the processes of eating and thinking can be represented as follows:

```
eat
    self printState: 'eating'.
    (rand randInteger: 15) timesRepeat: [selfProcess yield]

think
    self printState: 'thinking'.
    (rand randInteger: 15) timesRepeat: [selfProcess yield]
```

In order to present a finite solution, we introduce a counter *time*. This counter represents the number of times a philosopher will eat in a day. Thus one day in the life of a philosopher is represented by the following:

```
time timesRepeat:
    [ self think.
      self getChopSticks.
      self eat.
      self releaseChopSticks
    ].
self sleep.
```

Putting everything together gives us the class **Philosopher** shown in Figure 10.9. The Class **DiningPhilosophers** (Figure 10.10) can be used to initialize the chopsticks semaphores and the philosophers appropriately. The argument to the message *new:* is the number of philosophers and that of the message *dine:* is the number of times the philosopher will eat in a day. A representative output for five philosophers eating two times a day is as follows:

Figure 10.9 ☐ *The class Philosopher*

```
Class Philosopher
| rand leftChopStick rightChopStick name |
[
    new: aNumber
        rand ← Random new.
        rand randomize.
        name ← aNumber

    leftChopStick: lchop rightChopStick: rchop
        leftChopStick ← lchop.
        rightChopStick ← rchop.
```

Program Continued

```
|
    getChopSticks
        self printState: 'moving'.
        ((name \ \ 2) = = 0)
            ifTrue: [ leftchopStick wait. rightChopStick wait]
            ifFalse: [rightChopStick wait. leftChopStick wait]
|

    printState: state
        ('Philosopher ', name, ' is ', state) print
|

    releaseChopSticks
        self printState: 'finished'.
        leftChopStick signal.
        rightChopStick signal.
|

    think
        self printState: 'thinking'
        (rand randInteger: 15) timesRepeat: [selfProcess yield]
|

    eat
        self printState: 'eating'.
        (rand randInteger: 15) timesRepeat: [selfProcess yield]
|

    philosophize: time
        [ time timesRepeat:
            [ self think.
              self getChopSticks.
              self eat.
              self releaseChopSticks
            ].
        self printState: 'sleeping'
        ] fork
]
```

```
Philosopher 1 is thinking.
Philosopher 2 is thinking.
Philosopher 3 is thinking.
Philosopher 4 is thinking.
Philosopher 1 is eating.
Philosopher 5 is thinking.
Philosopher 3 is eating.
```

Philosopher 5 is eating.
Philosopher 2 is eating.
Philosopher 4 is eating.
Philosopher 1 is thinking.
Philosopher 2 is thinking.
Philosopher 3 is thinking.
Philosopher 4 is thinking.
Philosopher 1 is eating.
Philosopher 5 is thinking.
Philosopher 3 is eating.
Philosopher 5 is eating.
Philosopher 2 is eating.
Philosopher 4 is eating.
Philosopher 1 is sleeping.
Philosopher 2 is sleeping.
Philosopher 3 is sleeping.
Philosopher 4 is sleeping.
Philosopher 5 is sleeping.

Figure 10.10 □ *The class DiningPhilosophers*

Class **DiningPhilosophers**
| numberDiners chopSticks philosophers |
[
    new: aNumber

        numberDiners ← aNumber.
        chopSticks ← Array new: numberDiners.
        philosophers ← Array new: numberDiners.
(1 to: numberDiners) do:
        [:p | chopSticks at: p put: (Semaphore new: 1).
          philosophers at: p put: (Philosopher new: p)].
     (1 to: numberDiners) do:
       [:p | (philosophers at:
          leftChopStick: (chopSticks at:p)
          rightChopStick: (chopSticks at: ((p \ \ numberDiners) + 1)]
|
    dine: time
      (1 to: number Diners) do:
        [:p | (philosophers at: p) philosophize: time]
]

 **Further Reading**

Many of the concepts discussed in this chapter, for example the notion of mailboxes, are adapted from a paper by L. Peter Deutsch in the special issue of Byte devoted to Smalltalk (*Byte* 81).

The dining philosophers problem was originally stated and solved by Dijkstra (Dijkstra 65). It is discussed in most operating systems textbooks. The version used here is taken from Peterson and Silberschatz (Peterson 83).

EXERCISES

1. Explain why the method for **place:** in Figure 10.7 could not be written as follows:

    place: anItem
        counter signal.
        mutex critical: [items addLast: anItem]

2. Explain why the method for **retrieve** in Figure 10.7 could not be written as follows:

    retrieve
        counter wait.
        mutex critical: [↑ items removeLast]

3. Write a solution to the Dining Philosophers problem in which each philosopher is allowed to pick up his chopsticks only if both of them are available. Note that the easiest way to do this would be to introduce a monitor for the chopsticks semaphores, and modify the values of the chopsticks array only in a critical section.

4. How might processes be used to provide an alternative method for doing simulations, such as those described in Chapter 7? Produce a simulation for the Ice Cream store of Chapter 7 using processes.

P A R T
TWO

The Implementation

CHAPTER

11

Implementation Overview

In order to better understand the reasons for many of the design features of the Little Smalltalk system it is important to first consider what features of the Smalltalk language force the implementation to be different from, say, a Pascal compiler or an interpreter for BASIC. Among the more important aspects of the language, from the implementor's point of view, are the following:

☐ Smalltalk is typeless
There is no notion of a "declaration" of identifier type in Smalltalk. Any identifier can be used to refer to objects of any type and can be changed at any time to refer to objects of a different type.

☐ Objects have unscoped lifetimes.
In an Algol-like language, such as Pascal, variables are either global or local. Global identifiers exist all during execution and can thus be assigned static memory locations. Local identifiers exist only as long as the procedure in which they are declared is active. Since procedures activate and deactivate in a stack-like fashion, a stack (sometimes called "an activation record stack") can be used to maintain local memory locations. In Smalltalk, on the other hand, objects exist outside of procedure invocation (if we take message passing to be the Smalltalk equivalent of procedure invocation) and may persist for indefinite periods of time. Thus, in Smalltalk, a stack-like allocation scheme is not appropriate, and a different memory allocation policy must be used.

☐ Smalltalk is interactive.
In common with implementations for many other modern programming languages, such as APL, B, Prolog, or SETL, Little Smalltalk is an interactive system. This means that not only is the user free to create or modify identifiers at run time, but such basic features as class descriptions may change dynamically during execution. Thus, if run time execution speed is to be kept fairly consistent, no portion of the system may be tied too strongly to any particular feature (such as a class description) that may later be modified.

☐ Smalltalk is a multi-processing language.
As we saw in the last chapter, it is possible for a user to specify a number of different processes and have them execute concurrently. Thus the Little Smalltalk system must make it easy to transfer control from one process to another.

The following sections will outline some of the more important ways in which the design of Little Smalltalk deals with these features. The remaining chapters will then deal with the implementation in more detail.

Identifier Typelessness

In an Algol-like language, such as Pascal, all identifiers must have a declared type known at the time the program is parsed, during compilation. Thus, as memory locations are set aside, either at load time or at run time, it is necessary to allocate space only for the values, since the type information is known to the compiler and code can be generated accordingly.

value

In a typeless language, such as Smalltalk, the type of an identifier generally cannot be determined at the time a program (or class description) is parsed. The conventional solution is to associate with the memory for each identifier a small *tag* that indicates the type of object being held in the value field.

tag	value

In languages where the number of data types is fixed and rather small (such as many LISP implementations), this tag field can be similarly small, for example, eight bits. In Smalltalk, on the other hand, the only notion at all comparable to the concept of type is the class of the object indicated by the identifier; the number of different classes that could be defined is virtually limitless. Fortunately, for every class there is a unique object maintaining information about the class, namely the class object. Thus each object in the Little Smalltalk system can be tagged with a pointer to the appropriate class object.

class pointer	value

To determine if some operation (message) is appropriate for some object, the system uses the class pointer to examine the class (and, via another pointer in the class object, any superclasses) to search for an appropriate method. The next chapter will explain the internal structure of Little Smalltalk objects in more detail.

Unscoped Lifetimes

In Pascal, as in many other languages, memory for variables in a procedure is allocated when the procedure is invoked and can be released when the procedure returns. If, for example, a procedure P calls a procedure Q, the memory for Q will be allocated after the memory for P and can be released prior to that of P (since Q must return before P can return). Thus a stack can be used, with new memory being allocated on top of the stack as each procedure is entered (Figure 11.1).

In Smalltalk, we have already noted, objects can be created at any time and may persist for an indefinite period of time. This calls for a more sophisticated memory allocation protocol. Since physical memory is, on most systems, rather limited, it is important that memory for objects no longer being accessed be reused for new objects. Thus, at any time, memory can be viewed as a sequence of locations, some of which are being used and others unused (Figure 11.2).

The memory manager is thus an important component of the Little Smalltalk system. The memory manager handles all requests for memory and notes when memory is no longer being used. This important portion of the system will be described in more detail in Chapter 12.

Figure 11.1 □   *Static view of Pascal memory usage*

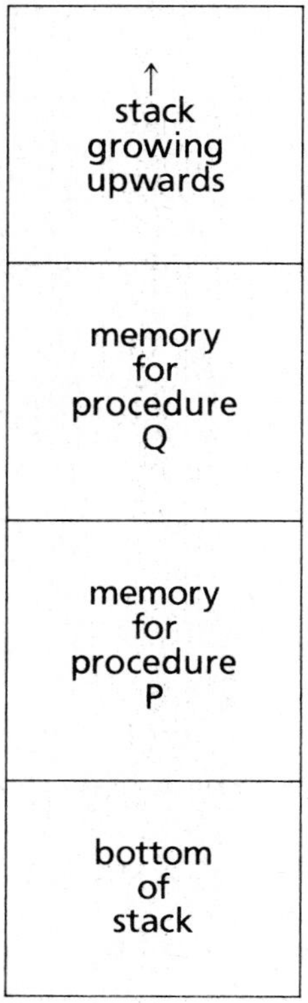

Figure 11.2 ☐ *Static view of Smalltalk memory usage*

memory for object nil
unused
memory for object x
unused
memory for object true
memory for object false
unused

An Interactive System

The internal representation of Little Smalltalk objects represents a compromise between two competing goals. On the one hand, the representation must be flexible enough to provide ease in creation, modification, and removal of objects. On the other hand, it cannot be so general as to greatly degrade efficiency. For example, if methods were kept in their original textual form they could be easily modified. This, however, would seriously slow the interpreter, requiring that it repeatedly parse statements prior to execution.

The internal representation of objects was briefly discussed in an earlier section and will be explained in more detail in the next chapter. An important special case, however, is the representation of objects of class **Class,** which must include a representation of class methods. Note that an interactive system, such as the Little Smalltalk system, must keep a great deal more information around than a batch-like system, such as a traditional compiler. Whereas a compiler can ignore and delete the textual representation as soon as an adequate internal form has been constructed, an interactive system must be able to regenerate the original text, if necessary. This is most obvious in the case of class descriptions, where three options present themselves. The first option is to re-generate a textual class description from the internal form if required, for example, to edit the class description. Another option is to keep both the internal representation and the original source level textual representation in memory. This, however, would require too much memory for small machines. An efficient, although slightly less general option is to keep as part of the internal form of a class object the name of the file from which the class description was read. The only restriction then is that class descriptions cannot be created, but must exist in some file. If the user wishes to edit the class description, the file is opened and edited, using a conventional editor.

Like most interpretive systems, the internal representation of the procedural (or executable) portion of a class, namely the class methods, can be thought of as an assembly language for a special purpose virtual machine. Whereas the real machine on which the system is executing deals with resources such as bytes and words, the virtual machine can deal with higher level concepts, such as stacks, objects, and symbols. The assembly language for this virtual machine is called *bytecode* and is discussed in Chapter 13. The interpreter for bytecodes is described in Chapter 14.

A Multi-Processing Language

The fact that Smalltalk is a multi-processing language produces a number of difficulties. You might think that if Smalltalk did not permit multiple processes, even though objects could persist indefinitely, at least the message passing protocol would exhibit a stack-like behavior. For example, if the message *one* is passed to an object *a,* and the method associated with that message passes a second message *two* to another object *b,* then the second message must return before the first message returns. Thus storage incurred as part of message passing, such as storage for arguments or temporary variables, could be allocated and deallocated in a stack-like fashion similar to activation records in a conventional language.

Unfortunately, this view is too simplistic. Even without multiple processes, the implementation of blocks causes problems. In order to execute properly, a block must have access to the environment (including argument and temporary variables) in which it was defined. Also, a block can be passed back as a result of a message or assigned to an identifier and thus outlive the message in which it was defined. Even in the single process case temporary and argument variables do not necessarily come into existence and die in a stack-like fashion.

The solution is to uniformly apply the techniques of the memory manager to those objects corresponding to values that the user can see, such as identifiers, as well as to internally generated objects, such as those that correspond to conventional activation records. When a message is to be sent, an object of class **Context** is created. A context (Figure 11.3) is an array-like object that points to the receiver of the message and the argument objects passed with the message. The context also provides space for any temporary identifiers or internal parameters (such as for blocks) that will be needed by the message.

A search is then made of the class descriptions to locate the bytecodes associated with the method for the message. Once the bytecodes are found, a second type of object, called an **Interpreter,** is created. The name **Interpreter** is a slight misnomer; a better name might have been **InterpretableMethodReadyForExecution.** Instances of class **Interpreter** point to the bytecodes they will execute, the context they will use during execution, and an interpreter stack used by the virtual machine that is executing the bytecodes (Figure 11.4).

When an interpreter executes a bytecode instruction that involves sending a new message, a new instance of **Interpreter** is created and linked to the existing interpreter, which then becomes inactive until the message returns:

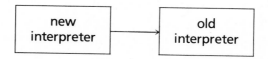

A **Process** is then merely a pointer to an active interpreter. Since there can be many processes, all active processes are linked together (Figure 11.5). The structure of the process handler will be discussed in Chapter 14.

Figure 11.3 □ *A typical instance of class Context*

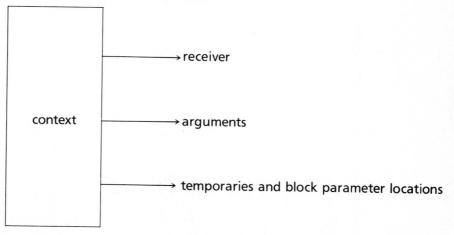

Figure 11.4 □ *An instance of class Interpreter*

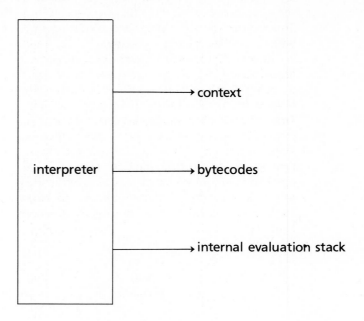

Figure 11.5 □ *A linked list of Processes*

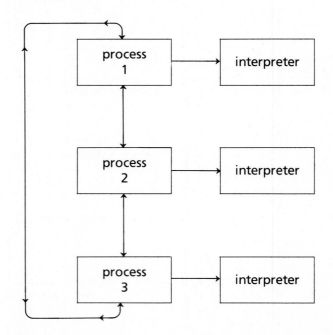

System Overview

The implementation of the Little Smalltalk system, like almost any large software system, is a collection of interacting components. This section will describe in broad terms the various components and their interrelationships.

Figure 11.6 illustrates the major components of the Little Smalltalk system and their control flow relationships. Central to the entire system is the **process manager.** As we saw in Chapter 10, a process is a sequence of Little Smalltalk statements plus the context information necessary to interpret them correctly. The process manager maintains a queue of active processes (recall that multiple processes can be created by using the message *fork* or *newProcess),* insuring that each process is given a fair share of execution time. One special process is the **driver.** The driver reads the commands typed at the terminal by the user, creates a process to execute

Figure 11.6 □ *An overview of the Little Smalltalk system*

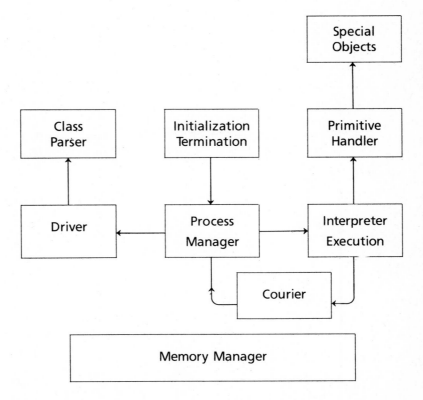

each, and places the process on the queue managed by the process manager. Subordinate to the driver is a special module for reading and translating class descriptions into the form used internally by the Little Smalltalk system.

Internally, Little Smalltalk statements are kept in an internal form called **bytecodes.** The **interpreter** is in charge of executing bytecodes and updating the context for each process in an appropriate fashion. Bytecodes representing primitive operations are processed by a special module called the **primitive handler.** The primitive handler is the main interface between the Little Smalltalk system and the underlying operating system. Also the primitive handler manipulates objects, such as integers, reals, strings, and symbols, for which the underlying representation is different from that of "normal" Little Smalltalk objects. To do this, the primitive manager uses a set of special object routines, each particular to a different type of object.

One of the most common tasks of the interpreter is the sending of a message from one object to another. To accomplish this, instructions describing the message to be sent are given to the **courier.** The courier creates an interpreter to evaluate the message and places it on the process manager queue, suspending the sending interpreter until the receiving interpreter has returned a value and terminated.

Underlying and pervading all portions of the system is the **memory manager.** The memory manager is in charge of creating objects and keeping track of which objects are currently in use and more importantly, which objects are no longer in use and thus can have their storage reclaimed to create subsequent objects.

Finally, the **initialization and termination** module is the routine first given control when the Little Smalltalk system is started. The task of this module is to set the values of certain global variables to the correct initial states, including reading in the standard library of Little Smalltalk classes, creating the driver process and placing it on the process manager queue, and starting execution. When the user indicates that execution can terminate, this routine then cleans up various object references kept in global variables and, if required, produces statistics on memory utilization.

Subsequent chapters will describe in detail the design and implementation of each of these components.

≡

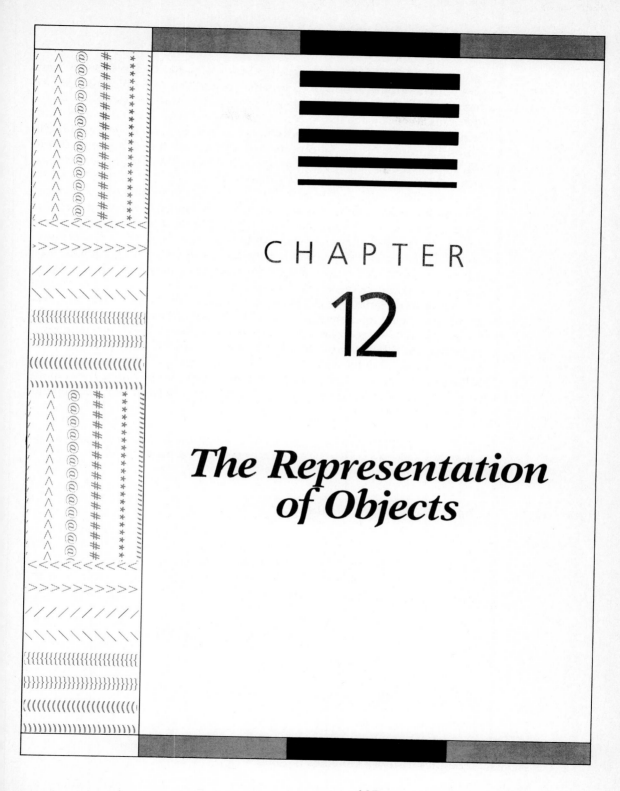

CHAPTER

12

The Representation of Objects

Fundamental to understanding the operation of the Little Smalltalk system is an understanding of how objects are represented internally. This chapter starts by describing the internal representation of most Smalltalk objects. A few classes of objects, the so-called *special objects,* have a slightly different representation since their memory must be able to contain non-Smalltalk values. Examples of special objects are instances of class **Integer** or **Symbol.** Following the description of special objects, this chapter concludes with a description of the memory manager.

As an illustrative example of the representation of objects, consider a class **Aclass** that includes, as part of its definition, instance variables i, j. and k. Assume that class **Aclass** is a subclass of **Bclass,** which defines instance variables k, l, and m. Class **Bclass,** in turn, is a subclass of **Cclass,** which defines instance variables n, p, and r. Finally, class **Cclass** is a subclass of **Object** (which defines no instance variables). This class — superclass structure is shown in Figure 12.1.

Suppose variable **a** refers to an instance of class **Aclass.** Next suppose we pass a message, **dobedo,** to **a.** This message, however, is not implemented as part of the class description for **Aclass** but is inherited from class **Bclass.** When we execute the associated method in class **Bclass,** the only instance variables available to that method will be those of class **Bclass** not those of either classes **Aclass** or **Cclass.**[1] It would be convenient if the representation of instances of **Bclass** (or **Aclass**) did not depend

---

1. Little Smalltalk differs from the Smalltalk-80 language in this respect. In the Smalltalk-80 system the instance variables from class **Cclass** are accessible.

Figure 12.1   □   *The class–superclass hierarchy*

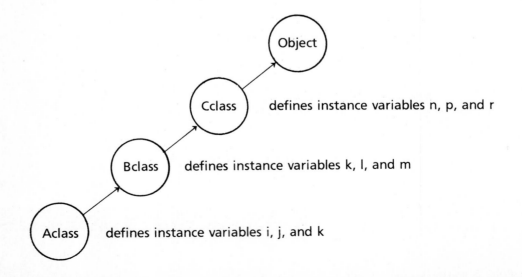

upon the representation of **Cclass,** since at any time the class description for **Cclass** could be modified, even to the extent of eliminating instance variables.

Thus a basic problem in constructing an internal representation for classes and objects is devising a scheme that permits the representation of a method for a class in a manner that is independent of superclasses. For example, how can we represent methods in class **Bclass** so that changes to class **Cclass** do not force us to make changes also to class **Bclass.** The solution in Little Smalltalk is for the structure of each object to mirror its class structure. That is, the object **a** possesses a pointer to an unnamed object that is an instance of class **Bclass.** (Since it is difficult to discuss unnamed objects, let us call the unnamed object *b-object.*) Similarly *b-object* would contain a pointer to an instance of class **Cclass.** Finally *c-object* contains a pointer to an instance of class **Object.** Thus the structure of an object can be described as shown in Figure 12.2. In an analogy to the class—superclass relationship, we call *b-object* a *superobject* for **a** and, similarly, *c-object* a superobject for *b-object.* Henceforth our terminology will be somewhat ambiguous. We will sometimes refer to the complete structure as shown in Figure 12.2 as an "object" and other times use the same term for each of the individual components. The context will determine the exact meaning of the term.

Each of the objects in Figure 12.2 may contain instance variables but only variables appropriate to the class of the object. When creating an object, we need determine only the number of instance variables for the class of the object and need not consider any information contained in

---

Figure 12.2 ☐ *The object–superobject relationship*

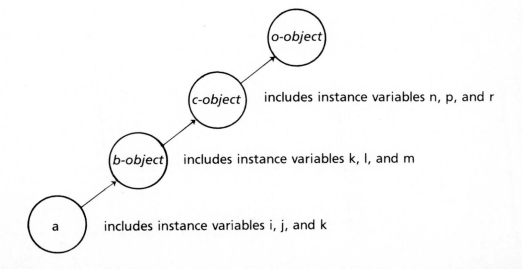

o-object

c-object   includes instance variables n, p, and r

b-object   includes instance variables k, l, and m

a   includes instance variables i, j, and k

the superclasses. The structure of each object in the Little Smalltalk system can therefore be described as follows:

reference count
number of instance variables
class pointer
super object pointer
instance variable *1*
...
instance variable *n*

The reference count field maintains a count of the number of pointers to the object and is used by the memory manager to discover when the memory used by an object can be recovered (when the reference count reaches zero). We will discuss this in more detail later in this chapter. The class pointer points to the instance of class **Class** that contains the description of the class of which the current object is an instance. The super-object pointer points to the instance of the superclass of the current object class, as just described. (As a special case, instances of class **Object** contain a null pointer in this field). An integer is contained in the object indicating the number of instance variables the current object contains. The final portion of each object is a list containing the values for each of the instance variables in the object (which are, in truth, pointers to other objects).

Since C does not generate code to perform subscript checking on array bounds, a single structure can be used to represent structures of any size, as follows:

```
struct obj_struct {
    int                 ref_count;
    int                 size;
    struct class_struct *class;
    struct obj_struct   *super_obj;
    struct obj_struct   *inst_var[1];
};
```

The inst_var array can be indexed arbitrarily to obtain any desired instance variable.[2]

There are two objects that can "represent" a receiver of a message. The

---

2. The purposeful abuse of arrays shown here is not presented as a principle to be widely applied. It is in fact quite easily a source of very inscrutable errors, and great care must be taken to insure that each time we index into the inst_var array valid information will be found there. Tricks of this kind should only be used after careful consideration has removed all more transparent alternatives. And, during development, code where tricks such as this are used must be all the more carefully examined to insure each use of the inst_var array is correct.

first is the object to which the message was actually sent. The second is the internal object which is an instance of the class in which the method executed was found. In the example we have been using, **a** would be an example of the first type, and the unnamed *b-object* would be an example of the second. Both objects are important in understanding the meaning of messages sent to **self** and to **super.** If the method for **dobedo** sent a message to **self,** the search for the corresponding method would begin in class **Aclass.** A message sent to **super,** on the other hand, would require a search to begin in class **Cclass.** The class of the receiver of the original message gives the location of the search for the former, whereas the class (actually the superclass) of the object that actually responded to the original message gives the location of the search for the latter. Thus both objects must be available to the interpreter. We will discuss this more in a later chapter.

Special Objects

Note that the instance variables in the objects described in the last section are, at the level of C structures, merely pointers to other objects. Nevertheless, there must exist some objects in the Little Smalltalk universe with memory containing not other objects but values that mimic values in the underlying machine representation. Examples of such objects are integers, floating point numbers, or symbols. Fortunately the number of such *special objects* is small and cannot be increased by the user without modifying the system. Figure 12.3 lists the special objects in the Little Smalltalk system. We will illustrate special objects by using the example of the class **Float,** instances of which must be able to contain a C "double" value. Since each instance of class **Float** is an object, it must contain a reference count. At the very least, then, structures for class **Float** must contain the following:

```
struct float_struct {
    int              f_ref_count;
    ...
    double           f_value;
};
```

The f_ prefix on the ref_count field and others is used in deference to those C compilers that demand unique field names on structures.

Although the variety of special objects is small, the number of instances of these objects can be quite large, usually far exceeding all other types of objects. Therefore, a concise representation for these objects can reduce substantially the size of the entire data area and, in many cases, dramatically alter the speed of the system or the size of the programs that can be executed.

A basic problem is how to tell if an object is or is not a special object, and, if it is, what type of object it represents. The "obvious" solution is to

Figure 12.3 ☐ *Special objects in the Little Smalltalk system*

Class	Use
Block	code blocks
ByteArray	bytecode arrays
Char	single characters
Class	class descriptions
file	external files
Float	floating point quantities
Integer	integer quantities
Interpreter	interpreters (bytecodes in execution)
Process	processes
String	string values
Symbol	symbolic values

keep a table with the class for each special object. By looking up the class of any particular object in this table we can tell if it is special and what type of object it is. This solution, however, is unworkable. The Little Smalltalk system makes no distinction between classes for special objects and other classes, and, therefore, there is nothing that prevents a user from altering a special value class. If the user does modify one of these classes such as **Float,** then new instances of class **Float** should point to the new class description. Nevertheless, instances of the old class **Float** must also be recognized as special objects. In a single table it would be difficult to keep enough information to recognize that both of these instances were indeed special objects.

    A non-obvious but more workable solution is to use the "size" field to mark special objects. Normal objects will always have a size field that is zero or greater. Since the memory of special objects does not provide for the use of the inst_var array (and, by implication, special objects cannot include instance variables), we can use a *negative* number to designate special objects. Different negative numbers can be used to distinguish the different types of special objects. Special objects are created either by the driver calling C routines or by invoking primitive methods, and thus it is easy to insure that proper numbers are maintained. Testing to see if a size field is less than zero is sufficient to determine if an object is a special object or not. Testing to see if it is a particular value will tell what type of object it is. We can define macros to perform these operations. For example, suppose we choose − 31415 to represent the special objects of class **Float** (the choice of number is unimportant, as long as it is distinct from the numbers for all other special objects). We can define the following macros:

```
# define FLOATSIZE —31415

# define is_bltin(x) (((object *) x) − >size < 0)
# define check_bltin(obj, type) (((object *) obj) − >size = = type)

# define is_float(x) check_bltin(x, FLOATSIZE)
```

The macro is_bltin tests to see if an object is special. Note the use of a *cast* to insure that the size field can be applied to the object. The macro is_float determines if an object represents a instance of class **Float.**

Should special objects contain a class and/or a superobject pointer? Arguments can be made both ways. For the sake of uniformity and consistency the answer should clearly be yes. However, the class description of special objects is not likely to change during execution (in contradiction to some comments made earlier). Since special objects are by far the most common form of object in the system, a small reduction in the memory requirements for special objects may have a considerable impact on the total amount of memory needed for execution. By keeping a table of special object classes and superobjects, we can eliminate the necessity of keeping this information with every object. This, of course, has the unfortunate consequence that *should* the user redefine a class such as **Float,** all floating point values that existed prior to the change will have their classes altered. Nevertheless after considerable debate on this issue, it was decided to use the more space-efficient representation in Little Smalltalk.[3]

Internally, an instance of class **Float** has the following structure:

```
# define FLOATSIZE —31415

struct float_struct {
    int            f_ref_count;
    int            f_size;
    double         f_value;
    };
```

The f_size field should always be FLOATSIZE. All other special objects are treated similarly. The superobject and class of any special object can be determined by a pair of procedures: fnd_super( ) and fnd_class( ), respectively.

---

3. The fact that we wanted Little Smalltalk to run on machines with very limited memory, such as the DecPro 350 or the IBM PC, was a major factor in this decision. Also note that this scheme works only because the superclasses for classes representing special objects do not contain instance variables. In the one case where this is not true (the class **String**), the representation for each object must contain a superobject pointer.

Memory Management

As execution progresses, objects are continually being constructed, used, and discarded. If new memory were allocated each time an object was constructed, the system would very quickly exhaust all available memory.[4] Therefore in the Little Smalltalk system great care is taken to reuse memory as much as possible. A method known as *reference counting* is used to accomplish this. A *reference* to an object is simply a pointer pointing to the object. Each object maintains a count of the number of currently existing references that point to the object. Care is taken to keep these counts accurate. When a reference count reaches zero, there are no remaining pointers that can reach the object, and therefore the memory it occupies can be recycled for use by another object.[5]

Free memory is maintained on *free lists*. A free list is a linear-linked list of free memory structures. When memory for a new object is desired, the free list for the object type is examined first. If a structure is found on the free list, it is removed and used for the new object, otherwise, a general memory allocation routine is called to allocate new storage for the object. When the reference count on an object reaches zero, the object is returned to an appropriate free list.

For normal Little Smalltalk objects (i.e., not special objects), a free list is maintained for all objects containing less than a certain number of instance variables. An array is defined, the elements of the array being the head for a free list of objects of the given size. This array is obj_free_list, shown in Figure 12.4.

Objects are created by calling a procedure new_obj( ), shown in Figure12.4. New_obj takes three parameters. The first is a pointer to one of the special objects representing a class, the second an integer indicating the number of instance variables to be allocated in the object, and the third a flag indicating whether the instance variables should be initialized to the value of the pseudo variable **nil**.[6]

---

4. Virtual memory systems postpone this problem but do not eliminate it. In addition, since objects have different lifetimes, unless some provision is made for reusing object memory on a virtual system, serious thrashing can result.

5. There are two main classes of memory management algorithms, *reference counting* schemes and *garbage collecting* methods. Reference counting has the advantage of simplicity, which is the main reason it is used in the Little Smalltalk system. It has the disadvantage that cycles can cause memory to be marked as being used when in fact it is not. A good discussion of memory management algorithms can be found in (Knuth 81).

6. Careful readers will note a bit of circularity here. The pseudo variable **nil** is an object and is therefore presumably created by calling new_obj. Can **nil** be initialized to **nil?** Similarly **nil** is presumably an instance of some class **(UndefinedObject)** that contains fields that must be initialized to some value. Which comes first, the instance **nil** or the class **UndefinedObject?** This difficulty is known as *bootstrapping* and is indeed one of the tricky aspects of the Little

Figure 12.4 □ *The procedure new_obj( )*

```
# define MAXOBJLIST 100

struct obj_struct *obj_free_list[ MAXOBJLIST ] ;

# define sizeobj(x) (sizeof(object) + ((x) − 1) * sizeof(object *) )

struct obj_struct *new_obj(nclass, nsize, alloc)
struct class_struct *nclass;
int nsize, alloc;
{    struct obj_struct *new;
     int i;

     if (nsize < 0)
         cant happen(2);
     if (nsize < MAXOBJLIST && obj_free_list[ nsize ] ) {
         new = obj_free_list[nsize];
         obj_free_list[nsize] = new−>super_obj;
         }
     else {
         new = (object *) o_alloc(sizeobj(nsize));
     }
     new−>super_obj = (object *) 0;
     new−>class = nclass;
     if (nclass)
         obj_inc((object *) new−>class );
     new−>ref_count = 0;
     new−>size = nsize;
     if (alloc)
         for (i = 0; i < nsize; i+ +) {
             obj_inc(new−>inst_var[ i ] = o_nil);
         }
     return(new);
}
```

The value nsize should never be negative (special objects are created by other means, to be described shortly). The procedure cant_happen( ) is a bit of "defensive programming," designed to trap impossible situations that somehow do happen. This routine is used throughout the Little

----

Smalltalk initialization sequence. The solution involves first creating some objects that do not have a class and using them to create other objects which then can be used to overwrite the first object. Eventually a complete system is produced.

Smalltalk system. If cant_happen( ) is ever called, an informative error message is produced and execution is halted.

After checking that the size is positive, the procedure new_obj( ) next examines the object free list of the appropriate size. If there is some object on the free list, it is removed, and the list is updated. Note the use of the super_obj field as the link in maintaining the free list. If the number of instance variables is too large or if there is nothing on the free list, a new object is created by calling a general purpose memory allocation routine.

When the reference count on an object indicates that its memory can be reclaimed, the routine free_obj( ) (Figure 12.5) is called. Free_obj frees the instance variables used in the object and then either places the object on the free list or, if it is too large, returns it using the system memory deallocation routine.

Each special object maintains its own free list. We illustrate this with the free list routines for the class **Float.** The routine new_float( ) shown in Figure 12.6 takes a C floating point value and returns a Smalltalk object representing the equivalent value. The variable fr_float contains the free list for these objects and is declared to be of type mem_struct, since the fields of the floating structure do not contain anything that could be used as a link. A cast is used to insure that variables are assigned values of the correct type.

Figure 12.5 □ *The procedure free_obj( )*

```
free_obj(obj, dofree)
struct obj_struct *obj;
int    dofree;
{   int size, i;

    size = obj—>size;
    if (dofree)
        for (i = 0; i < size; i + + )
            obj_dec(obj—>inst_var[i]);
    if (obj—>class)
        obj_dec((object *) obj—>class);
    if (size < MAXOBJLIST) {
        obj—>super_obj = obj_free_list[size];
        obj_free_list[size] = obj;
        }
    else {
        free(obj);
        }
}
```

Everytime a new reference to an object is created, we must increment the reference count field for that object. This is accomplished by a macro obj_inc( ) shown in Figure 12.7. Similarly, whenever an object reference is deleted, the routine obj_dec( ) is called. The procedure obj_dec( ) decrements the reference count for the object. If the resulting value is still positive, nothing further needs be done, since there are still valid refer-

Figure 12.6 ☐ *Memory allocation routines for the class **Float***

```
struct mem_struct {
    struct mem_struct *mlink'
    };

struct mem_struct *fr_float = 0;

/* new_float - produce a new floating point number */
struct obj_struct *new_float(val)
double val;
{   struct float_struct *new;

    if (fr_float) {
        new = (struct float struct *) fr_float;
        fr_float = fr_float—>mlink;
        }
    else {
        new = (struct float_struct *)
            o_alloc(sizeof(struct float_struct));
        }

    new—>f_ref_count = 0;
    new—>f_size = FLOATSIZE;
    new—>f_value = val;
    return( (struct obj_struct *) new);
}
free_float(f)
struct float_struct *f;
{
    if (! is_float(f))
        cant_happen(8);
    ((struct mem_struct *) f)—>mlink = fr_float;
fr_float = (struct mem_struct *) f;
}
```

Figure 12.7 ☐ *Object reference increment and decrement routines*

```
# define obj_inc(x) ((x)->ref_count + +)

obj_dec(x)
struct obj_struct *x;
{
    if (--(x->ref_count) > 0) return;
    if (x->ref_count < 0) cant_happen(12);
    if (is_bltin(x)) {
        switch(x->size) {
            ...
            case FLOATSIZE:
                free_float((struct float_struct *) x);
                break;
            default: cant_happen(6);
            }
        }
    else {
        if (x->super_obj)
            obj_dec(x->super_obj);
        free_obj(x, 1);
        }
}
```

ences. If the resulting value is negative, something is wrong with the system, and cant_happen( ) is called. Otherwise the reference count field is zero, and the space is recovered by calling either a routine specific to the type of the object or the general memory recovery routine.

Optimizations

Memory management is a central task in the Little Smalltalk system. Because a large percentage of execution time is spent in performing this task, a great deal of attention has been devoted to speeding up the operation of the memory manager. In this section we will merely mention some of the approaches taken, leaving the details of implementation to the imagination of the reader or to those ambitious enough to dig through the code.

1. The underlying operating system memory allocation routines are slightly more efficient on large blocks of memory than on small blocks.

One scheme is to allocate a large block initially, for example a block equal to 100 floating point structures, and then to carve it up into little pieces and place them on the free list. Almost all free lists used in Little Smalltalk are initialized in this manner.

2. Some constants, such as small integers or the pseudo variable **nil,** occur frequently and seldom change. A single value can be maintained and reused as called for.

3. According to the superobject scheme described in this chapter, all objects should end in an unnamed instance of class **Object.** Since class **Object** does not define any instance variables, we can reduce memory requirements substantially by keeping a single instance of this class and sharing references. A similar trick is used for numbers, which share a common instance of class **Magnitude** and **Number.**

≡

CHAPTER

13

Bytecodes

Like most interpretive systems, the Little Smalltalk interpreter represents programs (in this case, class descriptions) internally in an intermediate representation. The word *intermediate* refers to the fact that the code is between the very high level class description and the low level language in which the machine is actually operating. There are several reasons for this type of representation. One is compactness; the internal representation of a class description can be much smaller than the character representation used by the creator of the class. This is important since, for example, there are over 300 methods defined in the standard library alone. A second reason is efficiency; by translating the class description once into an intermediate representation and thereafter using the internal form, we avoid having to reparse the class description each time a method is invoked. With a good intermediate representation, it will be possible to construct a very fast interpreter.

This chapter will describe the intermediate representation for methods used by the Little Smalltalk interpreter. This intermediate representation is known as a *bytecode* format.[1]

A traditional approach in designing interpreters is to define a *virtual machine* for a simpler language and then translate the high-level language into instructions for this simpler machine. Consider what such a virtual machine might look like for the Smalltalk language. Assume that at run time context information, such as the values of instance variables or temporary variables, will be available in the form of an array. We can arrange for this to be true and can define even the mapping between instance variables (for example) and an index into the context array when the class description is parsed. A convenient form of virtual machine is a *stack-based* architecture. In this style, intermediate results and temporary values are pushed onto or removed from a stack as required. Given these assumptions, the actions we would like to perform are as follows:

1. Access or modify instance variables.
2. Access or modify temporary variables.
3. Access arguments.
4. Access literals. Two special subcases of this are pseudo variables (since the meaning of **self** or **super** is context dependent and cannot be assigned at the time the method is defined), and class variables (since the class may not exist when the method is defined and the meaning of class variables can only be established at run time).

---

1. Note that the bytecode format used in the Little Smalltalk system is different from that used in the Xerox Smalltalk-80 system.

5. Send messages. A special case of this is sending a message to **self** and to **super.**

6. Perform a return of some expression. A special case of this is the implicit return of **self** at the end of every method.

7. Create a block.

8. Perform a primitive operation.

So there are approximately a dozen types of operations we would like to perform. We will eventually define a few more to permit some optimizations, but a limit of 16 different operations is sufficient. In each case the operation can be described as a tag, or opcode (to pursue the virtual machine analogy), followed by some other information. In many cases the other information is simply an integer (an offset into the instance variable array, for example). In other cases the value is more complicated (a literal or a class name, for example).

First let us consider how we might represent an operation such as referencing an instance variable. We have hypothesized at least 12, and no more than 16, different types of operations. So four bits are both necessary and sufficient to represent the operation type. Since we will want to sequence easily through a list of opcodes/values pairs and in these cases the opcodes and values can be represented by small integers, an array of bytes can be an attractive representation. It seems rather wasteful to devote an entire byte to each opcode, since each opcode requires only four of the eight bits in the byte. One scheme, therefore, is to encode *both* the opcode and the value fields in a single byte, placing the opcode in the upper four bits and the value field in the lower four bits. (Each four-bit sequence can be called a "nibble" since it is a small byte.) Pictorially, this can be represented as follows:

width	4	4
field	opcode	value

If, for example, we let 1, mean "access an instance variable," then the instruction to access instance variable number 3 would be the single byte with value l * 16 + 3, or 19.

An obvious problem with this scheme is that it permits the manipulation of only 16 instance variables. Classes can have more, but that is quite uncommon. A simple solution to this, and related problems is to have an "extended size" instruction. This would involve having some opcode (say, zero) which takes another opcode as a value. The entire next byte following this instruction is then taken to be the value field for the extended instruction. Pictorially, the instruction "access instance variable number 37" could be given as follows:

width	4	4	8
value	0	1	37

The advantage of this scheme is that it can apply to more than just one type of opcode, and, furthermore, it allows us to keep the very short description in the large number of cases where the extended form is not necessary. Of course, the disadvantage is that we are still limited to 256 instance variables, but that is a reasonable compromise.

A simple solution to the problem of literals is to associate a literal array with each method. At parse time this array can be defined with whatever literals are needed by the method. The value field for those instructions that require a literal is then just an index into this array.

The following sections present a description of each of the instructions in our internal representation.

Extended Instruction Format – opcode 0

width	4	4	8
value	0	*opcode*	*value*

The low order 4 bits of the first byte are used as the opcode for the next instruction. The following byte (all 8 bits) are taken to be the value field for the next instruction.

Access an Instance Variable – opcode 1

width	4	4
field	1	*index*

The instance variable indexed by the value field is pushed onto the stack. The extended instruction format can be used for instance variables with indices greater than 16.

Access an Argument or Temporary Variable – opcode 2

width	4	4
field	2	*index*

Both arguments and temporary variables are kept in a single array called the *context* (Chapter 11). The element of this array indexed by the value field is pushed onto the stack. As with the instance variable opcode, the extended instruction format can be used for indices greater than 15. By convention the receiver (the zeroth argument) is placed in the first position of the context.

Access a Literal — opcode 3

width	4	4
field	3	*index*

The element of the literal array indexed by the value field is pushed onto the stack. Note that, since the literal array can hold any literal value known at parse time, this works for all types of literals (characters, integer, string, symbol, or arrays) with the exception of classes, which must be generated at run time.

Access a Class Object — opcode 4

width	4	4
field	4	*index*

At parse time, a symbol representing the name of the desired class is placed into the literal array. The value field then contains the index in the literal array of this symbol. During execution the class description corresponding to this symbol is retrieved and pushed onto the stack.

Store into an Instance Variable — opcode 6

width	4	4
field	6	*index*

The current value contained in the top of the stack is popped and stored into the instance variable indexed by the value field.

Store into a Temporary Variable — opcode 7

width	4	4
field	7	*index*

The current value contained in the top of the stack is popped and stored into the position of the context indexed by the value field. Although both arguments and temporary variables are stored in the context, the parser can make certain that no instruction which would overwrite an argument location is generated.

Send a Message — opcode 8

width	4	4	8
value	8	argcount	message index

It is assumed that prior to this instruction the receiver of the message plus the necessary argument values have been pushed onto the stack. The value field contains the number of arguments to be passed along with the message. The extended instruction format can be used for messages with more than 16 arguments. The following byte is interpreted as an index into the literal array. The symbol stored at that location is taken to represent the message selector to be sent.

Send a Message to super – opcode 9

The fields are the same as in the previous message. Note that the object representing both **self** and **super** is the same and is given by the first position in the context array.

Create a Block – opcode 14

width	4	4	8	8
value	14	argcount	argument location	block size

The value field of the first byte contains the number of arguments for the block. If this value is nonzero, the second byte contains the position in the context where the arguments for the block should be placed. If there are no arguments for the block, the second byte is omitted. The third byte contains the size (in bytecodes) of the instructions contained in the block. The instructions for the block follow immediately after this byte.

Special instruction – opcode 15

width	4	4
field	15	value

The value field is used to indicate a variety of instructions that either do not require arguments or usually require arguments greater than 16, and thus would not benefit from the short encoding. These can be described as follows:

value	meaning
1	Duplicate top of stack.
2	Pop top of stack and discard it.
3	Return top of stack.
4	Return from inside of block.
5	Return receiver.
6	Pop top of stack. If it is **true**, skip the number of bytes indicated by the next byte and push **nil** onto the stack.

7	Pop top of stack. If it is **false,** skip the number of bytes indicated by the next byte and push **nil** onto the stack.
8	Skip forward the number of bytes indicated by the byte immediately following this instruction.
9	Skip backwards the number of bytes indicated by the byte immediately following this instruction.
10	Perform a primitive operation. The following byte indicates the number of arguments to accompany the primitive; and the byte after that, the primitive number.
11	Pop top of stack. If it is **true,** skip the number of bytes indicated by the next byte and push **true** onto the stack.
12	Pop top of stack. If it is **false,** skip the number of bytes indicated by the text byte and push **false** onto the stack.

The Representation of Methods

Opcodes 5 and 10 through 13 are used to provide a succinct representation for common operations, and they will be described in the next section. The class of special objects **ByteArray** is used to represent arrays of bytes. Instances of **ByteArray** are created using a syntax similar to normal arrays, with a square bracket instead of parenthesis:

#[17 23 36]

Internally, a method is translated into an array containing two elements. The first element is a **ByteArray** containing the bytecodes for the method. The second element is the literal array associated with the method. Thus, for example, the method:

isEmpty
   ↑ self size = 0

would be represented in the bytecode format in the following way:

highBits	lowBits	Meaning
2	1	Push the first element of context (self) onto stack.
8	0	Send a message with no arguments.
	1	Message is at first location of literal array.
4	2	Push the literal in location two onto stack.
8	1	Send a message with one argument.

	3	Message is in third location of literal array.
15	3	Return top of stack.

literal array
#(# size 0 # =)

This would be rendered entirely in Smalltalk format as follows:

#(#[33 128 1 66 129 3 243] #(#size 0 # =))

Optimizations

There are two classes of optimizations. The first type reduces the size of the internal representation of methods. Since the standard Smalltalk library is represented in the internal form, and is of considerable size, any savings in size will greatly decrease the amount of memory that must be devoted to storing the standard library and thus increase the size of programs the user can execute. The second class of optimizations increases the speed of the Little Smalltalk system, while possibly limiting generality.

To understand why more succinct representation is necessary, consider the representation of the method for *isEmpty* described in the last section. Some constants, such as 0, 1, or **nil,** occur with much greater regularity than do any other constants. One way to reduce size, therefore, is to encode with a special opcode a few of the most common integers, classes, and the pseudo variables. This is essentially trading a small increase in the complexity of the interpreter for a reduction in the size of many methods. The value field of this special opcode should be able to represent the most common integers (−1, 0, 1, 2), common classes **(Array, Collection),** and the pseudo variables **nil, true, false** and **smalltalk.** We will use opcode 5 for this purpose. The following table shows how each of the values is interpreted.

0–9	The integer value.
10	The integer − 1.
11	The pseudo variable **true.**
12	The pseudo variable **false.**
13	The pseudo variable **nil.**
14	The pseudo variable **smalltalk.**
15	The pseudo variable **selfProcess.**
30	One of the classes **Array, Arrayedcollection, Bag, Block, Boolean, ByteArray, Char, Class, Collection, Complex, Dictionary, False,**

File, Float, Integer, Interpreter, Interval, KeyedCollection, Magnitude, Number, Object, Point, Radian, Random, SequenceableCollection, Set, String, Symbol, True, or **UndefinedObject**

Note that the class constants have value fields greater than 16 and thus must use the extended instruction form. Nevertheless, there is still a net size reduction since these constants are much less common than the integer values, and the form still eliminates the need for a position in the literals array.

In a similar fashion, when we examine the bytecode representation of a few classes, we note that some messages occur with much greater frequency than others. For example, in the class **Collection** the messages **new new: value: do: class** and **error:** comprise almost a third of all messages relayed. The distribution of messages sent will, of course, differ from class to class, but the following messages seem to be most common:

unary messages
new isNil notNil size class value first next print printString strictlyPositive currentKey
binary and binary keyword messages
new: at: to: do: value: = = ~~ timesRepeat: whileTrue: whileFalse: ifTrue: ifFalse: error: add: coerce: removeKey: addFirst: addLast: reverseDo: addAll: addAllLast: occurrencesOf: remove: binaryDo: keysDo: inRange:
arithmetic messages
+ − * \ \ bitShift: bitAnd: bitOr: < < = = ~= >= >
ternary keyword messages
at:put: ifTrue:ifFalse: ifFalse:ifTrue: value:value: to:by: at:ifAbsent: indexOf:ifAbsent: inject:into: remove:ifAbsent: removeKey:ifAbsent:

A very powerful scheme for reducing the size of the internal bytecode representation of many methods is to encode the sending of these common messages by a single instruction, using the value field to indicate which instruction is desired. Note that this does not alter the meaning of the message or the way in which the message is processed by the receiver; it merely reduces the size of the bytecodes and of the literal arrays. We will use opcode 10 to represent unary messages, opcode 11 for binary messages, opcode 12 for arithmetic messages, and opcode 13 for ternary keyword messages.

If we use these new opcodes, the bytecode representation for **isEmpty** becomes the following:

highBit	lowBit	Meaning
2	1	Push the first element of context (self) onto stack.
10	4	Send unary message "size."
5	0	Push constant 0.

| 12 | 10 | Send arithmetic message "=." |
| 15 | 3 | Return top of stack. |

literal array
#( )

So the size of the bytecode array has been reduced from 7 to 5 and, more importantly, the literal array has been eliminated altogether.

Dynamic Optimizations

The optimizations we have been considering so far have been concerned with reducing the *size* of the internal representation. An even more important type of optimization is concerned with increasing the *speed* of the Smalltalk system. The next section will consider several of these optimizations.

A great percentage of all messages processed by the Smalltalk system are represented by *ifTrue:*, *ifFalse:*, or their combinations. Conditionals and loops can be implemented using nothing more than message passing. While this contributes to the simplicity and elegance of the Smalltalk language, from a practical point of view a considerable amount of time is being needlessly used by the system in the overhead involved in message passing.

One scheme that improves the speed of the Smalltalk system is to process conditionals and some loops with in-line code.[2] Consider the sequence of actions to be performed in a conditional expression:

(3 < 7) ifTrue: [9]

In the process of interpreting this expression, the boolean expression would be evaluated and pushed onto the stack. The top element of the stack would then be removed, and the message *ifTrue:* would be sent to it along with a block argument. Either the block would be evaluated and its result returned or **nil** would be returned by the appropriate subclass of **Boolean.** In either case, the result would be pushed back onto the stack.

---

2. There is, of course, a great philosophical debate concerning whether this is desirable. According to some, in Smalltalk the user should be able to change arbitrarily the meaning of any message, interchanging the meanings of **ifTrue:** and **ifFalse:** for example. Furthermore, since there is no notion of types in Smalltalk, the parser cannot be certain that the recipient of any **ifTrue:** or **ifFalse:** message will be an instance of **Boolean.** In some other class, the meanings of these messages could be radically different. Nevertheless, the speed increases are so dramatic that some compromise must be made between maintaining the elegance and increasing the efficiency of the language.

Instead of using message passing, the interpreter can simulate these actions by using a "skip" instruction, called "skip on false." The value field of this instruction encodes the number of bytes to skip. The meaning of this instruction would be to pop and examine the top of the stack, and, if it is **true,** the instruction terminates and the next bytecode is examined. If, on the other hand, the top of the stack is not **true,** the value **nil** is pushed onto the stack and the location counter is incremented by the amount in the value field. There is a similar "skip on true" instruction. The body of the argument block can then be placed immediately after the skip instruction without creating a block.

Unfortunately, there are no remaining opcodes. Using opcode 15 we therefore define skip on true and skip on false to be special instructions. The following byte is then taken to be the value field, just as it is in the extended instruction format. Note that even with this format, the representation of a conditional is still shorter than the previous representation using blocks and message passing.

Given this scheme, the internal representation of our example would be as follows:

highBit	lowBit	Meaning
5	3	Push the constant 3 onto the stack.
5	7	Push the constant 7.
12	8	Send the message # <.
15	7	Skip on **false.**
	1	Amount to skip.
5	9	Push the constant 9 onto the stack.
15	2	return top of stack

The implementation of the logical connectives **and:** and **or:** is similar to that of conditionals, except that, instead of pushing **nil** onto the stack when a skip is taken, either **true** or **false** is used. To accomplish this another pair of special instructions, *and-skip* or *or-skip,* is used.

Finally by introducing another pair of instructions, which merely branch forward or backward by a specified amount, it is possible to encode **whileTrue:** or **whileFalse:.** The statement

[*block one*] **whileTrue:** [*block two*]

can be represented internally as

bytecode representation of block one
skip on false
bytecode representation of block two
skip back to the beginning of block one

C H A P T E R

14

The Process Manager

As Chapters 10 and 11 noted, the process manager is a central component in the Little Smalltalk system. Acting as a controller, the process manager schedules the different tasks to be performed and insures that every process is given a fair share of execution. This chapter describes the interface between the process manager and the rest of the Little Smalltalk system, and it explains the tasks the various routines perform.

In a certain sense, the process manager can be thought of as an abstract datatype manipulating a circularly (and doubly) linked list of process objects (instances of class **Process**). There is a global variable, *running-Process,* that points to the process currently being given control of execution. Each process points to a linked list of interpreters. The interpreter indicated by *runningProcess* points to the bytecodes, and it is the bytecodes that are actually being executed at any time.[1] This situation is shown in Figure 14.1. The doubly linked list controlled by the process manager is known as the *process queue.*

---

1. Except when the current interpreter is the *driver,* which we will describe shorty. In the Little Smalltalk system, the actions of the driver are controlled by C code and not by bytecodes.

Figure 14.1 □ *The process queue*

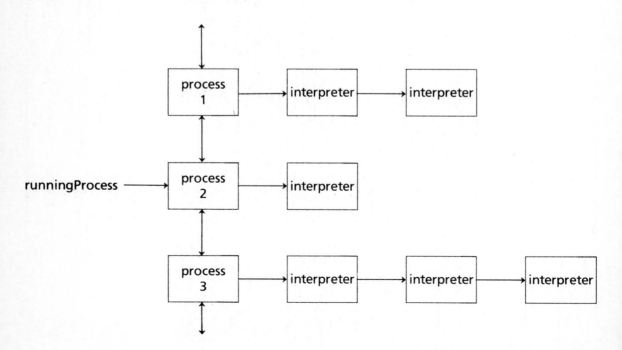

Processes (instances of class **Process**) are special objects and thus can have an internal structure different from other types of objects. The internal C structure of a process is shown in Figure 14.2. The global variable *runningProcess* has already been described. A second variable, *current Process*, is slightly different. The variable *currentProcess* is guaranteed always to point to a process that is on the process queue. If the currently running process becomes terminated, the value of *runningProcess* will not change until control is returned to the process manager; however, the value of *currentProcess* will be moved to the next value in the process chain.

Processes can exist without being on the process queue. Passing the message *newProcess* to a block, for example, creates a process but does not schedule it for execution. Processes are said to be in one of four *states*. These states are:

Active   An active process is one that is on the process queue and will be scheduled for execution.

Figure 14.2   □   *The internal representation of processes*

```
struct process_struct {
    int                     p_ref_count;
    int                     p_size;
    struct interp_struct    *interp;
    int                     p_state;
    struct process_struct   *next;
    struct process_struct   *prev;
    } ;

extern struct process_struct *runningProcess;

extern struct process_struct *currentProcess;

extern struct obj_struct *o_drive;

# define is_driver(x) (x_drive = = (object *) x)

/* process states */

# define ACTIVE          0
# define SUSPENDED       1
# define READY           ˜ SUSPENDED
# define BLOCKED         2
# define UNBLOCKED       ˜ BLOCKED
# define TERMINATED      4
```

Figure 14.3   □   *Process manager interface*

init_process( )	create initial process queue
start_execution ( )	start process manager
link_to_process(anInterpreter)	change interpreter link on current processs
cr_process(anInterpreter)	create a new process
flush_processes( )	remove all remaining processes from queue
set_state(aProcess, state)	set the state on the given process

Suspended A suspended process is not on the process queue but can be scheduled for later execution by passing it the message *resume*. Newly created processes using the *newProcess* message are initially in the suspended state.

Blocked A process can be blocked by a semaphore (see Chapter 10). Like a suspended process, a blocked process is not scheduled for execution. A blocked process may be restarted by the blocking semaphore.

Terminated A terminated process is one that has halted either because it finished execution or because it received an explicit *terminate* message. A terminated process cannot be restarted.

A process that is not suspended is said to be *ready*. A process that is not blocked is said to be *unblocked*. In terms of C subroutine calls, the interface to the process manager is shown in Figure 14.3. The next section will describe the purpose of each routine by going through a typical sequence of calls.

Initially, when the Little Smalltalk system is started, there are no objects on the process queue. The initialization module creates an interpreter object (an instance of class **Interpreter**). This special interpreter is known as the *driver*. It is unique because, instead of having its actions controlled by bytecodes, the actions of the driver are produced by a C subroutine that reads commands from the terminal and creates other interpreters to execute them. Internally, the driver is pointed to by a global variable named *o_drive*.

Figure 14.4 □ *Routines for performing process initialization*

```
/* init_process – initialize the process module */
init_process ( )
{       struct process_struct *p;
        int i;

        /* make the process associated with the driver */
        currentProcess = cr_process(o_drive);
        assign(currentProcess –>next, currentProcess);
        assign(currentProcess –>prev, currentProcess);
        currentProcess –>p_state = ACTIVE;
{

/* cr_process – create a new process with the given interpreter */
struct process_struct *cr_process (anInterpreter)
struct interp_struct *anInterpreter;
{       struct process_struct *new;

        /* get a process either from the free list or from memory */
    if (fr_process) {
        new = (process *) fr_process;
        fr_process = fr_process –>next;
    }
    else
        new = structalloc(process_struct);

    new –>p_ref_count = 0;
    new –>p_size = PROCSIZE;

    sassign(new –>interp, anInterpreter);
    new –>p_state = SUSPENDED;
    sassign(new –>next, (process *) o_nil);
    sassign(new –>prev, prev, (process *) o_nil);

    return(new);
}
```

The initialization module calls init_process( ), which in turn calls cr_process( ) to create a new process (Figure 14.4). The procedure init_process( ) then creates the initial process queue, with the single process and interpreter, as follows:

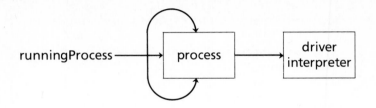

The initialization code then calls start_execution( ). The procedure start_execution( ) loops over the process queue and for the remainder of execution will select items from the process queue and execute them (Figure 14.5). The flag *atomcnt* is used to provide "atomic" (i.e., uninterruptible) execution and will be described shortly. When the user indicates there are no further commands (by typing control—D), start_execution( ) will return to the initialization routine. The initialization routine will call flush_processes( ), which will remove any remaining processes from the process queue and execution will halt (Figure 14.6).

Before that happens, however, it is likely the user will type a number of commands. When the driver is given control (via test_driver( ), as shown

---

Figure 14.5   □   *The main execution loop*

```
/* start_execution - main execution loop */
start_execution ( )
{    struct interp_struct *presentInterpreter;

     atomcnt = 0;
     while (1) {
         /* advance to the next process unless atomic action flag is on */
         if (!atomcnt)
             runningProcess = currentProcess = currentProcess—>next;

         if (! is_driver(runningProcess—>interp)) {
         /* not the driver, resume executing the bytecodes */
         sassign(presentInterpreter, runningProcess—>interp);
         resume(presentInterpreter);
         }
     /* test driver is passed 1 if it is the only process
         or if the atomic action flag is enabled */
     else if (! test_driver((currentProcess = = currentProcess—>next) || (atomcnt > 0)))
         break;
     }
}
```

Figure 14.6 □ *Process termination*

```
/* flush_processes — flush out any remaining process from queue */
flush_processes ( )
{
    while (currentProcess != currentProcess->next)
        remove_process(currentProcess);
    /*prev link and next link should point to the same place now.
        In order to avoid having memory recovered while we are
        manipulating pointers, we increment reference count, then change
        pointers, then decrement reference count */

    obj_inc((object *) currentProcess);
    safeassign(currentProcess->prev,(process *) o_nil);
    safeassign(currentProcess->next, (process *) o_nil;
    obj_dec((object *) currentProcess);
}

/* remove_process - remove a process from process queue */
static remove_process (aProcess)
process *aProcess;
{
    if (aProcess = = aProcess->next)
        cant_happen(15);           /* removing last active process */

    /* currentProcess must always point to a process that is on the process queue, make
sure this remains true */

    if (aProcess = = currentProcess)
        currentProcess = currentProcess->prev;

    obj_inc((object *) currentProcess); obj_inc((object *) aProcess);
    safeassign(aProcess->next->prev, aProcess->prev);
    safeassign(aProcess->prev->next, aProcess->next);
    obj_dec((object *) currentProcess); obj_dec((object *) aProcess);
}
```

in Figure 14.5; the procedure test_driver( ) will be described in the next section) it waits for a command to be entered at the terminal. When the user has typed a command, a new instance of **Interpreter** is created to evaluate it. (The next chapter will discuss how interpreters are created and executed in response to messages). The driver sets a pointer in the new interpreter to point back to itself and then calls link_to_process( ), giving the new interpreter as argument.

The procedure link_to_process( ) changes the interpreter pointer on the currently executing process (the one pointed to by *runningProcess*) to be the argument (Figure 14.7). Thus, we have the following picture:

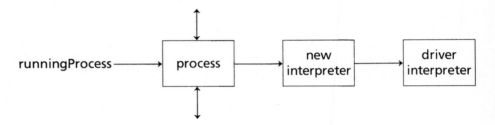

Control then returns to start_execution( ) which, if there were other processes on the queue, would give control to the next process. If there are no other ready processes, the newly created interpreter is given control.

Suppose the method being executed by the interpreter requires a message to be sent. The interpreter signals the courier that a message is required. After determining the recipient of the message, the courier creates a new instance of **Interpreter** to respond to the message and links this interpreter to the sending interpreter. The courier then calls link_to_process( ) to modify the current processes interpreter chain, giving us the following picture:

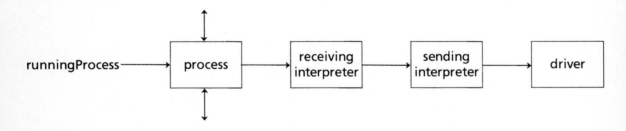

Figure 14.7 □ *The procedure link_to_process*

```
/* link_to_process – change the interpreter for the current process */
link_to_process (anInterpreter)
struct interp_struct *anInterpreter;
{    struct obj_struct *temp;

     safeassign(runningProcess—>interp, anInterpreter);
}
```

The execution of a block (generated by sending the message *value* to an instance of class **Block**) causes a similar sequence of events. A new interpreter is created to execute the statements within the block and then is linked into the current interpreter chain.

When the interpreter encounters a bytecode indicating that a return should be performed, it again calls link_to_process( ); this time however, it passes as argument the interpreter to which control is being returned.

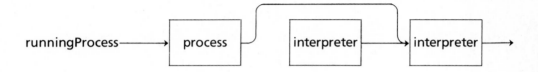

A return from within a block is slightly more complicated because the return must take place from the context in which the block was defined. This context corresponds to an interpreter that may be several positions higher in the interpreter chain. A search is made of the interpreter chain until the correct interpreter is found, and then a return is performed from that location.

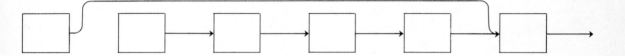

Passing the message *newProcess* to a block causes both a new interpreter and a new process to be created. Unlike the original interpreter chain, the interpreter chain for this new process ends not with the driver, but simply with a null pointer for the calling interpreter. Passing the message *resume* to this new process will place the process on the process queue. When an interpreter chain ending in a null pointer is terminated (for example, by finishing execution) the assoociated process is removed from the process queue. The message *fork* passed to a block is simply a combination of *newProcess* and *resume*.

The final procedure describe in Figure 14.3, set_state( ), is used by the classes **Process** and **Semaphore** (via primitives) to insert or remove processes from the process queue and to terminate processes in error conditions (attempting to return from a block when the creating context is no longer in existence, for example). The procedure set_state( ) is shown in Figure 14.8. Because the classes **Semaphore** and **Process** themselves manipulate the process queue, there is the potential for dangerous interaction should the process queue change while a method in one of these classes is

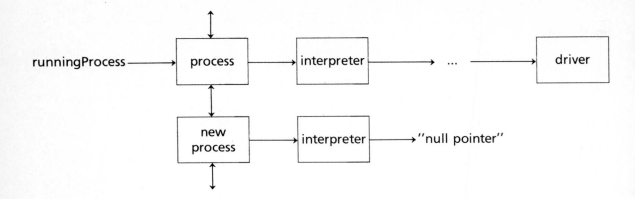

executing. For this reason, there is a flag called the *atomic action flag* that can be set by processes. If the atomic action flag is set by invoking the proper primitive no other process will be given control of execution until the atomic action flag is reset. Thus the class **Semaphore,** for example, will enable atomic actions, insert or delete a process from the process queue, and disable atomic actions. In terms of the process management routines, atomic actions are controlled by the global variable *atomcnt* (Figure 14.5).

The Driver

The structure of the driver module is shown in Figure 14.9. The interface to this module is through the single procedure test_driver( ),[2] which, as we saw in Figure 14.5, was called by the start up routine. The procedure test_driver( ) is called by the process manager to determine if a command has been entered by the user at the keyboard. To do this, test_driver( ) calls upon the procedure line_grabber( ). The line grabber routine buffers characters typed by the user until a complete line has been entered. When the line grabber indicates that a complete line has been entered (by returning a nonzero value), the first character of the line is examined by the test_driver( ) routine. If the first character is a right parentheses, the line is assumed to represent a system directive and is passed to the command module for processing. See Figure 14.10.

The command module examines the second character of the line to determine the command type and then processes the command. This may have the side effect of altering the location from which the line grabber

---

2. This is not quite true. The initialization module uses some of the subroutines from the commands submodule during initialization, for example, to read in the standard library.

Figure 14.8 □ *The procedure set_state( )*

```
/* set_state - set the state on a process, which may involve inserting or
removing it from the process queue */
int set_state (aProcess, state)
struct process_struct *aProcess;
int state;
{
    switch (state) {
        case BLOCKED:
        case SUSPENDED:
        case TERMINATED:
            if (aProcess—>p_state = = ACTIVE)
                remove_process(aProcess);
            aProcess—>p_state | = state;
            break;

        case READY:
            case UNBLOCKED:
            if ((aProcess—>p_state^state) = = ~ACTIVE)
                schedule_process(aProcess);
            aProcess—>p_state &= state;
            break;

        case CUR_STATE:
            break;
        default:
            cant_happen(17);
        }
    return(aProcess—>p_state);
}
```

reads input (in the case of the)i,)e and)r commands, for example), or of totally changing the values in memory (for the)l command. The)i command will generate a new Unix process to parse the class description given in the command and then change the file examined by the line grabber to be the output of the class parser. This will be described in more detail in the next section.

If the line returned by the line grabber is not a command line, it is passed to the command line parser for decoding. The task of the parser is to decipher the command line and produce an interpreter that will have the effect of performing the actions desired by the user. To accomplish

Figure 14.9 ☐ *Structure of the driver module*

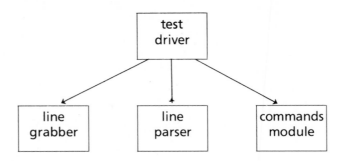

this, a simple recursive descent parser is used. If no errors are found during parsing, the parser calls upon the interpreter module to create a new interpreter and then calls link_to_process( ) to place the interpreter onto the process queue, as described in the last section.

The sources for the line_grabber, the parser, the lexical commands module, and the class parser described in the next section will not be presented here since they are quite lengthy.

The Class Parser

Class descriptions are handled in a rather novel way in the Little Smalltalk system. Instead of complicating the driver by requiring it to read and understand the syntax of classes, the system creates a separate Unix process that parses the class descriptions and translates them into sequences of simple Little Smalltalk statements. Since the class parser lives in its own Unix process, its size does not increase the size of Little Smalltalk itself, and the Little Smalltalk system can run on machines with very limited address spaces.[3] The limitation of this technique, however, is that class descriptions must be read in from a file and cannot be created directly at the terminal.

The class parser uses an LALR parsing algorithm, generated automatically from the grammar by a sophisticated parser generator. Since the grammar is much larger, the class parser is many times more complex than the simple parser used in the driver module. The class parser reads

---

3. The tradeoff is that the Little Smalltalk system will work only under operating systems that permit multiple-user processes.

Figure 14.10 □ *The procedure test_driver( )*

```
/* test_driver - see if the driver should be invoked */
int test_driver(block)
int block; /* indicates whether to use block or non-blocking input */
{
    switch(line_grabber( block )) {
        default: cant_happen(17);
        case —1:
            /* return end of file indication */
            return(0);
        case 0:
            /* enqueue driver process again */
            return(1);
        case 1:
            if (*lexptr = = ')') {
                dolexcommand(lexptr);
                return(1);
                }
            parse( );
            return(1);
        }
}
```

and parses a class description. If there are no errors encountered during parsing, it then produces a file of Little Smalltalk statements that together create the objects of class **Class** corresponding to the class descriptions. The file containing these commands is then read by the line grabber module, and the class is defined.

To understand how instances of class **Class** can be created using Little Smalltalk statements, it is necessary first to see how objects of class **Class** are represented internally in the Little Smalltalk system. Instances of class **Class** are special objects (see Chapter 12), and thus are permitted to have internal representations different from other Little Smalltalk objects. In particular, the internal structure of **Class** objects is given by the following C structure definition:

```
struct class_struct {
    int                c_ref_count;
    int                c_size
    struct obj_struct  *class_name;
    struct obj_struct  *super_class;
    struct obj_struct  *file_name;
```

```
struct obj_struct      *c_inst_vars;
int                    context_size;
struct obj_struct      *message_names;
struct obj_struct      *methods;
int                    stack_max;
};
```

As we noted in Chapter 12, the c_size field is always a designated negative integer, the value of which indicates that this is an object of class **Class.** The class_name, super_class and file_name fields are each pointers to objects of class **Symbol,** representing, respectively, the name of the class, the name of the super class, and the name of the file from which the class description was read.

The c_inst_vars and message_names fields are both pointers to arrays of symbols. The first represents the names of the instance variables defined by the class (and, by the size of this array, the number of instance variables used by the class). The second contains the names of the messages to which the class will respond.

The methods field is a pointer to an array containing the internal representation of the method associated with each message. This array runs in parallel with the message_names arrays, so to find the method associated with a particular message you first look up the message name in the message_names array and then, using the same index, extract the associated method. As we noted in the last chapter, each method is represented internally by an array of two elements. The first element is a **ByteArray** containing the bytecodes for the method. The second element is an array of literal values used by the method.

The final two fields, context_size and stack_max, are used in constructing interpreters to respond to messages accepted by the class. They give the maximum size of the context and the stack needed to respond to any message defined in the class. As the next chapter will describe in more detail, each instance of class **Interpreter** independently maintains its own stack of intermediate values.

Instances of class **Array** and class **Class** can be created by using primitive operations. For this is important for bootstrapping purposes because the first classes created cannot have access to any methods defined in other classes. In particular, four primitives are important. Primitive number 110 creates an array of a specified size. Primitive number 112 assigns a value to a given position in an array. Primitives 97 and 98 create new instances of class **Class** and insert them in the class dictionary. Thus for a class description such as the following:

```
Class test1 :Test2
| a b c |
[
    first: x
```

```
            a ← x + 3
  |
      second          | i |
          i ← a * 7.
          ↑ i − 33
  ]
```

The following Little Smalltalk statements are generated. First primitive 110 generates an array of sufficient size to hold the methods for the class. Primitive 112 then places the description of each method into the appropriate location in this array. Note that no message passing is involved and so these commands can be the very first ones executed by the Little Smalltalk system.

```
temp ← < primitive 110 2 >
<primitive 112 temp 1          " second " \
    #( #[ 16 87 194 113 33 48 193 243 245] \
    #( 33 ) ) >

<primitive 112 temp 2          " first: " \
    #( #[33 83 192 96 245] \
    #( )) >
```

Primitive number 97 creates a new instance of class **Class,** initializing it with the values taken from its arguments. Primitive number 98 takes an object of class **Class** and places it into the internal class dictionary maintained by the Little Smalltalk system. Together, these two primitives can define a new class, as follows:

```
<primitive 98 #Test1 \
    <primitive 97 #Test1 #Test2 #test1.st \
    #( #a #b #c) \
    #( #second #first: ) \
temp 2 3 > >
```

When read by the Little Smalltalk system, these commands will define the class **Test1** and provide it with the methods given by the class description.

CHAPTER

15

The Interpreter

As we have previously noted, methods are internally represented by byte-code format (Chapter 13). When a message is sent, an instance of class **Interpreter** is constructed. This object collects the necessary components for executing the method associated with the message, namely the byte-codes for the method, the receiver of the message,[1] the literals and context needed by the method, and the stack to be used by the virtual machine executing the method.

The internal C structure for instances of class **Interpreter** is shown in Figure 15.1. Note that there are several more fields in addition to the ones alluded to in the last paragraph. The *sender* field points to the sending interpreter, that is, the interpreter that was active at the point the message was sent which caused the current interpreter to be created. The *creator* field is usually null, except in the case of interpreters created to execute blocks. In this case, the creator points to the interpreter in which the block was originally defined, and thus the interpreter to be returned from in the case of a block return. The *currentbyte* pointer indicates the next bytecode to be evaluated when execution continues. In fact it is a pointer into the array associated with the *bytecode* field (Figure 15.2). In a similar fashion, the *stacktop* is a pointer into one entry of the array stored in the object pointed to by the *stack* field.

---

1. Actually both of them, since, as we saw in Chapter 11, there are two objects that can be said to represent the receiver of a message. In Little Smalltalk the named receiver is represented by the first position in the Context array. The actual receiver (i.e., the object in which class the method was found) is explicitly pointed to by the *receiver* field in the interpreter.

Figure 15.1 □ *The internal representation for class* **Interpreter**

```
struct interp_struct      {
        int               t_ref_count;
        int               t_size;/* should always be INTERPSIZE */
        struct            interp_struct *creator;
        struct            interp_struct *sender;
        object            *bytecodes;
        object            *receiver;
        object            *literals;
        object            *context;
        object            *stack;
        object            **stacktop;
        uchar             *currentbyte;
        };
```

Figure 15.2 □ *CurrentByte points into the bytecode array*

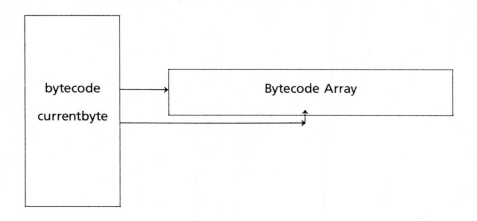

The interface to the interpreter module is shown in Figure 15.3. The procedure cr_interpreter( ) creates a new instance of class **Interpreter,** initializing it with the values given by the arguments. The bytecode pointer is set to the first byecode in the method, and the size of the stack is determined by examining the class of the receiver.

The routine copy_arguments( ) is used to copy an array of argument values into the context for an interpreter. It is used both by the courier when the interpreter is first defined, and by the block execution module to pass arguments to interpreters associated with instances of class **Block.**

When a message returns, the response to the message must be passed back to the sender. This is accomplished by pushing the response onto the senders stack and then resuming execution of the sender interpreter. The routine push_object( ) performs the first of these actions, pushing an object onto the stack of an interpreter, both of which are passed as arguments. Normally the interpreter involved is the sender although in the case of a block return it will be the sender of the creator.

The actual interpretation of bytecodes is performed by the process resume( ). The procedure is so called because, when called by the process manager, it resumes execution from the point it last left off. It then executes bytecodes until either the method terminates or until a message is sent. In the former case the interpreter is taken off the process manager queue and the sender process moves to the top from where it will be subsequently resumed by the process manager. In the second case the courier is called. The courier then finds a method to match with a message, creates a new instance of class **Interpreter,** and places the new interpreter in the front of the sender interpreter in the process queue.

Figure 15.3   □   *The interface to the interpreter module*

```
cr_interpreter(sender, receiver, literals, bitearray,context)
    struct interp_struct *sender;
    struct obj_struct *literals, *bitearray, *receiver, *context;
    creates a new instance of class Interpreter

copy_arguments(anInterpreter, argLocation, argCount, argArray)
    struct interp_struct *anInterpreter;
    int argLocation, argCount;
    object **argArray;
    takes a pointer to an array of arguments, and loads the argu-
    ments into the context for the interpreter at the specified loca-
    tions

push_object(anInterpreter, anObject)
    struct interp_struct *anInterpreter;
    struct obj_struct *anObject;
    pushes the object onto the stack associated with the interpreter

resume(anInterpreter)
    struct interp_struct *anInterpreter;
    resumes (or begins) evaluation of the bytecodes associated with
    an instance of class Interpreter
```

The structure of the procedure resume( ) is very regular. It is merely a large infinite loop (exited by a return from within the loop) surrounding a switch statement (Figure 15.4). The loop reads each bytecode in turn, and the switch selects which actions to take to execute the opcode. The macro nextbyte places the next byte in the argument and advances the currentbyte pointer. By modular arithmetic the byte is then converted into the high order and low order four-bit portions.

We can divide the bytecodes into groups with similar functions. These groups are those that push objects on the stack (opcodes 1 to 5), pop an object from the stack (opcodes 6 and 7), send a message (opcodes 8 through 13), block creation (opcode 14), and special instructions (opcode 15).

≡ **Push Opcodes**

Writing the code for those actions that manipulate the stack is greatly simplified by a number of macros that select various fields from the interpreter object:

Figure 15.4   □   *The structure of the procedure* **resume( )**

```
resume(anInterpreter)
struct interp_struct *anInterpreter
{   local declarations

    int highBits, lowBits;

    while(1) {
    nextbyte(highBits);
    lowBits = highBits % 16;
    highBits / = 16;

    switch(highBits) {
        default:
            cant_happen(9);

        case0:
            actions for opcode 0
            break;

        ...
        case 15:
            actions for opcode 15
            break;
        }
    }
}


# define push(x) {assign(*(anInterpreter—>stacktop), x); \
    anInterpreter—>stacktop + + ;}
# define instvar(x) (anInterpreter—>receiver)—>inst var[ x ]
# define tempvar(x) (anInterpreter—>context)—>inst var[ x ]
# define lit(x)     (anInterpreter—>literals)—>inst_var[ x ]
```

These macros make the code for the first three opcodes trivial:

```
case 1: /*push instance variable */
    push(instvar(lowBits));
    break;

case 2: /* push context value */
    push(tempvar(lowBits));
    break;
```

```
case 3: /* push a literal */
    push(lit(lowBits));
    break;
```

Opcode 4, which pushes a class object onto the stack, is complicated slightly by the fact that the object in the value field is a symbol, and first the associated class object must be found. This is achieved by calling the primitive manager with the message FINDCLASS. A later section will describe the primitive manager in more detail.

```
case /* push class */
    tempobj = lit(lowBits);
    if (! is_symbol(tempobj)) cant_happen(9);
    tempobj = primitive(FINDCLASS, 1, &tempobj);
    push(tempobj);
    break;
```

Opcode 5 selects either an integer, a pseudo variable, or a class and pushes it onto the stack. The routine new_int returns an object of class **Integer,** sharing multiple copies if the object occurs more than once. Each of the pseudo variables has an internal C pointer associated with it. Otherwise, to get a class a new symbol is created, and the primitive manager is called as for opcode 4.

```
case 5: /* special literals */
    if (lowBits < 10)
        tempobj = new_int(lowBits);
    else if (lowBits == 10)
        tempobj = new int( —1 );
    else if (lowBits == 11)
        tempobj = o_true;
    else if (lowBits == 12)
        tempobj = o_false;
    else if (lowBits == 13)
        tempobj = o_nil;
    else if (lowBits == 14)
        tempobj = o_smalltalk;
    else if (lowBits == 15)
        tempobj = (object *) runningProcess;
    else if ((lowBits >= 30) && (lowBits < 60)) {
        /* get class */
        tempobj = new_sym(classspecial[lowBits — 30]);
        tempobj = primitive(FINDCLASSS, 1, &tempobj);
        }
    else tempobj = new_int(lowBits);
    push(tempobj);
    break;
```

Pop Opcodes

Like the push opcodes, the writing of the code for the instructions that pop objects from the stack is greatly simplified by first defining useful macros, in this case a macro to pop an object off the stack and return it:

```
# define popstack( ) (*(--anInterpreter − >stacktop))
```

This makes Opcodes 6 and 7 easy.

```
case 6: /* pop and store instance variable */
    assign(instvar(lowBits), popstack( ));
    break;

case 7: /* pop and store in context */
    assign(tempvar(lowBits), popstack( ));
    break;
```

Message-Sending Opcodes

To send a message will usually require several instructions in bytecode. First, the receiver for the message is pushed on the stack, followed by the arguments in order. Finally, a send message instruction is given. When the send message opcode is read, therefore, the stack looks as follows:

top of stack

argument n

...

argument 1
receiver

bottom of stack

In the most general case, opcodes 8 and 9, the low-order bits of the opcode give the number of arguments associated with the message. The next byte is then a pointer into the literal table where a symbol corresponding to the message is stored. The code for opcodes 8 and 9 is shared by first placing the receiver into a local variable and executing an unconditional jump to a common section of code.[2]

```
case 8; /* send a message */
    numargs = lowBits;
    nextbyte(i);
    tempobj = lit(i);
    if (! is_symbol(tempobj)) cant_happen(9);
    message = symbol_value(tempobj);
    goto do_send;

case 9: /* send a message to super */
    numargs = lowBits;
    nextbyte(i);
    tempobj = lit(i);
    if (! is_symbol(tempobj)) cant_happen(9);
    message = symbol_value(tempobj);
    receiver = fnd_super(anInterpreter->receiver);
    goto do_send2;


/* do_send - call courier to send a message */
do_send:
    receiver = *(anInterpreter->stacktop - (numargs + 1));
do_send2:
    decstack(numargs + 1);
    send_mess(anInterpreter, receiver, message, anInter-
preter->stacktop , numargs);
    return;
```

---

2. The use of the goto in this case might be considered with horror by those who do not understand the principles of structured programming. The closer one gets to an actual machine, the greater the necessity for unconditional jumps becomes. (Think how difficult it would be to do assembly language programming without jumps.) Most user programs, fortunately, do not have to be described at this level, and thus the avoidance of gotos usually results in programs that are cleaner and easier to understand. Writing a virtual machine, such as the interpreter, is in many ways similar to writing for an actual machine. In this case, the sin of the "unstructured" goto seems less serious than the problems that could arise from duplicating the code and thereby running the risk of doing two different things where only one is intended, or from placing the duplicated code in a procedure since the amount of sharing between the interpreter and the procedure would have to be so great. (This is, in fact, one of those rare occasions when true block-structured subprocedures would be useful in C since so much information must be shared by the two routines.)

The local variable *numargs* holds the number of arguments for the message. The variable *receiver* contains the receiver for the message, and the variable *message* contains the character string representing the message name. (Note this is a pointer to a character sting and not an object.) The code at label do_send: looks into the stack to find the receiver; whereas, in the case of opcode 9, the receiver is taken to be the superobject of the current receiver.

The courier is then called via the procedure send_mess( ). The courier creates a new interpreter and places it in front of the current interpreter in the process queue. Upon returning from the courier, the stack is decremented and pointers in the stack are changed to point to **nil.** (This insures that objects no longer being used are quickly recovered, instead of having useless references to them left lying around). Control is then passed back to the process manager. When the current process is restarted, the interpreter given control will be the new one placed in front of the present interpreter by the courier.

Opcodes 10 through 13 avoid looking up the message, taking it instead from a built-in table of messages.

```
case 10: /* send a special unary message */
    numargs = 0;
    message = unspecial[lowBits];
    goto do_send;

case 11: /* send a special binary message */
    numargs = 1;
    message = binspecial[lowBits];
    goto do_send;

case 13: /* send a special ternary keyword message */
    numargs = 2;
    message = keyspecial[lowBits];
    goto do_send;
```

Opcode 12 could be handled similarly. However, by far the greatest number of these messages sent and a sizable percentage of *all* messages sent, involve arguments that are both integers. One completely transparent optimization, therefore, and a very cost-effective one, is to perform these operations in the interpreter if the arguments are both instances of class **Integer.** If not, then the standard calling sequence is followed. The macro decstack( ) merely pops the specified number of locations from the stack.

```
case 12: /* send a special arithmetic message */
    tempobj = *(anInterpreter->stacktop - 2);
    if (! is_integer(tempobj)) goto ohwell;
    i = int_value(tempobj);
    tempobj = *(anInterpreter->stacktop - 1);
    if (! is_integer(tempobj)) goto ohwell;
```

```
            j = int_value(tempobj);
            decstack(2);
            switch(lowBits) {
                case 0: i + = j; break;
                case 1: i − = j; break;
                case 2: i * = j; break;
                case 3: if (i < 0) i = -i;
                    i % = j; break;
                case 4: if (j < 0) i > > = (-j);
                    else i < < = j; break;
                case 5: i & = j; break;
                case 6: i | = j; break;
                case 7: i = (i < j); break;
                case 8: i = (i < = j); break;
                case 9: i = (i = = j); break;
                case 10: i = (i ! = j); break;
                case 11: i = (i > j); break;
                case 12: i = (i > j); break;
                case 13: i % = j; break;
                case 14: i / = j; break;
                case 15: i = (i <j) ? i : j;
                    break;
                case 16: i = (i < j) ? j : i;
                    break;
                default: cant_happen(9);
                }
        if ((lowBits < 7) || (lowBits > 12))
            tempobj = new_int(i);
        else tempobj = (i ? o_true : o_false);
        push(tempobj);
        break;

        ohwell: /* oh well, send message conventional way */
        numargs = 1;
        message = arithspecial[lowBits];
        goto do_send;
```

Block Creation

In the bytecode format, the low-order bits of the block creation instruction give the number of arguments to the block. If the number is non-zero, the next byte gives the location in the context where the arguments should be stored when the block is invoked. The byte following then gives the size in bytes of the bytecodes containing the statements for the block. The actual bytecodes for the statements in the block follow immediately the block creation instruction.

The procedure new_block( ) is called to create a block. A later section will describe this in more detail. For now, it is sufficient to say that it creates and initializes an instance of class **Block,** which is then pushed onto the stack. The current bytecode pointer is then advanced over the text of the block by using the macro skip( ).

```
case 14: /* block creation */
    numargs = lowBits;
    if (numargs)
        nextbyte(arglocation);
    nextbyte(i);   /* size of block */
    push(new_block(anInterpreter, numargs, arglocation));
    skip(i);
    break;
```

Special Instructions

The code for opcode 15 is the largest of all the opcode sections because there are so many different cases to be handled. Nonetheless, once the macros used in the previous instructions have been defined, the code is rather tediously simple. The two exceptions to this are the code for those instructions that return an object and the code to handle the primitive instructions. There are three instructions that return an object. In the first, Opcode (15.3) returns the object currently on the top of the stack, opcode (15.4) performs a block return (which also takes its argument from the top of the stack), and opcode (15.5) returns the receiver. Block returns will be described in a later section. The other two place the object to be returned in the local variable tempobj, and then branches to a common return section.

```
case 15: /* special bytecodes */
    switch(lowBits) {

    case 0: /* no-op */
        break;

    case 1: /* duplicate top of stack */
        push(*(anInterpreter—>stacktop) – 1));
        break;

    case 2: /* pop top of stack */
        assign(*(anInterpreter—>stacktop),o_nil);
```

```
            anInterpreter—>stacktop--;
            break;

case 3: /* return top of stack */
        tempobj = popstack( ):
        goto do_return;

case 4: /* block return */
        block_return(anInterpreter, popstack( ));
        return;

case 5: /* self return */
        tempobj = tempvar(0);
        goto do_return;

case 6: /* skip on true */
        nextbyte(i);
        tempobj = popstack( );
        if (tempobj = = o_true) {
            skip(i);
            push(o_nil);
            }
        break;

case 7; /* skip on false */
        nextbyte(i);
        tempobj = popstack( );
        if (tempobj = = o_false) {
            skip(i);
            push(o_nil);
            }
        break;

case 8: /* skip forward */
        nextbyte(i);
        skip(i);
        break;

case 9: /* skip backward */
        nextbyte(i);
        skip( – i );
        break;

case 10: /* execute a primitive */
        nextbyte(numargs);
```

```
            nextbyte(i); /* primitive number */
            decstack(numargs);
            tempobj = primitive(i, numargs, anInterpreter − >stacktop);
            push(tempobj);
            break;

    case 11: /* skip true, push true */
            nextbyte(i);
            tempobj = popstack( );
            if (tempobj = = o_true) {
                skip(i);
                anInterpreter − >stacktop + + ;
                }
            break;

    case 12: /* skip on false, push false */
            nextbyte(i);
            tempobj = popstack( );
            if (tempobj = = o_false) {
                skip(i);
                anInterpreter − >stacktop + + ;
                }
            break;

    default:
            cant_happen(9);
    }
    break;

    /* do_return-return from a message */
do_return:
    sender = anInterpreter − >sender;
    if (is_interpreter(sender)) {
        if (! is_driver(sender))
            push_object(sender, tempobj);
        link_to_process(sender);
        }
    else {
        terminate_process(runningProcess);
    }
    return;
```

The code at do_return first checks to see if there is a sender. If there is, and if the sender is not the driver, the object in tempobj is pushed onto the stack in the sender. The sender is then made the first interpreter in the process queue by calling the procedure link_to_process( ). If there is no sender, the current process is terminated.

The code to execute a primitive (case 10), first decrements the stack over the arguments. It then calls the primitive handler, passing it the primitive number, number of arguments, and a pointer to the location in the stack where the arguments (which have not been overwritten) are to be found.

The Courier

The courier is so called because it carries a message, determines to whom it should be sent and how it will be transmitted, but does not itself read the messages. The interface to the courier is through the procedure_ send_mess( ), which we have already described. Once called, the courier walks up the super-object chain of the receiver, examining the classes of each object in turn. In each class it looks at the list of messages to which the class will respond, searching for one that will match the message being sent.

If it finds a class that will respond to the message, it creates a context for the message (the size of the context can be determined by the class description) and an interpreter for the message. Calling the process manager, the new interpreter is then linked to the head of the interpreter chain for the currently running process. The courier afterwards returns to the interpreter, which immediately returns back to the process manager. When the process manager again restarts the process, the new interpreter will be resumed.

If the courier cannot find a class that will respond to the message, it produces an error message and a trace of the previous messages sent in the current process. This trace is easily constructed by following back the interpreter chain from the current interpreter back to an interpreter with no sender, which must be the start of the interpreter chain. The pseudo variable **nil** is then pushed onto the stack of the calling interpreter, which is then restarted. Unfortunately, **nil** is seldom an appropriate value to be used in this circumstance, and such errors have an annoying way of cascading.

The Primitive Handler

The primitive handler is the interface between the Smalltalk world and the world of the underlying virtual machine. Any operation that cannot be specified in Smalltalk, such as adding two floating point values together, concatenating a pair of strings, or converting an integer into a floating point value, must ultimately be performed via the primitive handler. In principle only the primitive handler has detailed knowledge of the internal representations of special objects and can manipulate the various fields in these objects.[3]

The structure of the primitive handler (Figure 15.5) is rather complicated but very regular. This complex structure is dictated by the necessity to combine some common operations to reduce the size of the primitive handler as much as possible. (It is already the largest module in the Little Smalltalk system) Appendix 4 will show that primitive operations seem to be collected in groups of ten. For example binary integer operations have numbers between 10 and 29, unary integer operations have numbers between 30 and 39, character operations numbers between 40 and 49, and so on. Dividing the primitive number by ten will tell which *group* the primitive falls into. From this information you can check type to insure the arguments to the primitive are correct (for example, that character primitives are indeed presented with character arguments) can be performed. Also the internal values (for example, the integer values from instances of class **Integer**) can be placed into local variables within the primitive handler. Thus the start of the primitive handler is a large switch statement to perform type checking.

Once type checking has been performed, a several-page switch statement is used to find the appropriate action for each primitive type. After performing the correct actions, the primitive handler will return an object. This object can be of any type (**Symbol, String, Float,** etc.), and once more an attempt is made to combine similar actions so as to reduce the necessity for duplicating code. Each of the individual code sections for the various primitive operations ends by an unconditional jump to a return section of the appropriate type.

Blocks

The routine new_block( ), introduced in the discussion of opcode 14, creates a new instance of class **Block**. Instances of **Block** are special objects with an internal structure as shown in Figure 15.6. The interpreter field in each block points to a copy of the interpreter in which it was created.

---

3. In practice this is not quite true, as the memory manager must also know about the internal structure of all objects. Also some complex operations are handled by special routines in the modules for different types of objects, such as symbols or classes. These are called by the primitive handler, however, and logically can be considered to be part of the primitive handler module.

Figure 15.5 □ *The structure of the primitive handler*

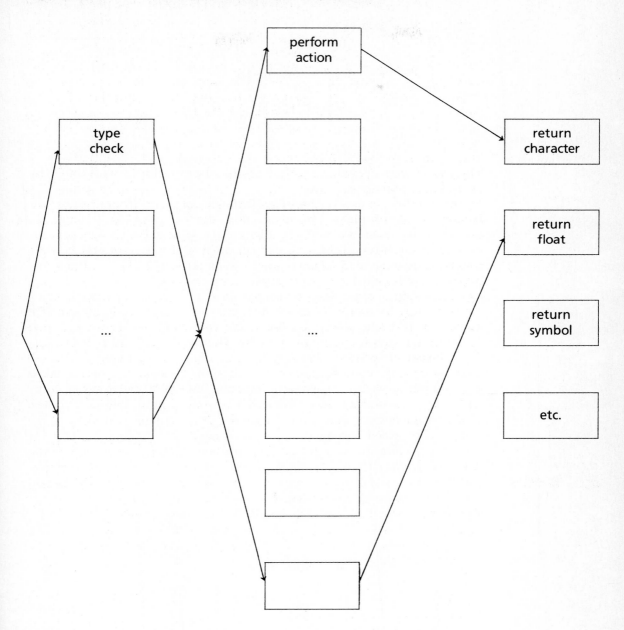

Figure 15.6 □ *The structure of instances of class **Block***

```
struct block_struct {
    int           b_ref_count;
    int           b_size;
    struct interp_struct*b_interpreter;
    int           b_numargs;
    int           b_arglocation;
} ;
```

The copy shares everything with the original except for the stack and the currentbyte pointer.

In response to a *value* message, instances of class **Block** execute the **BlockExecute** primitive. This instruction, after verifying that the number of arguments matches the number of arguments defined by the block, again copies the interpreter for the block, copies the arguments into the context for the interpreter, and appends the interpreter to the front of the interpreter chain for the current process.

Returning a value from a block (in the absence of an explicit block return) therefore requires exactly the same sequence of events as a normal return. In fact, the class parser and the command line driver generate bytecodes so that the same mechanism is used.

In order to perform a block return, the interpreter chain is examined, searching for the creating interpreter. If found, the same actions are taken as would if the creator itself were returning the object being returned by the block. The creator, and all interpreters following it, will be removed from the interpreter chain, and the sender of the creator will move to the top to be resumed next by the process manager.

If the creator is not found in the interpreter chain (if a block containing a return is placed into a variable or returned from a message and thus outlives its creator), an error message is produced and the value that would have been returned is returned to the sender of the *value* message which invoked the block.

References

Abelson, H., and diSessa, A. [1981] *Turtle Geometry: The Computer as a Medium for Exploring Mathematics.* Boston: MIT Press.

Almes, G. T.; Black, A. P.; Lazowska, E. D.; and Noe, J. D. [1985] "The Eden System: A Technical Review." *IEEE Transactions on Software Engineering*, SE-11: 43–59.
> Presents an overview of a modern object-oriented operating system.

Birtwistle, G. M.; Dahl, O.-J.; Myhrhaug, B.; and Nygaard, K. [1973] *Simula Begin.* Lund, Sweden: Studentlitteratur.
> Simula is a language of the Algol family designed for simulation and is a very important ancestor of Smalltalk. The concept of Classes was inherited from Simula.

Birtwistle, G. M. [1979] *DEMOS; A System for Discrete Event Modelling on Simula.* London: MacMillan.
> A comprehensive description of how the language Simula can be used in producing discrete event models of the type described in Chapter 7.

Budd, T. A. [1982] "An Implementation of Generators in C." *Computer Languages*, 7: 69–88.
> Describes how a simple form of generators can be implemented in the language C.

Byte [1981] *Special Issue on Smalltalk* 6: 14–378.
> A special issue of the programming magazine *Byte* containing a large number of articles on Smalltalk-80 written by members of the Xerox Learning Research Group.

Campbell, J. A., (ed.) [1984] *Implementations of PROLOG.* New York: Wiley & Sons.
> PROLOG is a language for logic programming. This collection of papers describes many different aspects of the implementation of the language.

Dahl, O.-J.; Dijkstra, E.; and Hoare, A. [1972] *Structured Programming.* London: Academic Press.
> Introduced the notion of structured programming. Includes an article by O-J Dahl on the language Simula.

Dijkstra, E. W. [1965] "Cooperating Sequential Processes." *Technical Report EWD-123.* Eindhoven, the Netherlands: Technological University.

An early paper on sychronization, describes the "Dining Philosophers" problem discussed in Chapter 10.

Ghezzi, C., and Jazayeri, M. [1982] *Programming Language Concepts*, New York: Wiley & Sons.
Describes the features typically found in languages of the ALGOL family and their conventional implementations.

Gibbs, G. I., ed. [1974] *Handbook of Games and Simulation Exercise.* Beverly Hills, Cal.: Sage Publications, Inc.
Presents references to a large number of games and simulation exercises.

Goldberg, A., ed., and Kay, A., ed. [1976] *Smalltalk-72 Instruction Manual,* Xerox PARC Technical Report
Describes the language Smalltalk-72, one of the first in the evolution of Smalltalk languages.

Goldberg, A., and Robson, D. [1983] *Smalltalk-80: The Language and Its Implementation.* Reading, Mass.: Addison-Wesley.
The definitive description of Smalltalk. Contains many extensive examples of simulations and use of the graphics features of the Smalltalk-80 language.

Goldberg, A. [1983] *Smalltalk-80: The Interactive Programming Environment.* Reading, Mass.: Addison-Wesley.
The Smalltalk-80 Programming system developed at Xerox Parc is much more than just the Smalltalk language. This book describes features of the programming environment developed for Smalltalk-80.

Greenberg, S. [1972] *GPSS Primer.* New York: Wiley & Sons.
An introduction to the computer simulation language GPSS.

Griswold, R. E.; Poage, J. F.; and Polonsky, I. P. [1971] *The SNOBOL4 Programming Language.* Englewood Cliffs, N. J.: Prentice-Hall.
Snobol4 is one of the earliest attempts at a language for nonnumeric programming.

Griswold, R. E., and Griswold, M. T. [1983] *The Icon Programming Language.* Englewood Cliffs, New Jersey: Prentice-Hall.
Icon is a language for nonnumerical problems and a descendant of Snobol4 (Griswold 71). Many of the ideas concerning generators described in Chapter 8 were derived from Icon.

Griswold, R. E., and O'Bagy, J. [1985] "Seque: A Language for Programming with Streams." *TR 85-2.* Tucson, Arizona: The University of Arizona Department of Computer Science.
The language Seque is derived from Icon (Griswold 83) and attempts to deal with sequences as a formal object, rather than with generators.

Hanson, D. R., and Griswold, R. E. [1978] "The SL5 Procedure Mechanism." *Communications of the ACM,* 21: 392–400.

> The programming language SL5 provides a great deal of flexibility in the area of procedure activation and parameter passing. The concept of *filters,* described in Chapter 8, is taken from SL5.

Hewitt, C.; Bishop, P.; and Steiger, R. [1973] "A Universal Modular Actor Formalism for Artificial Intelligence." *Proceedings of the 3rd International Joint Conference on Artificial Intelligence.*

> Actors is a technique for describing object-oriented programming in Lisp.

Ingalls, D. H. [1978] "The Smalltalk-76 Programming System: Design and Implementation." *Proceedings of the Fifth Principles of Programming Languages Symposium,* January 1978: 9–16.

> The language Smalltalk-76 was the immediate predecessor to the language Smalltalk-80 on which Little Smalltalk is based.

Kay, A. [1969] "The Reactive Engine" Ph.D. Thesis, University of Utah. (available on University Microfilms).

> Describes the Flex system, an important predecessor of Smalltalk.

Kay, A. [1977] "Microelectronics and the Personal Computer." *Scientific American,* 237: 230–244.

> A good introduction to the philosophy behind the development of the Smalltalk-80 programming system. Describes some early experiments involving teaching Smalltalk to children.

Knuth, D. [1981] *The Art of Computer Programming.* Fundamental Algorithms, Vol. 1; Seminumerical Algorithms, Vol. 2; Sorting and Searching, Vol. 3. Reading, Mass: Addison-Wesley.

> These three volumes (the first of a planned seven-volume collection) present an extremely complete analysis of most of the important algorithms used in computer science.

Krasner, G., ed. [1983] *Smalltalk-80 Bits of History, Words of Advice.* Reading, Mass.: Addison-Wesley.

> A collection of papers describing various aspects of the implementation of the Smalltalk-80 system.

Koved, L. [1984] "The Object Model: A Historical Perspective." *Technical Report TR-1443.* College Park, Md.: The University of Maryland Department of Computer Sciences, September 1984.

> Describes how the object-oriented model has influenced machine architecture, operating systems, and language design. Includes a lengthy reference list.

LaLonde, W. R.; Thomas, D. A.; and Pugh, J. R. [1984] "Teaching Fifth Generation Computing: The Importance of Smalltalk." *Technical Report SCS-TR-64.* Ottawa, Ontario: Carleton University School of Computer Science, October 1984.

Argues that the Smalltalk language will be as important as Prolog in developing fifth-generation computer systems. Includes a lengthy reference list of associated literature.

Liskov, B.; Atkinson, R.; Bloom, T.; Moss, E.; Schaffert, J. C.; Scheifler, R.; and Snyder, A. [1981] *CLU Reference Manual.* New York: Springer-Verlag.

CLU is a modern language in the Algol family. Although the language includes a concept called *generators,* they are considerably different from generators in Little Smalltalk.

Maryanski, F. [1980] *Digital Computer Simulation.* Rochelle Park, N.J.: Hayden Book Company, Inc.

A rather general introduction to computer simulation models illustrated with examples from the languages GPSS, Simscript, CSMP, and Dynamo.

Ord-Smith, R. K., and Stephenson, J. [1975] *Computer Simulation of Continuous Systems.* Cambridge, England: Cambridge University Press.

Papert, S. [1980] *MindStorms: Children, Computers and Powerful Ideas.* City: Basic Books.

Introduces the language LOGO.

Peterson, J., and Silberschatz, A. [1983] *Operating System Concepts.* Reading, Mass.: Addison-Wesley.

A good introductory operating systems textbook. Discusses various solutions to the "Dining Philosophers" problem discussed in Chapter 10.

Pinnow, K. W.; Ranweiler, J. G.; and Miller, J. F. [1982] "The IBM System/38 Object-Oriented Architecture" in *Computer Structures: Principles and Examples.* pp 537–540. New York: McGraw-Hill.

Describes some of the object-oriented features of a modern processor and its associated operating system.

Rattner, J., and Cox, G. [1980] "Object-Based Computer Architecture." *Computer Architecture News* 8: 4–11.

Describes the influence of the object-oriented viewpoint on machine architecture.

Reynolds, C. W. [1982] "Computer Animation with Scripts and Actors." *Computer Graphics* 16: 289–296.

Describes how object-oriented techniques (the Actor model) can be used for computer animation.

Shaw, M. [1980] "The Impact of Abstraction Concerns in Modern Programming Languages." *Proceedings of the IEEE* 68: 1119–1130.

Describes abstraction techniques for several modern languages.

Shaw, M. ed. [1981] *Alphard: Form and Content.* New York: Springer-Verlag.

A collection of papers on the language Alphard, a modern language in the Algol family

Smith, D. C., and Enea, H. K. [1973] "Backtracking in MLISP2." *Proceedings of the 3rd International Joint Conference on Artificial Intelligence,* August 1973: 677–685.

Weinreb, D., and Moon, D. [1980] "Flavors: Message Passing in the Lisp Machine." *MIT AI Memo Number 602,* November 1980.
Describes a technique for adding the ability to represent objects and message passing to the computer language LISP.

Wulf, W. A.; Cohen, E.; Corwin, W.; Jones, A.; Levin, R.; Pierson, C.; and Pollack, F. [1974] "HYDRA: The Kernel of a Multiprocessor Operating System." *Communications of the ACM,* June 1974, pp. 337–345.
Describes the HYDRA operating system, which is based on objects communicating via messages.

Zeigler, B. P. [1976] *Theory of Modelling and Simulation.* New York: Wiley & Sons
A rather theoretical overview of simulation methods.

Projects

This section contains a series of projects suitable for graduate or advanced undergraduate students in a one-term course based on the material in this book. Some of the projects involve working only in Smalltalk and therefore can be attempted by students with knowledge only of the first part of the book. Other projects involve making modifications to the actual implementation and therefore require knowledge of the second half of the book.

1. Card Games

Instances of the following class when properly initialized can be used to represent single playing cards from a conventional deck of cards.

```
Class Card
| suit face |
[
    suit: suitValue face: face Value
        suit ← suitValue
        face ← faceValue
|
    printString          | print |
        Switch new: face ;
            case: 1 do: [ print ← 'ace' ] ;
            case: 10 do: [ print ← 'jack' ] ;
            case: 11 do: [ print ← 'queen' ] ;
            case: 12 do: [ print ← 'king' ] ;
            default: [ print ← face printString ] .
        print ← print , ' of ' ,
            ( #('hearts' 'clubs' 'diamonds' 'spades') at: suit)
        ↑ print
]
```

Implement the class **Deck,** which represents a deck of playing cards. Instances of **Deck** respond to the following messages:

shuffle   The deck of cards is shuffled into random order. The order can either be determined a priori in response to this message or produced as each card is dealt out.

deal   One card is dealt from the deck and is not replaced. That is, once a card is dealt from the deck it cannot be dealt again until after the deck has been *shuffled* again.

deal: As many cards as indicated by the argument are dealt out. Deal returns an array of cards.

Using **Deck,** devise a simulation for a simple card game such as Solitaire or Blackjack. You may wish to add further messages to class **Card** or to make it a subclass of **Magnitude.**

2. Arbitrary Precision Arithmetic

Implement the class **BigInteger** (subclass of **Number**). Instances of class **BigInteger** represent integers of arbitrary size. Internally, integers larger than can be accommodated in the underlying machine representation are encoded as an array of values. For example, suppose only values less than 100 could be represented in machine words. A larger value, say 1476632, could be represented by the array #(1 47 66 32). (Actually, depending upon the algorithms selected, it may be preferable to keep the values in *reverse* order).

Instances of class **BigInteger** should respond to the following messages:

coerce: The argument should be an instance of class **Integer.** Return a **BigInteger** with the same magnitude.

\+   If the argument is a **BigInteger,** return a new **BigInteger** representing the sum. If the argument is not a **BigInteger,** pass the message up to the superclass **(Number).** Similar messages for —, *, <, = and <=.

printString   Return a string representation of the integer value.

Other messages may be necessary, depending upon your implementation.

It is suggested that you start with an easy approximation. For example, produce a class that works only for positive numbers and the message +. Later add negative values and other messages. (Volume 2 of (Knuth 81) describes some algorithms that might be useful for this project.)

3. Polynomials

Implement the class **Polynomial.** Instances of **Polynomial** represent polynomial values with numerical coefficients. As with the last project, the class **BigInteger,** polynomial coefficients are maintained internally by an array of coefficients. Instances of **Polynomial** should respond to the following messages:

coerce: Return a new polynomial of degree zero with the argument as coefficient.

degree	Return the degree of the polynomial.
coefficient:	Return the value of the named coefficient, or zero if no coefficient matches the argument.
eval:	Return the numerical result produced by evaluating the polynomial on the argument value.
+	If the argument is a **Polynomial,** return a new **Polynomial** representing the sum. If the argument is not a **Polynomial,** pass the message up to the superclass **(Number).** Similar messages for —, $*$, $<$, $=$ and $<=$.
printString	Return a string representation of the polynomial value.

Other messages may be necessary, depending upon the implementation technique.

4. Matrices

The class **Array** provides protocol for vectors, that is, one-dimensional arrays. Matrices of higher dimension can be thought of as being composed of two vectors, a *shape* vector giving the dimension of the array and a *values* vector maintaining the values in the array. For example, the two-dimensional array

```
10    3    13
12    7     9
 6   14    21
```

can be thought of as being composed of the following two vectors

shape #(3 3)
values #(10 3 13 12 7 9 6 14 21)

Notice the values are stored in row major, or ravel order.

Define a class for manipulating matrices of arbitrary dimension. Values in the matrix can be defined either by giving them an explicit shape or values array or by modifying a single element. What functionality should matrices exhibit? Possibilities include pointwise multiplication or addition by a scalar or by another matrix, matrix multiplication, inner or cross products, or others.

5. APL

The programming language APL provides a rich repertoire of operations that can be performed on multidimensional arrays. Because the class **Matrix** was defined in the last project, many of the APL operations can be easily simulated in Smalltalk (ignoring syntax, of course).

6. Lisp

The class **List** provides a simple list structure. Show how this class could be modified to accept the LISP-like messages *car, cdr,* and *cons.* What other classes would have to be changed? What other Lisp-like features could be simulated?

7. Numerical Generality

One can envision a class **Fraction** representing rational values. Instances of class **Fraction** would be represented internally by a pair of integers representing a numerator and denominator. A fraction could be produced by the division of two integers. Operations involving two fractions or a fraction and an integer would produce a new fraction. Operations involving a fraction and a floating point value would produce a floating point value.

One difficulty of implementing the class **Fraction** is the built-in notion of numerical generality. The numerical generality hierarchy is **Integer,** then **Float,** then any user-defined classes. In the case of **Fraction,** one would like the generality to come between **Integer** and **Float.**

Investigate how numerical generality (primitive number 6) is implemented. Suggest and implement an alternative scheme that permits numerical generality to be assigned at run-time rather than having a built-in hierarchy. Using this new scheme, implement the class **Fraction.**

8. Cursor Motions

On many terminals the cursor can be moved to an arbitrary location on the screen by sending a special sequence of characters (usually a sequence of unprintable characters). Note that a "character" can be constructed for any nonzero value using an integer and the message *asCharacter.*

If you have a terminal with such a capability, describe how to modify the class **String** to respond to the following message

    aString printAt: aPoint

The point is taken to be a pair of coordinates, and the receiver string should be printed at that location.

9. Bar Graphs

Instances of the class **Bar Graph** should respond to messages setting a header and/or a footer and providing an array of values and, optionally, an array of titles associated with each value. It should then produce a graph, such as that shown below, where the number of stars printed is proportional to the value of the given item.

```
                                    header
title1            value1      *************
title2            value2      *********
...
titlen            value2      *******************
                                    footer
```

10. Function Plots

Describe a class, **Plot,** that will produce plots of functions. You may wish to augment your plot with headers, footers, or other informative indications as in the bar graphs just described. Instances of class **Plot** should respond to either a message giving an ordered collection of points or a message giving the function to be graphed. For example, the following might be a typical session:

```
graph ← Plot new
graph from: − 10 to: 20
graph function: [:x | (3 * (x ↑ 2) ) + ( 2 * x) + 5 ]
graph plot
```

11. Pens

This project assumes you have access to an output device on which you can draw lines between pairs of coordinates. If you have such a device, implement the class **Pen,** a tool for investigating "turtle geometry." (See (Papert 80), (Abelson 81), and Goldberg 83); the name "turtle" describes the drawing instrument in the Abelson system.) Instances of class **Pen** represent a writing instrument on the terminal screen. Such instruments have a state (either up, off the screen; or down, on the screen) and a direction (between 0 and 2π radians).

Pens can be directed to move either a given distance (*go:*) or to a specific location (*goto:*) If the pen is down, a line is drawn on the terminal screen. If the pen is up, no drawing takes place.

Instances of class **Pen** should respond to the following messages:

location	Return the location of the pen as a **Point.**
up	Set the state of the pen to up. When up, a pen does not write on the surface as it moves.
down	Set the state of the pen to down. When down, a pen writes on the surface as it moves.
turn:	The argument is an amount in radians. The direction of the pen is moved the indicated amount.
go:	The argument gives the distance the pen should move.
goto:	The argument is a **Point** the pen should move to.

Other messages may suggest themselves to you. As an example, the following script:

```
bic ← Pen new
bic down
(3 to: 6) do: [:nsides | nsides timesRepeat: [ go: 1 . bic turn: ( 2 pi /
nsides ) radians] ]
```

would produce the following picture:

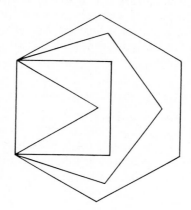

12. Collections

The basic types of collections in Little Smalltalk are represented by classes **Bag, Set, Dictionary, List,** and **Array.** There are various different schemes to implement methods for these classes. Important considerations are the speed with which objects can be inserted, tested, or removed from the collection; the size (number of auxiliary objects required) to implement an instance of the collection; and the ease with which the implementation can be realized (for instance, the number of primitive operations required). An attractive implementation technique is to make some classes "fundamental" in the sense that instances of the class may be represented by special objects (chapter 11) and/or may use primitive operations to respond to insertion or deletion messages. Other types of collections can then be implemented by internally using instances of fundamental classes. Examples showing how this might be done are as follows:

A **Set** can be implemented using a **Bag** by merely checking to see if each entry is already in the set before it is in serted.

An **Array** can be implemented, using a **Dictionary** with integer keys. (Nothing is said about this being efficient, merely possible).

A **Set** or **Bag** can be implemented by a **Dictionary**. The element can be used as the key for the dictionary and (in the case of **Bag**) the value field used to store the number of times the element is repeated.

Conversely, a **Dictionary** can be implemented using a **Set** by storing each key-value pair as an instance of class **Point**.

A **Set** (also a **Dictionary**) can be implemented using an **Array** and instances of **List**. The array is used as a hash table (there is a primitive to produce a hash value from any object) and each entry in the array is a **List** containing all elements in the set that hash to the same value.

Investigate these possibilities and any others you can think of. Compare the number of operations involved to do insertions or deletions in the various methods. If possible, implement the various techniques and produce actual timings comparing them. Examine the implementation of the classes used in the Little Smalltalk system and explain the techniques used there. Look at the implementations described in (Goldberg 83) and contrast them with the techniques used in the Little Smalltalk system.

13. Opcode Design

Modify the parser so that it can be used to produce a static analysis of bytecode frequency, including the frequency of each of the special opcodes (opcode 15) and the frequency of each message corresponding to a built-in value (opcodes 10–13). Using the altered parser, recompile each of the classes in the standard prelude and tabulate the results. Are there any surprises? Based on these figures, should primitives have been given their own opcode? Which other opcode should be eliminated?

Modify the interpreter to measure the frequency of bytecode execution while a program is running. Using the altered system, execute a large set of programs (say the programs used to perform installation testing). How closely do the dynamic figures match the static figures?

Modify the courier to tabulate the number of messages sent while executing a given set of programs. What messages occur most frequently? Is there any way execution could be optimized for these messages?

14. Windows

Windows is a technique for organizing a single *physical* terminal screen into a larger number of different *logical* screens. Each window serves as a separate entity and can display data independently of all other windows. If you have access to a software system supporting windows (such as the

Curses package[1] or the Maryland Windows package[2]) implement the class **Window.**

Instances of the class **Window** should respond to the following messages:

> from aPoint to: aPoint
>> Specifies the upper left and lower right extent of the window.
>
> put: aString
>> Places the string as output in the window, scrolling the window up if necessary (just as on a terminal).
>
> moveToFront
>> May move the window, or other windows, so that the receiver window is completely exposed (i.e., not covered by other windows).

In addition, the class **Smalltalk** should be modified so that the pseudo variable **smalltalk** will respond to the following messages:

> smalltalk inputWindow: aWindow
>> Specifies that all future input should be taken from the specified window. This will require modifications in several places internally to insure that the cursor is always sitting on the given window when input is expected.
>
> smalltalk outputWindow: aWindow
>> Specifies that standard output (output produced via the *print* message) should appear on the designated window.

In order to accomplish the implementation of this class, you may need to create a special object for class **Window** (see Chapter 12). Since window operations are produced by calling C routines, they will necessarily have to be implemented via primitive calls, and thus the primitive handler will have to be modified. You may also require many more internal messages.

15. Context Saving

When an object is no longer being referenced, that is, when its reference count reaches zero, the storage for the object is reclaimed and the object effectively disappears. Thus it is clear that every accessible object must be pointed to by at least one other object. If this were uniformly true, all of memory would be one large cycle. Fortunately, there are exceptions.

Three sets of objects can exist without being pointed to:

---

1. Kenneth Arnold, *Screen Updating and Cursor Movement Optimization: A Library Package,* Unix 4.1 distribution, Berkeley, California, 1981.

2. Mark Weiser, Chris Torek, and Richard J. Wood, *Three Window Systems,* University of Maryland Technical Report TR-1444, 1985.

1. The driver maintains a pair of arrays (var_names and var_values) containing the names and values of all instance variables known at the command level.

2. An internal dictionary (in file cldict.c) is maintained, recording the objects representing each known class.

3. Pseudo variables (such as true and false) each have a corresponding globar variable (o_true or o_false, for example) in the internal C universe.

Knowing that these are the only pointers into memory, develop an algorithm that will save the current value of all known objects. Your algorithm should produce a script of Smalltalk commands that when read will recreate the state of the machine at the time the script was produced. This may require adding one or more fields to the internal structure of every object (although the fewer changes required, of course, the better). Make sure your algorithm works properly in the case of multiple copies of any object. You will probably have to make extensive use of the primitives 111 and 112 that extract or set an arbitrary field in any object.

You may wish to start with a simpler case, such as not dealing with classes or built-in objects.

16. Garbage Collection

The preceding project description explained how to access every object along a path headed by one of a small number of starting locations. This is one of the major requirements necessary in order to replace the current reference-counting memory management system with a scheme using garbage collection. Investigate at least one garbage collection algorithm and describe what changes would be required to both the internal representation of objects and to the Little Smalltalk implementation to incorporate this system. A description of simple garbage collection techniques is presented in (Ghezzi 82); schemes directed more specifically at Smalltalk are given in (Krasner 83).

17. Processor Scheduling

Chapter 14 describes the Process manager. In the Little Smalltalk system all processes have the same priority, and each new process is merely selected in turn form a circular list. An alternative scheme would permit the user to dynamically assign priorities to processes, with processing having a higher priority because of executing more frequently.

Describe a workable priority scheme. Describe what changes would have to be made to the Little Smalltalk system to implement your scheme.

18. Inheritance of Variables

In the Smalltalk-80 programming system (the Smalltalk language available from Xerox) not only are *methods* inherited from a superclass, but *variables* may be inherited as well. That is, suppose A is a subclass of B. An instance variable used in B may also be accessed or modified by methods in class A.

Given that, when class A is parsed, class B may not exist or may be modified later, devise a scheme to implement variable inheritance. (Hint, define new special opcodes which, like the class opcode, point to a literal value).

19. Multiple Inheritance

Multiple inheritance is a term used to describe a situation where an object inherits methods from two or more super classes. An example will illustrate this concept. In the standard classes for the Little Smalltalk system, the class **SequenceableCollection** is rather artificially placed as a subclass of **KeyedCollection.** As a result, the class **List,** which does not have keys, is nevertheless a subclass of **KeyedCollection.** A better organization might have been the following:

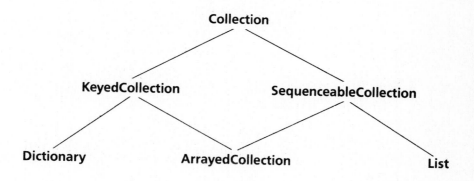

Here the classes **SequenceableCollection** and **KeyedCollection** are both subclasses of **Collection.** The class **List** is sequenceable, but not keyed, thus it is a subclass of **SequenceableCollection.** Similarly, the class **Dictionary** is keyed, but not sequenceable, and is thus a subclass of **KeyedCollection.** The class **ArrayedCollection,** however, is both sequenceable and keyed, and thus instances of **ArrayedCollection** inherit from *both* the classes **KeyedCollection** and **SequenceableCollection.**

Chapter 12 described how inheritance was implemented both in the structure of class objects (using a symbol representing the name of the superclass) and in the internal representation of objects (using the super-object pointer). One approach in both these instances is to use an *array* of objects to represent the information about superclasses. In the class **object** this would be an array of symbols indicating the super objects. In each individual object this would be an array of superobjects.

Describe what effect this change would have on the internal structure of the Little Smalltalk system. Show in detail how the courier could be modified to determine the receiver of a message in the case of multiple inheritance.

≡

Appendix 1

Running Little Smalltalk

The Little Smalltalk system is invoked by typing the command st. The system is interactive —that is, the user types an expression at the keyboard, and the system responds by evaluating the expression and typing the result. For example, when the expression **3 + 4** is typed, the value 7 is displayed on the output. Execution is terminated by typing control—D. A sample execution session is shown in Figure 1.

Whenever the system is waiting for the user to type a command, the cursor is slightly indented. Normally output appears immediately following the command unless it is written to a file or redirected by a Unix directive.

Instance variables for the command level can be created by assigning a value to a new variable name. Thereafter that variable can be used at the command level although it is not known within the scope of any method. The variable "last" always contains the value returned by the last expression typed. Figure 2 shows the creation of a variable. Note that the assignment arrow is formed as two-character sequence.

The default behavior is for the value of expressions, with the exception of assignments, to be typed automatically as they are evaluated. This behavior can be modified either by using the -d flag (see below), or by passing a message to the pseudo variable **smalltalk** (see the description of the class **Smalltalk** in Appendix 3).

Class descriptions must be read from files, they cannot be entered interactively. Class descriptions are entered by using a system directive.

Figure 1 □ *A sample Little Smalltalk session*

```
% st
Little Smalltalk
    3 + 4
7
    ^ D
%
```

209

Figure 2 □ *Creating variables*

```
    newvar < - 2 / 3
    newvar
0.666667
    2 raisedTo:newvar + (4 / 3)
4
    last
4
```

For example, to include a class description contained in a file named
newclass.st, the following system directive should be issued:

>   )i newclass.st

A list of files containing class descriptions can also be given as arguments
to the st command. The command

>   %st file₁ ... fileₙ

is equivalent to the sequence

>   %st
>   Little Smalltalk
>   )i file₁
>   ...
>   )i fileₙ

A table of system directives is given below.

)e filename   Edit the named file. The Little Smalltalk system will sus-
              pend, leaving the user in an editor for making changes to
              the named file. Upon leaving the editor, the named file will
              automatically be included, as if the)i directive had been
              typed.

)g filename   Search for an entry in the system library area matching the
              filename. If it is found, the class descriptions in the library
              entry are included. This command is useful for including
              commonly-used classes that are not part of the standard
              prelude, such as classes for statistics applications or graph-
              ics. Directions for setting up library entries can be found in
              the Little Smalltalk installation notes.

)i filename   Include the named file. The file must contain one or more
              class descriptions. The class descriptions are parsed, and if
              they are syntactically legal, new instances of class **Class** are
              added to the Smalltalk system.

)l filename   Load a previously-saved environment from the named file. The current values of all variables are overridden. The file must have been created using the)s directive (below).

)r filename   Read the named file. The file must contain Smalltalk statements as they would be typed at the keyboard. The effect is the same as if the lines of the file had been typed at the keyboard. The file cannot contain class descriptions.

)s filename   Save the current state in the named file. The values of all variables are saved and can later be reloaded using the)l directive (above).

)!string   Execute the remainder of the line following the exclamation point as a Unix command. Nothing is done with the output of the command nor is the returning status of the command recorded.

Note that the)e system directive invokes an editor on a file containing class descriptions and then automatically includes the file when the editor is exited. Classes also respond to the message edit, which will have the same effect as the)e directive applied to the file containing the class description. Thus the typical debug/edit/debug cycle involves repeated uses of the)e directive or the **edit** message until a desired outcome is achieved. The editor invoked by the)e directive can be changed by setting the EDITOR variable in the user's environment.

The st command can be followed by any of the following options:

—a   If the —a option is given, statistics on the number of memory allocations will be displayed following execution.

—d*digit*

    If the *digit* is zero, only those results explicitly requested by the user will be printed. If 1, the values of expressions typed at the keyboard will be displayed (this is the default). If 2, the values of expressions and the values assigned in assignment statements will be displayed.

—f   The —f option indicates that fast loading should be used, it loads a binary save image for the standard library.

—g   The next argument is taken to be the name of an additional library stored in the system library area. The library is loaded following the standard prelude, as if a '')g'' directive were given at the beginning of execution.

—l   The next argument is taken to be the name of a file containing a binary image saved using the)s directive. This binary image is loaded prior to execution.

—m   Do not perform fast loading. (Used when fastloading is the default.)

—n   The —n option, if given, suppresses the loading of the standard library. Since this gives you a system with almost no functionality, it is seldom useful except during debugging.

—r   The next argument is taken to be the name of a file of Smalltalk commands. The file is included prior to execution, as if a ")r" directive were given at the beginning of execution.

—s   In normal operation, the number of reference count increments and decrements is printed at the end of execution just prior to exit. In the absence of cycles, these increments should equal decrements. Since cycles can cause large chunks of memory to become unreachable and seriously degrade performance, this information is often useful in debugging. The —s option, if given, suppresses the printing of this information.

After the options, you can list any number of files. The files, if given, must contain class descriptions. Appendix 2 gives the syntax for class descriptions. Any classes so defined are included along with the standard library of classes before execution begins.

Appendix 2

Syntax Charts

Syntax charts for the language accepted by the Little Smalltalk system are described on the following pages. The following is a sample class description:

```
Class Set :Collection
| dict |
[
    new
        dict < − Dictionary new

|   add: newElement
        dict at: newElement
            ifAbsent: [dict at: newElement put: 1]

|   remove: oldElement ifAbsent: exceptionBlock
        dict removeKey: oldElement ifAbsent: exceptionBlock

|   size
        ↑ dict size

|   occurencesOf: anElement
        ↑ dict at: anElement ifAbsent: [0]

|   first
        dict first.
        ↑ dict currentKey

|   next
        dict next.
        ↑ dict currentKey

]
```

Class Description

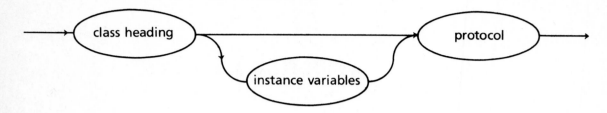

Class Heading

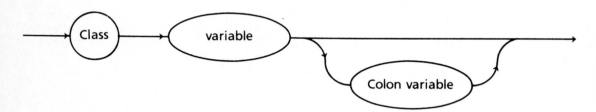

The keyword **Class** must begin with an uppercase letter and consist of lowercase letters, as shown.

The **variable** is the class name and must begin with an uppercase letter.

The **colon variable** defines the superclass for the class and, if not given, will default to class **Object.**

Colon Variables

The colon must immediately precede the variable.

Instance Variables

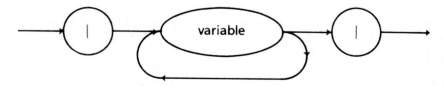

Instance variables must begin with a lowercase letter.

Protocol

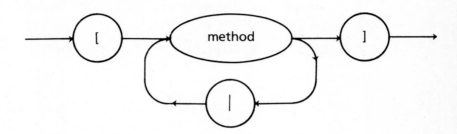

The vertical bar separating methods **must** be placed in column 1.

Method

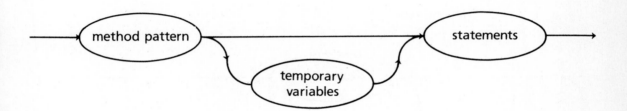

Method Pattern

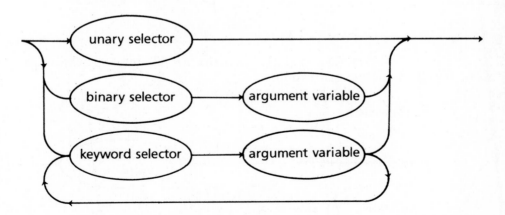

A unary selector is simply an identifier beginning with a lowercase letter, for example *sign*.

A binary selector is one or two adjacent nonalphabetic characters, except parenthesis, square braces, semicolon, or period, for example +.

A keyword selector is an identifier beginning with a lowercase letter and followed by a colon, for example *after:*.

Argument variables must begin with a lowercase letter and must be distinct from instance variables.

Temporary Variables

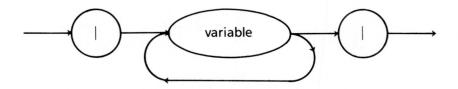

Temporary variables must begin with lowercase letters and must be distinct from both instance and argument variables.

Statements

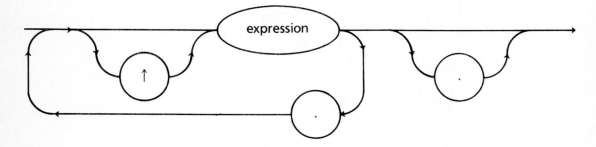

An expression preceded by an up arrow cannot be followed by a period and another expression.

Expression

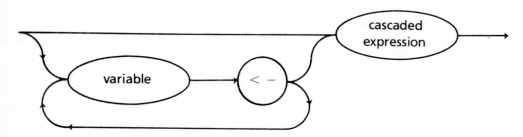

The assignment arrow is a two-character sequence formed by a less than sign ($<$) followed by a minus sign ($-$).

Cascaded Expression

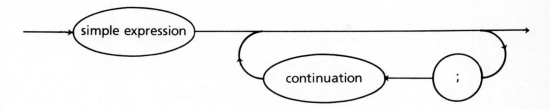

Simple Expression

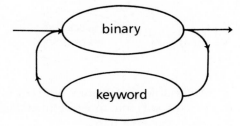

Binary

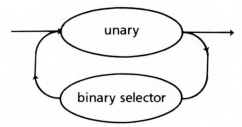

Unary

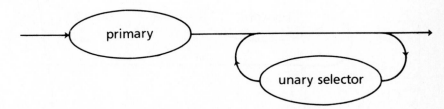

Primary

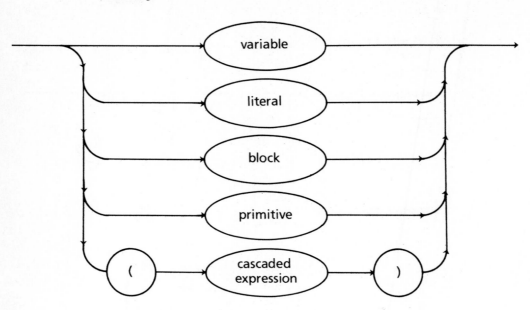

A variable that begins with an uppercase letter is a class name; otherwise, the variable must be instance, argument or temporary variable or a pseudo variable name.

Continuation

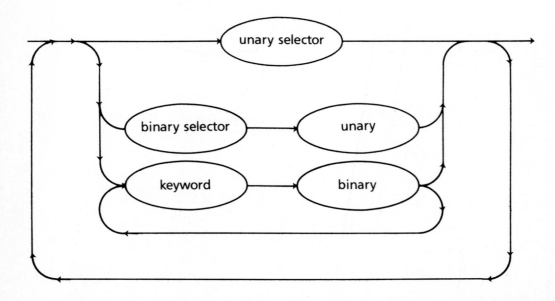

Block

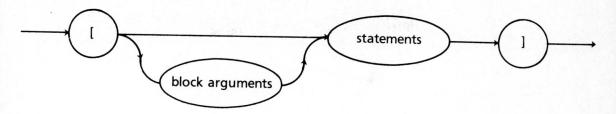

The last statement in a block cannot be followed by a period.

Block Arguments

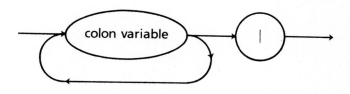

Literal

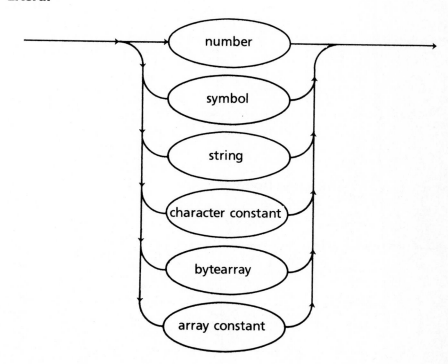

Number

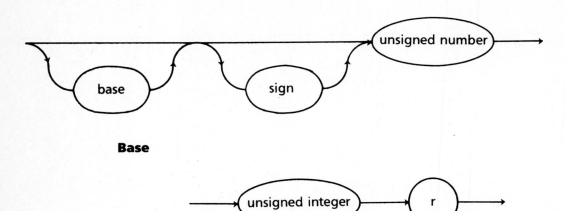

Base

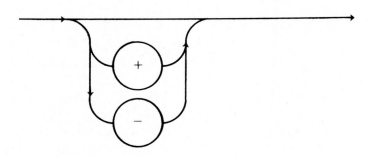

The integer value must be in the range 2 through 36.

Sign

Unsigned Number

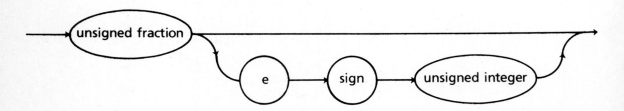

Unsigned Fraction

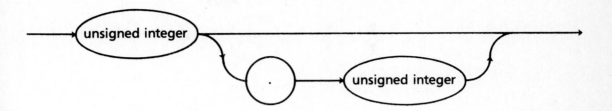

Unsigned Integer

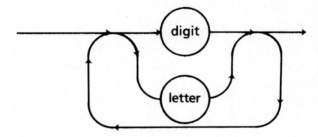

Uppercase letters are used to represent the digits 11-36 in bases greater than 10.

Symbol

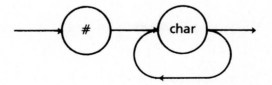

The character sequence following the sharp sign includes all nonspace characters except period, parenthesis, or square braces.

String

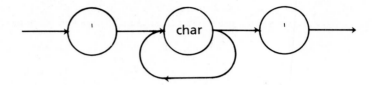

To include a quote mark in a string, use two adjacent quote marks.

Character Constant

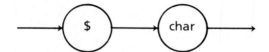

Bytearray

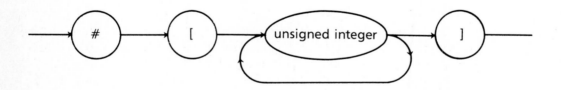

The unsigned integer must be in the range 0 through 255.

Array Constant

Array

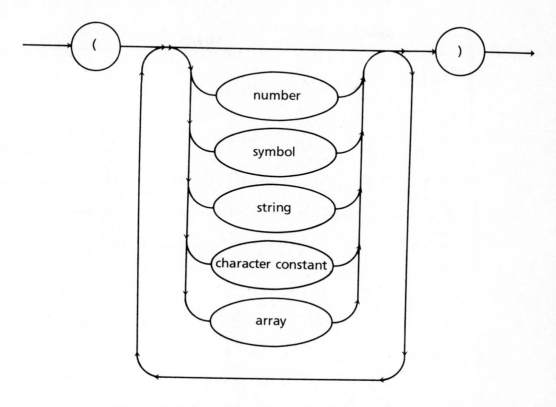

The leading sharp sign can be omitted in symbols and arrays inside of an array list. Binary selectors, keywords, and other sequences of characters are treated as symbols inside of an array.

Primitive

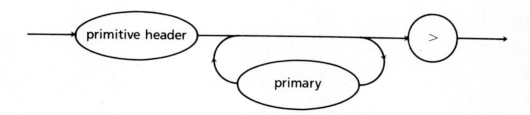

Primitive Header

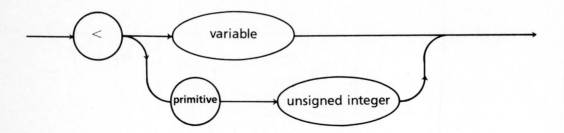

The variable must correspond to one of the primitive names. (See Appendix 4.)

The keyword **primitive** or the primitive name must immediately follow the angle bracket.

The unsigned integer must be a number in the range 0–255.

Appendix 3

Class Descriptions

The messages accepted by the classes included in the Little Smalltalk standard library are described in the following pages. A list of the classes defined, where indentation is used to imply subclassing, is given below:

Object
    UndefinedObject
    Symbol
    Boolean
        True
        False
    Magnitude
        Char
        Number
            Integer
            Float
        Radian
        Point
    Random
    Collection
        Bag
        Set
        KeyedCollection
            Dictionary
                Smalltalk
            SequenceableCollection
                Interval
                List
                    Semaphore
                File
                ArrayedCollection
                    Array
                    ByteArray
                    String
    Block
    Class
    Process

In the descriptions of each message the following notes may occur:

d   Indicates the effect of the message differs slightly from that given in (Goldberg 83).

n   Indicates the message is not included as part of the language defined in (Goldberg 83).

r   Indicates that the protocol for the message overrides a protocol given in some superclass. The message given a second time only where the logical effect of this overriding is important. Some messages, such as copy, are overridden in many classes but are not described in the documentation because the logical effect remains the same.

Object

The class **Object** is a superclass of all classes in the system and is used to provide a consistent basic functionality and default behavior. Many methods in class **Object** are overridden in subclasses.

Responds to

	= =	Return **true** if receiver and argument are the same object; **false** if not.
	~~	Inverse of = =. Return **true** if receiver and argument are different ofjects; **false** if not.
	asString	Return a string representation of the receiver; by default this is the same as *printString*, although one or the other is redefined in many subclasses.
	asSymbol	Return a symbol representing the receiver.
	class	Return object representing the class of the receiver.
	copy	Return *shallowcopy* of receiver. Many subclasses redefine *shallowCopy*.
	deepCopy	Return the receiver. This method is redefined in many subclasses.
d	do:	The argument must be a one-argument block. Execute the block on every element of the receiver collection. Elements in the receiver collection are enumerated using *first* and *next* (below), so the default behavior is merely to execute the block using the receiver as argument.
	error:	Argument must be a String. Print argument string as error message. Return **nil.**

n	first	Return first item in sequence, which is, by default, simply the receiver. See *next*, below.
	isKindOf:.	Argument must be a **Class.** Return **true** if class of receiver, or any superclass thereof, is the same as argument.
	isMemberOf:	Argument must be a **Class.** Return **true** if receiver is instance of argument class.
	isNil	Test whether receiver is object **nil.**
n	next	Return next item in sequence, which is, by default, **nil.** This message is redefined in classes which represent sequences, such as **Array** or **Dictionary.**
	notNil	Test if receiver is not object **nil.**
	print	Display print image of receiver on the standard output.
	printString	Return a string representation of receiver. Objects which do not redefine printString and which therefore do not have a printable representation, return their class name as a string.
	respondsTo:	Argument must be a symbol. Return **true** if receiver will respond to the indicated message.
	shallowCopy	Return the receiver. This method is redefined in many subclasses.

Examples

	Printed result
7~~7.0	True
7 asSymbol;	# 7
7 class	Integer
7 copy	7
7 isKindOf: Number	True
7 isMemberOf: Number	False
7 isNil	False
7 respondsTo: # +	True

Object
   UndefinedObject
The pseudo variable **nil** is an instance (usually the only instance) of the class **UndefinedObject.** The variable **nil** is used to represent undefined values and is also typically returned in error situations. The variable **nil** is also used as a terminator in sequences, as, for example, in response to the message *next* when there are no further elements in a sequence.

Responds to

r	isNil	Overrides method found in Object. Return **true**.
r	notNil	Overrides method found in Object. Return **false**.
r	print-String	Return "**nil**".

Examples

Printed result

nil isNil   True

Object
  Symbol

Instances of the class **Symbol** are created either by their literal representation, which is a pound sign followed by a string of nonspace characters
(for example #aSymbol), or by the message *asSymbol* being passed to an
object. Symbols cannot be created using *new*. Symbols are guaranteed to
have unique representations; that is, two symbols representing the same
characters will always test equal to each other. Inside of literal arrays, the
leading pound signs on symbols can be eliminated, for example: #(these
are symbols).

Responds to

r	= =	Return **true** if the two symbols represent the same characters; **false** otherwise.
r	asString	Return a string representation of the symbol without the leading pound sign.
r	printString	Return a string representation of the symbol, including the leading pound sign.

Examples

Printed result

#abc = = # abc	True
#abc = = # ABC	False
#abc ~ ~ # ABC	True
#abc printString	# abc
'abc' asSymbol	# abc

Object
   Boolean

The class **Boolean** provides protocol for manipulating true and false values. The pseudo variables **true** and **false** are instances of the subclasses of **Boolean: True** and **False,** respectively. The subclasses **True** and **False,** in combination with blocks, are used to implement conditional control structures. Note, however, that the bytecodes may optimize conditional tests by generating code inline, rather than using message passing. Note also that bit-wise boolean operations are provided by class **Integer.**

Responds To

     &   The argument must be a boolean. Return the logical conjunction (and) of the two values.

     | The argument must be a boolean. Return the logical disjunction (or) of the two values.

     and: The argument must be a block. Return the logical conjunction (and) of the two values. If the receiver is false, the second argument is not used; otherwise, the result is the value yielded in evaluating the argument block.

     or: The argument must be a block. Return the logical disjunction (or) of the two values. If the receiver is true, the second argument is not used; otherwise, the result is the value yielded in evaluating the argument block.

     eqv: The argument must be a boolean. Return the logical equivalence (eqv) of the two values.

     xor: The argument must be a boolean. Return the logical exclusive or (xor) of the two values.

Examples

	Printed result
(1 > 3) & (2 < 4)	False
(1 > 3) | (2 < 4)	True
(1 > 3) and: [2 < 4]	False

Object
   Boolean
      True

The pseudo variable **true** is an instance (usually the only instance) of the class **True.** In conjunction with blocks, the class **True** is used to implement conditional transfer of control.

Responds To

ifTrue:	Return the result of evaluating the argument block.
ifFalse;	Return **nil.**
ifTrue:ifFalse:	Return the result of evaluating the first argument block.
ifFalse:ifTrue:	Return the result of evaluating the second argument block.
not	Return **false.**

Examples

                                        Printed result

(3 < 5) not	False
(3 < 5) ifTrue: [17]	17

Object
    Boolean
        False
The pseudo variable **false** is an instance (usually the only instance) of the
class **False.** In conjunction with blocks, the class **False** is used to implement conditional transfer of control.

ifTrue:	Return **nil.**
ifFalse:	Return the result of evaluating the argument block.
ifTrue:ifFalse;	Return the result of evaluating the second argument block.
ifFalse:iftrue:	Return the result of evaluating the first argument block.
not	Return **true.**

Examples

                                        Printed result

(1 < e) ifTrue: [17]	17
(1 < 3) ifFalse; [17]	nil

Object
        Magnitude
The class **Magnitude** provides protocol for those subclasses possessing a
linear ordering. For the sake of efficiency, most subclasses redefine some
or all of the relational messages. All methods are defined in terms of the
basic messages <, = and >, which are in turn defined circularly in terms

of each other. Thus each subclass of **Magnitude** must redefine at least one of these messages.

<	Relational less than test. Returns a boolean.
< =	Relational less than or equal test.
=	Relational equal test. Note that this differs from = =, which is an object equality test.
~=	Relational not equal test, opposite of =.
> =	Relational greater than or equal test.
>	Relational greater than test.
between:and:	Relational test for inclusion.
max:	Return the maximum of the receiver and argument value.
min:	Return the minimum of the receiver and argument value.

Examples

Printed result

$A max: $a	$a
4 between: 3.1 and: (17/3)	True

Examples

Printed result

3 < 4.1	True
3 + 4.1	7.1
3.14159 exp	23.1406
0 gamma	40320
5 reciprocal	0.2
0.5 radians	0.5 radians
13 roundTo: 5	15
12 truncateTo: 5	10

Object
    Magnitude
        Char

The class **Char** defines protocol for objects with character values. Characters possess an ordering given by the underlying representation; however, arithmetic is not defined for character values. Characters are written literally by preceding the character desired with a dollar sign, for example: $a $B $$.

Responds to

r	= =	Object equality test. Two instances of the same character always test equal.
	asciiValue	Return an **Integer** representing the ASCII value of the receiver.
	asLowercase	If the receiver is an uppercase letter, returns the same letter in lowercase; otherwise, returns the receiver.
	asUppercase	If the receiver is a lowercase letter, returns the same letter in uppercase; otherwise, returns the receiver.
r	asString	Return a length one string containing the receiver. Does not contain leading dollar sign; compare to *printString*.
	digitValue	If the receiver represents a number (for example $9), return the digit value of the number. If the receiver is an uppercase letter (for example $B), return the position of the number in the uppercase letters + 10, ($B returns 11, for example). If the receiver is neither a digit nor an uppercase letter, an error is given and **nil** returned.
	isAlphaNumeric	Respond **true** if receiver is either digit or letter; **false** otherwise.
	isDigit	Respond **true** if receiver is a digit; **false** otherwise.
	isLetter	Respond **true** if receiver is a letter, **false** otherwise.
	isLowercase	Respond **true** if receiver is a lowercase letter; **false** otherwise.
	isSeparator	Respond **true** if receiver is a space, tab or newline; **false** otherwise.
	isUppercase	Respond **true** if receiver is an uppercase letter; **false** otherwise.
	isVowel	Respond **true** if receiver is $a, $e, $i, $o, or $u, in either upper- or lowercase.
r	printString	Respond with a string representation of the character value. Includes leading dollar sign; compare to *asString*, which does not include $.

Examples

	Printed result
$A < $0	False
$A asciiValue	65

$A asString	A
$A printString	$A
$A isVowel	True
$A digitValue	10
$ asciiValue radix: 8	8r40

Object
    Magnitude
        Number

The class **Number** is an abstract superclass for **Integer** and **Float**. Instances of **Number** cannot be created directly. Relational messages and many arithmetic messages are redefined in each subclass for arguments of the appropriate type. In general, an error message is given and **nil** returned for illegal arguments.

Responds To

	+	Mixed type addition.
	−	Mixed type subtraction.
	*	Mixed type multiplication.
	/	Mixed type division.
n	↑	Exponentiation, same as raisedTo:
	@	Construct a point with coordinates being the receiver and the argument.
	abs	Absolute value of the receiver.
	exp	e raised to the power.
n	gamma	Return the gamma function (generalized factorial) evaluated at the receiver.
	ln	Natural logarithm of the receiver.
	log:	Logarithm in the given base.
	negated	The arithmetic inverse of the receiver.
	negative	**True** if the receiver is negative.
n	pi	Return the approximate value of the receiver multiplied by (3.1415926...).
	positive	**True** if the receiver is positive.
n	radians	Argument converted into radians.
	raisedTo:	The receiver raised to the argument value.
	reciprocal	The arithmetic reciprocal of the receiver.
	roundTo:	The receiver rounded to units of the argument.

sign	Return -1, 0, or 1 depending upon whether the receiver is negative, zero, or positive.
sqrt	Square root, nil if the receiver is less than zero.
squared	Return the receiver multiplied by itself.
strictlyPositive	**True** if the receiver is greater than zero.
to:	Interval from receiver to argument value with step of 1.
to:by:	Interval from receiver to argument in given steps.
truncatedTo:	The receiver truncated to units of the argument.

Object
    Magnitude
        Number
            Integer

The class **Integer** provides protocol for objects with integer values.

Responds To

r = =	Object equality test. Two integers representing the same value are considered to be the same object.
//	Integer quotient, truncated towards negative infinity (compare to *quo:*).
\ \	Integer remainder, truncated towards negative infinity (compare to *rem:*).
allMask:	Argument must be **Integer**. Treating receiver and argument as bit strings, return **true** if all bits with value in argument correspond to bits with 1 value in the receiver.
anyMask:	Argument must be **Integer**. Treating receiver and argument as bit strings, return **true** if any bit with 1 value in argument corresponds to a bit with 1 value in the receiver.
asCharacter	Return the Char with the same underlying ASCII representation as the low order eight bits of the receiver.
asFloat	Floating point value with same magnitude as receiver.
bitAnd:	Argument must be **Integer**. Treating the receiver and argument as bit strings, return logical **and** of values.
bitAt:	Argument must be **Integer** greater than 0 and less than underlying word size. Treating receiver as a bit string, return the bit value at the given position, numbering from low order (or rightmost) position.
bitInvert	Return the receiver with all bit positions inverted.

bitOr:	Return logical **or** of values.
bitShift:	Treating the receiver as a bit string, shift bit values by amount indicated in argument. Negative values shift right; positive values shift left.
bitXor:	Return logical **exclusive-or** of values.
even	Return **true** if receiver is even; **false** otherwise.
factorial	Return the factorial of the receiver. Return as **Float** for large numbers.
gcd:	Argument must be **Integer.** Return the greatest common divisor of the receiver and argument.
highBit	Return the location of the highest 1 bit in the receiver. Return **nil** for receiver zero.
lcm:	Argument must be **Integer.** Return least common multiple of receiver and argument.
noMask:	Argument must be **Integer.** Treating receiver and argument as bit strings, return true if no 1 bit in the argument corresponds to a 1 bit in the receiver.
odd	Return true if receiver is odd; false otherwise.
quo:	Return quotient of receiver divided by argument.
radix:	Return a string representation of the receiver value printed in the base represented by the argument. Argument value must be less than 36.
rem:	Remainder after receiver is divided by argument value.
timesRepeat:	Repeat argument block the number of times given by the receiver.

Examples

Printed result

5 + 4	7
5 allMask: 4	True
4 allMask: 5	False
5 anyMask: 4	True
5 bitAnd: 3	1
5 bitOr: 3	7
5 bitInvert	−6
254 radix: 16	16rFE
−5 // 4	−2
−5 quo: 4	−1
−5 \ \ 4	1
−5 rem: 4	−1
8 factorial	40320

Object
    Magnitude
        Number
            Float

The class **Float** provides protocol for objects with floating point values.

Responds To

r	= =	Object equality test. Return **true** if the receiver and argument represent the same floating point value.
n	↑	Floating exponentiation.
	arcCos	Return a **Radian** representing the arcCos of the receiver.
	arcSin	Return a **Radian** representing the arcSin of the receiver.
	arcTan	Return a **Radian** representing the arcTan of the receiver.
	asFloat	Return the receiver.
	ceiling	Return the integer ceiling of the receiver.
	coerce:	Coerce the argument into being type Float.
	exp	Return e raised to the receiver value.
	floor	Return the integer floor of the receiver.
	fractionPart	Return the fractional part of the receiver.
n	gamma	Return the value of the gamma function applied to the receiver value.
	integerPart	Return the integer part of the receiver.
	ln	Return the natural log of the receiver.
	radix:	Return a string containing the printable representation of the receiver in the given radix. Argument must be an Integer less than 36.
	rounded	Return the receiver rounded to the nearest integer.
	sqrt	Return the square root of the receiver.
	truncated	Return the receiver truncated to the nearest integer.

Examples

                Printed result

4.2 * 3	12.6
2.1 ↑ 4	19.4481
2.1 raisedTo: 4	19.4481

0.5 arcSin	0.523599 radians
2.1 reciprocal	0.47619
4.3 sqrt	2.07364

Object
    Magnitude
        Radian

The class **Radian** is used to represent radians. Radians are a unit of measurement, independent of other numbers. Only radians will respond to the trigonometric functions such as *sin* and *cos*. Numbers can be converted into radians by passing them the message *radians*. Similarly, radians can be converted into numbers by sending them the message *asFloat*. Notice that only a limited range of arithmetic operations are permitted on Radians. Radians are normalized to be between 0 and 2π by adding or subtracting multiples of 2π.

Responds to

+	Argument must be a radian. Add the two radians together and return the normalized result.
−	Argument must be a Radian. Subtract the argument from the receiver and return the normalized result.
*	Argument must be a number. Multiply the receiver by the argument amount and return the normalized result.
/	Argument must be a number. Divide the receiver by the argument amount and return the normalized result.
asFloat	Return the receiver as a floating point number.
cos	Return a floating point number representing the cosine of the receiver.
sin	Return a floating point number representing the sine of the receiver.
tan	Return a floating point number representing the tangent of the receiver.

Examples

                        Printed result

0.5236 radians sin	0.5
0.5236 radians cos	0.866025
0.5236 radians tan	0.577352
0.5 arcSin asFloat	0.532599

Object
  Magnitude
    Point
Points are used to represent pairs of quantities, such as coordinate pairs.

Responds To

<	**True** if both values of the receiver are less than the corresponding values in the argument.
< =	**True** if the first value is less than or equal to the corresponding value in the argument, and the second value is less than the corresponding value in the argument.
> =	**True** if both values of the receiver are greater than or equal to the corresponding values in the argument.
*	Return a new point with coordinates multiplied by the argument value.
/	Return a new point with coordinates divided by the argument value.
/ /	Return a new point with coordinates divided by the argument value.
+	Return a new point with coordinates offset by the corresponding values in the argument.
abs	Return a new point with coordinates having the absolute value of the receiver.
dist:	Return the Euclidean distance between the receiver and the argument point.
max:	The argument must be a **Point.** Return the lower right corner of the rectangle defined by the receiver and the argument.
min:	The argument must be a **Point.** return the upper left corner of the rectangle defined by the receiver and the argument.
transpose	Return a new point with coordinates being the transpose of the receiver.
x	Return the first coordinate of the receiver.
x:	Set the first coordinate of the receiver.
x:y:	Sets both coordinates of the receiver.
y	Return the second coordinate of the receiver.
y:	Set the second coordinate of the receiver.

Examples

	Printed result
(10@12) < (11@14)	True
(10@12) < (11@11)	False

(10@12) max: (11@11)	11@12
(10@12) min: (11@11)	10@11
(10@12) dist: (11@14)	2.23607
(10@12) transpose	12@10

Object
Random

The class **Random** provides protocol for random number generation. Sending the message *next* to an instance of **Random** results in a **Float** between 0.0 and 1.0 randomly distributed. By default, the pseudo random sequence is the same for each object in class **Random.** This can be altered by using the message *randomize*.

Responds to

n	between:and:	Return a random number uniformly distributed between the two arguments.
n	first	Return a random number between 0.0 and 1.0. This message merely provides consistency with protocol for other sequences such as Arrays or Intervals.
	next	Return a random number between 0.0 and 1.0.
d	next:	Return an **Array** containing the next n random numbers where n is the argument value.
n	randInteger:	The argument must be an integer. Return a random integer between 1 and the value given.
n	randomize	Change the pseudo-random number generator seed by a time-dependent value.

Examples

Printed result

i ← Random new	
i next	0.759
i next	0.157
i next: 3	#(0.408 0.278 0.547)
i randInteger: 12	5
i between: 4 and 17.5	10.0

Object
Collection

The class **Collection** provides protocol for groups of objects such as **Arrays** or **Sets.** The different forms of collections are distinguished by several characteristics, among them whether the size of the collection is fixed or unbounded, the presence of absence of an ordering, and their insertion or access method. For example, an **Array** is a collection with a fixed size and ordering, indexed by integer keys. A **Dictionary,** on the other hand, has no fixed size or ordering and can be indexed by arbitrary elements. Nevertheless, **Arrays** and **Dictionary**s share many features in common such as their access method (*at:* and *at:put:*) and the ability to respond to *collect:*, *select:*, and many other messages.

The table below lists some of the characteristics of several forms of collections:

Name	Creation Method	Size fixed?	Ordered?	Insertion Method	Access Method	Removal Method
Bag/Set	**new**	no	no	add:	includes:	remove:
Dictionary	**new**	no	no	at:put:	at:	removeKey:
Interval	**n to: m**	yes	yes	none	at:	none
List	**new**	no	yes	addFirst: addLast:	first last	remove:
Array	**new:**	yes	yes	at:put:	at:	none
String	**new:**	yes	yes	at:put:	at:	none

The list below shows messages that are shared in common by all collections.

Responds to

addAll: The argument must be a **collection.** Add all the elements of the argument collection to the receiver collection.

asArray   Return a new collection of type **Array** containing the elements from the receiver collection. If the receive was ordered, the elements will be in the same order in the new collection; otherwise, the elements will be in an arbitrary order.

asBag   Return a new collection of type **Bag** containing the elements from the receiver collection.

n	asList	Return a new collection of type **List** containing the elements from the receiver collection. If the receiver was ordered, the elements will be in the same order in the new collection, otherwise the elements will be in an arbitrary order.
	asSet	Return a new collection of type **Set** containing the elements from the receiver collection.
	asString	Return a new collection of type **String** containing the elements from the receiver collection. The elements to be included must all be of type **Character.** If the receiver was ordered, the elements will be in the same order in the new collection; otherwise, the elements will be listed in an arbitrary order.
	coerce:	The argument must be a collection. Return a collection of the same type as the receiver containing elements from the argument collection. This message is redefined in most subclasses of collection.
	collect:	The argument must be a one-argument block. Return a new collection like the receiver containing the result of evaluating the argument block on each element of the receiver collection.
	detect:	The argument must be a one-argument block. Return the first element in the receiver collection for which the argument block evaluates **true.** Report an error and return **nil** if no such element exists. Note that in unordered collections (such as **Bags** or **Dictionary**s the first element to be encountered that will satisfy the condition may not be easily predictable.
	detect:ifAbsent:	Return the first element in the receiver collection for which the first argument block evaluates **true.** Return the result of evaluating the second argument if no such element exists.
	do:	The argument must be a one-argument block. Evaluate the argument block on each element in the receiver collection.
	includes:	Return **true** if the receiver collection contains the argument.
	inject:into:	The first argument must be a value, the second a two-argument block. The second argument is evaluated once for each element in the receiver collection, passing as arguments the result of the

previous evaluation (starting with the first argument) and the element. The value returned is the final value generated.

isEmpty	Return **true** if the receiver collection contains no elements.
occurrencesOf:	Return the number of times the argument occurs in the receiver collection.
remove:	Remove the argument from the receiver collection. Report an error if the element is not contained in the receiver collection.
remove:ifAbsent:	Remove the first argument from the receiver collection. Evaluate the second argument if not present.
reject:	The argument must be a one-argument block. Return a new collection like the receiver containing all elements for which the argument block returns false.
select:	The argument must be a one-argument block. Return a new collection like the receiver containing all elements for which the argument block returns **true.**
size	Return the number of elements in the receiver collection.

Examples

Printed result

```
i ← 'abacadabra'
i size                      10
i asArray                   #( $a $b $a $c $a $d $a $b $r $a )
i asBag                     Bag ( $a $a $a $a $a $r $b $b $c $d)
i asSet                     Set ( $a $r $b $c $d )
i occurencesOf: $a          5
i reject: [:x | x isVowel]  bcdbr
```

Object
    Collection
        Bag/Set
Bags and **Sets** are each unordered collections of elements. Elements in the collections do not have keys but are added and removed directly. The difference between a **Bag** and a **Set** is that in a **Bag** each element can occur any number of times; whereas only one copy is inserted into a **Set**.

Responds to

add:	Add the indicated element to the receiver collection.
add:withOccurences:	(**Bag** only) Add the indicated element to the receiver **Bag** the given number of times.
n first	Return the first element from the receiver collection. Because the collection is unordered, the first element depends upon certain values in the internal representation and is not guaranteed to be any specific element in the collection.
n next	Return the next element in the collection. In conjunction with *first*, this can be used to access each element of the collection in turn.

Examples

                                                        Printed result

```
i ← (1 to: 6) asBag                     Bag ( 1 2 3 4 5 6 )
i size                                  6
i select: [:x | (x \ \ 2) strictly Positive]   Bag ( 1 3 5 )
i collect: [:x | x \ \ 3]               Bag ( 0 0 1 1 2 2 )
j ← ( i collect: [:x | x \ \3] ) asSet  Set ( 0 1 2 )
j size                                  3
```

Note: Since **Bags** and **Sets** are unordered, there is no way to establish a mapping between the elements of the Bag i in the example above and the corresponding elements in the collection that resulted from the message collect: [:x | x \ \ 3].

Object
   Collection
      KeyedCollection

The class **KeyedCollection** provides protocol for collections with keys, such as **Dictionary**s and **Arrays.** Since each entry in the collection has both a key and value, the method *add:* is no longer appropriate. Instead, the method *at:put:*, which provides both a key and a value, must be used.

Responds to

asDictionary	Return a new collection of type **Dictionary** containing the elements from the receiver collection.

at:	Return the item in the receiver collection whose key matches the argument. Produce an error message and return nil if no item is currently in the receiver collection under the given key.
at:ifAbsent;	Return the element stored in the dictionary under the key given by the first argument. Return the result of evaluating the second argument if no such element exists.
atAll:put:	The first argument must be a collection containing keys valid for the receiver. Place the second argument at each location given by a key in the first argument.
binaryDo:	The argument must be a two-argument block. This message is similar to *do:,* however both the key and the element value are passed as argument to the block.
includesKey:	Return **true** if the indicated key is valid for the receiver collection.
indexOf:	Return the key value of the first element in the receiver collection matching the argument. Produces an error message if no such element exists. Note that, as with the message *detect:,* in unordered collections the first element may not be related in any way to the order in which elements were placed into the collection but is rather implementation dependent.
indexOf:ifAbsent	Return the key value of the first element in the receiver collection matching the argument. Return the result of evaluating the second argument if no such element exists.
keys	Return a set containing the keys for the receiver collection.
keysDo;	The argument must be a one-argument block. Similar to *do:* except that the values passed to the block are the keys of the receiver collection.
keysSelect;	Similar to *select* except that the selection is made on the basis of keys instead of values.
removeKey:	Remove the object with the given key from the receiver collection. Print an error message and return **nil** if no such object exists. Return the value of the deleted item.
removeKey:ifAbsent:	Remove the object with the given key from the receiver collection. Return the result of evaluating the second argument if no such object exists.

values   Return a Bag containing the values from the re-
                              ceiver collection.

Examples

                                        Printed result

i ← 'abacadabra'
i atAll: (1 to: 7 by: 2) put: $e   ebecedebra
i indexOf: $r   9
i atAll: i keys put: $z   zzzzzzzzzz
i keys   Set (1 2 3 4 5 6 7 8 9 10)
i values   Bag ($z $z $z $z $z $z $z $z $z $z)
#(how odd) asDictionary   Dictionary (1 @ #how 2 @ odd)

Object
    Collection
        KeyedCollection
            Dictionary
A **Dictionary** is an unordered collection of elements as are **Bags** and **Sets**.
However, unlike these collections, when elements are inserted and removed from a **Dictionary,** they must reference an explicit key. Both the
key and value portions of an element can be any object although commonly
the keys are instances of **Symbol** or **Number.**

Responds to

	at:put:	Place the second argument into the receiver collection under the key given by the first argument.
	currentKey	Return the key of the last element yielded in response to a *first* or *next* request.
n	first	Return the first element of the receiver collection. Return **nil** if the receiver collection is empty.
n	next	Return the next element of the receiver collection, or **nil** if no such element exists.

Examples

                        Printed result

i ← Dictionary new
i at: #abc put: # def
i at: # pqr put: # tus
i at: # xyz put: # wrt

i print	Dictionary (# abc @ # def # pqr @ # tus # xyz @ # wrt)
i size	3
i at: # pqr	# tus
i indexOf: # tus	#pqr
i keys	Set (# abc # pqr # xyz)
i values	Bag (# wrt # def # tus)
i collect: [:x | x asString at: 2]	Dictionary (# abc @ $e # pqr @ $u # xyz @ $r)

Object
    Collection
        KeyedCollection
           Dictionary
                Smalltalk

The class **Smalltalk** provides protocol for the pseudo-variable **smalltalk.** Since it is a subclass of Dictionary, this variable can be used to store information and thus provide a means of communication between objects. Other messages modify various parameters used by the Little Smalltalk system. Note that the pseudo-variable **smalltalk** is unique to the Little Smalltalk system and is not part of the Smalltalk-80 programming environment.

Responds To

n	date	Return the current date and time as a string.
n	display	Set execution display to display the result of every expression typed except assignments. Note that the display behavior can also be modified using the —d argument on the command line.
n	displayAssign	Set execution display to display the result of every expression typed including assignment statements.
n	doPrimitive:withArguments:	Execute the indicated primitive with arguments given by the second array. A few primitives (such as those dealing with process management) cannot be executed in this manner.
n	getString	Return text typed at the terminal as a String. All characters up to the next newline are accepted.
n	noDisplay	Turn off execution display (no results will be displayed unless explicitly requested by the user).

d	perform:withArguments:	Send indicated message to the receiver using the arguments given. The first value in the argument array is taken to be the receiver of the message. Results are unpredictable if the number of arguments is not appropriate for the given message.
n	sh:	The argument, which must be a string, is executed as a Unix command by the shell. The value returned is the termination status of the shell.
n	time:	The argument must be a block. The block is executed and the number of seconds elapsed during execution returned. Time is accurate to within only about one second.

Examples

Printed result

smalltalk date	Fri Apr 12 16:15:42 1985
smalltalk perform: # + withArguments: #(2 5)	7
smalltalk doPrimitive: 10 withArguments: #(2 5)	7

Object
    Collection
        KeyedCollection
            SequenceableCollection
The class **SequenceableCollection** contains protocol for collections that have a definite sequential ordering and are indexed by integer keys. Since there is a fixed order for elements, it is possible to refer to the last element in a **SequenceableCollection.**

Responds to

	Append the argument collection to the receiver collection, returning a new collection of the same type as the receiver.
copyFrom:to:	Return a new collection like the receiver containing the designated subportion of the receiver collection.
copyWith:	Return a new collection like the receiver with the argument added to the end.

copyWithout: ·	Return a new collection like the receiver with all occurrences of the argument removed.
equals:startingAt:	The first argument must be a **Sequenceable-Collection.** Return true if each element of the receiver collection is equal to the corresponding element in the argument offset by the amount given in the second argument.
findFirst:	Find the key for the first element whose value satisfies the argument block. Produce an error message if no such element exists.
findFirst:ifAbsent:	Both arguments must be blocks. Find the key for the first element whose value satisfies the first argument block. If no such element exists, return the value of the second argument.
findLast:	Find the key for the last element whose value satisfies the argument block. Produce an error message if no such element exists.
findLast:ifAbsent:	Both arguments must be blocks. Find the key for the last element whose value satisfies the first argument block. If no such element exists, return the value of the second argument.
firstKey	Return the first key valid for the receiver collection.
indexOfSubCollection: startingAt:	Starting at the position given by the second argument, find the next block of elements in the receiver collection which match the collection given by the first argument and return the index for the start of that block. Produce an error message if no such position exists.
indexOfSubcollection: startingAt:ifAbsent:	Similar to *indexOfSubCollection:startingAt:,* except that the result of the exception block is produced if no position exists matching the pattern.
last	Return the last element in the receiver collection.
lastKey	Return the last key valid for the receiver collection.
replaceFrom:to:with:	Replace the elements in the receiver collection in the positions indicated by the first two arguments with values taken from the collection given by the third argument.
replaceFrom:to:with: startingAt:	Replace the elements in the receiver collection in the positions indicated by the first two arguments with values taken from the collection

		given in the third argument, starting at the position given by the fourth argument.
n	reversed	Return a collection like the receiver with elements reversed.
	reverseDo:	Similar to *do:* except that the items are presented in reverse order.
n	sort	Return a collection like the receiver with the elements sorted using the comparison $<\ =$. Elements must be able to respond to the binary message $<\ =$.
n	sort:	The argument must be a two-argument block which yields a boolean. Return a collection like the receiver, sorted using the argument to compare elements for the purpose of ordering.
	with:do:	The second argument must be a two-argument block. Present one element from the receiver collection and from the collection given by the first argument in turn to the second argument block. An error message is given if the collections do not have the same number of elements.

Examples

                                                                    Printed result

```
i ← 'abacadabra'
i copyFrom: 4 to: 8                          cadab
i copyWith: $z                               abacadabraz
i copyWithout: $a                            bcdbr
i findFirst: [:x | x > $m]                   9
i indexOfSubCollection: 'dab 'startingAt: 1  6
i reversed                                   arbadacaba
i , i reversed                               abacadabraarbadacaba
i sort: [:x :y | x > = y]                    rdcbbaaaaa
```

Object
    Collection
        KeyedCollection
            SequenceableCollection
                Interval

The class **Interval** represents a sequence of numbers in an arithmetic sequence, either ascending or descending. Instances of **Interval** are created by numbers in response to the message *to:* or *to:by:*. In conjunction with the message *do:*, **Intervals** create a control structure similar to **do** or **for** loops in Angol-like languages. For example:

> (1 to: 10) do: [:x | x print]

will print the numbers 1 through 10. Although **Intervals** are a collection, additional values cannot be added. **Intervals** can, however, be accessed randomly by using the message *at:*.

Responds to

first	Produce the first element from the interval. In conjunction with *last*, this message may be used to produce each element from the interval in turn. Note that **Intervals** also respond to the message *at:*, which can be used to produce elements in an arbitrary order.
from:to:by:	Initialize the upper and lower bounds and the step size for the receiver. (This is used principally internally by the method for number to create new **Intervals**).
next	Produce the next element from the interval.
size	Return the number of elements that will be generated in producing the interval.

Examples

	Printed result
(7 to: 13 by: 3) asArray	# (7 10 13)
(7 to: 13 by: 3) at: 2	10
(1 to: 10) inject: 0 into [:x :y	x + y]	55
(7 to: 13) copyFrom: 2 to: 5	# (8 9 10 11)
(3 to: 5) copyWith: 13	# (3 4 5 13)
(3 to: 5) copyWithout: 4	# (3 5)
(2 to: 4) equals: (1 to: 4) startingAt:2	True

Object
   Collection
      KeyedCollection
         SequenceableCollection
            List

Lists represent collections with a fixed order but indefinite size. No keys are used, and elements are added or removed from one end or the other. Used in this way, Lists can perform as *stacks* or as *queues*. The table below illustrates how stack and queue operations can be implemented in terms of messages to instances of List.

stack operations		queue operations	
push	addLast:	add	addLast:
pop	removeLast	first in queue	first
top	last	remove first in queue	removeFirst
test empty	isEmpty	test empty	isEmpty

Responds to

add: Add the element to the beginning of the receiver collection. This is the same as *addFirst:*.

addAllFirst: The argument must be a SequenceableCollection. The elements of the argument are added, in order, to the front of the receiver collection.

addAllLast: The argument must be a SequenceableCollection. The elements of the argument are added, in order, to the end of the receiver collection.

addFirst: The argument is added to the front of the receiver collection.

addLast: The argument is added to the back of the receiver collection.

removeFirst   Remove the first element from the receiver collection, returning the removed value.

removeLast   Remove the last element from the receiver collection, returning the removed value.

Examples

                                                Printed result

```
i ← List new
i addFirst: 2 / 3                   List ( 0.6666 )
i add: $A
i addAllLast: (12 to: 14 by: 2)
i print                             List ( 0.6666 $A 12 14)
i first                             0.6666
i removeLast                        14
i print                             List ( 0.6666 $A 12 )
```

Object
    Collection
        KeyedCollection
            SequenceableCollection
                List

Semaphore

Semaphores are used to synchronize concurrently running **Processes.**

Responds To

new: If created using *new,* a **Semaphore** starts out with zero excess signals. Alternatively, a **Semaphore** can be created with an arbitrary number of excess signals by giving it an argument to *new:.*

critical: The argument must be a block. The block is executed as a critical section during which no other critical section using the same semaphore can execute.

signal   If there is a process blocked on the semaphore, it is scheduled for execution; otherwise, the number of excess signals is incremented by one.

wait   If there are excess signals associated with the semaphore, the number of signals is decremented by one; otherwise, the current process is placed on the semaphore queue.

Object
    Collection
        KeyedCollection
            SequenceableCollection
                File

A **File** is a type of collection where the elements are stored on an external medium, typically a disk. For this reason, although most operations on collections are defined for files, many can be quite slow in execution. A file can be opened on one of three *modes.* In *character* mode every read returns a single character from the file. In *integer* mode every read returns a single word as an integer value. In *string* mode every read returns a single line as a **String.** For writing, character and string modes will write the string representation of the argument, while integer mode must write only a single integer.

Responds To

at: Return the object stored at the indicated position. Position is given as a character count from the start of the file.

at:put: Place the object at the indicated position in the file. Position is given as a character count from the start of the file.

characterMode   Set the mode of the receiver file to *character.*

currentKey   Return the current position in the file, as a character count from the start of the file.

integerMode   Set the mode of the receiver file to *integer.*

open:	Open the indicated file for reading. The argument must be a **String**.
open:for:	The *for:* argument must be one of 'r', 'w' or 'r+' (see fopen(3) in the Unix programmer's manual). Open the file in the indicated mode.
read	Return the next object from the file.
size	Return the size of the file, in character counts.
stringMode	Set the mode of the receiver file to *string*.
write:	Write the argument into the file.

Object
    Collection
        KeyedCollection
            SequenceableCollection
                ArrayedCollection

The class **ArrayedCollection** provides protocol for collections with a fixed size and integer keys. Unlike other collections, which are created using the message *new*, instances of **ArrayedCollection** must be created using the one-argument message *new:*. The argument given with this message must be a positive integer representing the size of the collection to be created. In addition to the protocol shown, many of the methods inherited from superclasses are redefined in this class.

Responds to

=	The argument must also be an **Array**. Test whether the receiver and the argument have equal elements listed in the same order.
at:ifAbsent:	Return the element stored with the given key. Return the result of evaluating the second argument if the key is not valid for the receiver collection.
n padTo:	Return an array like the receiver that is at least as long as the argument value. Returns the receiver if it is already longer than the argument.

Examples

	Printed result
'small' = 'small'	True
'small' = 'SMALL'	False
'small' asArray	# ($s $m $a $l $l)

```
'small' asArray = 'small'     True
# (1 2 3) padTo:5             # (1 2 3 nil nil)
# (1 2 3) padTo: 2            # (1 2 3)
```

Object
    Collection
        KeyedCollection
            SequenceableCollection
            ArrayedCollection
                Array

Instances of the class **Array** are perhaps the most commonly used data structure in Smalltalk programs. **Arrays** are represented textually by a pound sign preceding the list of array elements.

Responds to

at: Return the item stored in the position given by the argument. An error message is produced and **nil** returned if the argument is not a valid key.

at:put: Store the second argument in the position given by the first argument. An error message is produced and **nil** returned if the argument is not a valid key.

Examples

                            Printed result

```
i ← # ( 110 101 97)
i size                               3
i ← i copyWith: 116                  # ( 110 101 97 116)
i ← i collect: [:x | x asCharacter]  # ( #n #e #a #t )
i asString                           neat
```

Object
    Collection
        KeyedCollection
            SequenceableCollection
            ArrayedCollection
                ByteArray

A **ByteArray** is a special form of array in which the elements must be numbers in the range 0 through 255. Instances of **ByteArray** are given a very compact encoding and are used extensively internally in the Little Smalltalk system. A **ByteArray** can be represented textually by a pound sign preceding the list of array elements surrounded by a pair of square braces.

Responds to

at: Return the item stored in the position given by the argument. An error message is produced and **nil** returned if the argument is not a valid key.

at:put: Store the second argument in the position given by the first argument. An error message is produced and **nil** returned if the argument is not a valid key.

Examples

	Printed result
i ← # [110 l0l 97]	3
i size	#[110 101 97 116]
i ← i copyWith: 116	# (#n #e #a #t)
i ← i asArray collect: [:x | x asCharacter]	neat
i asString	

Object
    Collection
        KeyedCollection
            SequenceableCollection
                ArrayedCollection
                    String

Instances of the class **String** are similar to **Arrays** except that the individual elements must be **Character. Strings** are represented literally by placing single quote marks around the characters making up the string. **Strings** also differ from **Arrays** in that Strings possess an ordering given by the underlying ASCII sequence.

Responds to

,   Concatenates the argument to the receiver string, producing a new string. If the argument is not a **String,** it is first converted using *printString*.

<   The argument must be a **String.** Test if the receiver is lexically less than the argument. For purposes of comparison, case differences are ignored.

< =   Test if the receiver is lexically less than or equal to the argument.

	> =	Test if the receiver is lexically greater than or equal to the argument.
	>	Test if the receiver is lexically greater than the argument.
n	asFloat	Return the string converted into a floating point value.
n	asInteger	Return the string converted into an integer.
r	asSymbol	Return a **Symbol** with characters given by the receiver string.
	at:	Return the character stored at the position given by the argument. Produce an error message and return **nil** if the argument does not represent a valid key.
	at:put:	Store the character given by second argument at the location given by the first argument. Produce an error message and return **nil** if either argument is invalid.
n	copyFrom:length:	Return a substring of the receiver. The substring is taken from the indicated starting position in the receiver and extends for the given length. Produce an error message and return **nil** if the given positions are not legal.
r	copyFrom:to:	Return a substring of the receiver. The substring is taken from the indicated positions. Produce an error message and return **nil** if the given positions are not legal.
n	print	A line consisting of the receiver is displayed on the terminal.
n	printAt:	The argument must be a **Point** which describes a location on the terminal screen. The string is printed at the specified location.
n	printNoReturn	The receiver is printed on the terminal without a newline/carriage return. A subsequent *printNoReturn* would follow immediately on the same line as the printed text.
	size	Return the number of characters stored in the string.
	sameAs:	Return **true** if the receiver and argument string match with the exception of case differences. Note that the boolean message = inherited from ArrayedCollection can be used to see if two strings are the same including case differences.

Examples

	Printed result
'example' at: 2	$x
'bead' at: 1 put: $r	read
'small' > 'BIG'	True
'small' sameAs: 'SMALL'	True
'tary' sort	arty
'12.3' asFloat	12.3
'Rats live on no evil Star' reversed	ratS live on no evil staR

Object
Block

Although it is easy for a programmer to think of blocks as a syntactic construct or a control structure they are actually objects and share attributes of all other objects in the Smalltalk system, such as the ability to respond to messages.

Responds to:

fork — Start the block executing as a **Process.** The value **nil** is immediately returned, and the **Process** created from the block is scheduled to run in parallel with the current process.

forkWith: — Similar to *fork*, except that the array is passed as arguments to the receiver block prior to scheduling for execution.

newProcess — A new **Process** is created for the block but is not scheduled for execution.

n newProcessWith: — Similar to *newProcess* except that the array is passed as arguments to the receiver block prior to being made into a process.

value — Evaluates the receiver block. Produces an error message and returns **nil** if the receiver block requires arguments. Return the value yielded by the block.

value: — Evaluates the receiver block. Produces an error message and returns **nil** if the receiver block does not require a single argument. Return the value yielded by the block.

value:value:	Two-argument block evaluation.
value:value:value:	Three-argument block evaluation.
value:value:value:value:	Four-argument block evaluation.
value:value:value: value:value:	Five-argument block evaluation.
whileTrue:	The receiver block is repeatedly evaluated. While it evaluates to **true,** the argument block is also evaluated. Return **nil** when the receiver block no longer evaluates to **true.**
whileTrue	The receiver block is repeatedly evaluated until it returns a value that is not true.
whileFalse:	The receiver block is repeatedly evaluated. While it evaluates to **false,** the argument block is also evaluated. Return **nil** when the receiver block no longer evaluates to **false.**
whileFalse	The receiver block is repeatedly evaluated until it returns a value that is not **false.**

Examples

                    Printed result

['block indeed'] value	block indeed
[:x :y | x + y + 3] value: 5 value: 7	15

Object
    Class

The class **Class** provides protocol for manipulating class instances. An instance of class **Class** is generated for each class in the Smalltalk system. New instances of this class are then formed by sending messages to the class instance.

Responds to

n	deepCopy:	The argument must be an instance of the receiver class. A *deepCopy* of the argument is returned.
n	edit	The user is placed into a editor, editing the file from which the class description was originally obtained. When the editor terminates, the class description will be reparsed and will override the previous description. See also *view* (below).

n	list	Lists all subclasses of the given class recursively. In particular, **Object** *list* will list the names of all the classes in the system.
	new	A new instance of the receiver class is returned. If the methods for the receiver contain protocol for *new,* the new instance will first be passed this message.
	new:	A new instance of the receiver class is returned. If the methods for the receiver contain protocol for *new:,* the new instance will first be passed this message.
n	respondsTo	List all the messages to which the current class will respond.
d	respondsTo:	The argument must be a Symbol. Return **true** if the receiver class or any of its superclasses contains a method for the indicated message. Return **false** otherwise.
n	shallowCopy:	The argument must be an instance of the receiver class. A *shallowCopy* of the argument is returned.
n	superClass	Return the superclass of the receiver class.
n	variables	Return an array containing the names of the instance variables used in the receiver class.
n	view	Place the user into an editor viewing the class description from which the class was created. Changes made to the file will not, however, affect the current class representation.

Examples

	Printed result
Array new: 3	# (nil nil nil)
Bag respondsTo: #add:	True
SequenceableCollection superClass	Keyed Collection
ArrayedCollection variables	#(#current)

Object
  Process
Processes are created by the system or by passing the message *newProcess* or *fork* to a block; they cannot be created directly by the user. The current process is always available as the value of the pseudo-variable **selfProcess.** (Note that the pseudo-variable **selfProcess.** (Note that the pseudo-variable **selfProcess** is unique to Little Smalltalk and is not part of the Smalltalk-80-programming environment.)

Responds To

block   The receiver process is marked as being blocked. This is usually the result of a semaphore wait. Blocked processes are not executed.

resume   If the receiver process has been *suspend*ed, it is rescheduled for execution.

suspend   If the receiver process is scheduled for execution, it is marked as suspended. Suspended processes are not executed.

state   The current state of the receiver process is returned as a Symbol.

terminate   The receiver process is terminated. Unlike a blocked or suspended process, a terminated process cannot be restarted.

unblock   If the receiver process is currently blocked, it is scheduled for execution.

yield   Returns **nil.** As a side effect, however, if there are pending processes, the current process is placed back on the process queue and another process is started.

≡

Appendix 4

Primitives

The following chart gives the function performed by each primitive in the Little Smalltalk system. The number to the left indentifies the primitive and is used in the longer form of primitive call, such as

<primitive 10 i j >

The identifier in bold following the number is the name of the primitive and is used in the more readable from of primitive call such as

<IntegerAddition i j >

Note that only the longer form (using numbers) is recognized at the command level.

Information about objects

0 (not used)

1 **Class** (one argument) Returns the class of the argument.

2 **SuperObject** (one argument) Returns the superobject of the argument.

3 **RespondsToNew** (one argument) Returns **true** if the argument (a class) responds to *new*.

4 **Size** (one argument) Returns the size of the argument. Size is the size of an array or the number of instance variables for a non-array.

5 **HashNumber** (one argument) Returns a hash value (integer) based on the argument.

6 **SameTypeOfObject** (two arguments) Returns **true** if the two arguments represent the same type of object.

7 **Equality** (two arguments) Returns **true** if the two arguments are equivalent (= =).

8 **Debug** (various arguments) Set or reset various toggle switches used during system development.

9 **GeneralityTest** (two arguments) Return either **true** or **false** depending upon the generality of the arguments.

Integer manipulation

In all cases there should be only two arguments, of which both must be integers.

10   **IntegerAddition** Return the integer sum of the two arguments.

11   **IntegerSubtraction** Return the integer difference.

12   **IntegerLessThan** Return **true** if the first argument is less than the second; **false** otherwise.

13   **IntegerGreaterThan** Integer > test.

14   **Integer LessThanOrEqual** Integer ≤ test.

15   **IntegerLessThanOrEqual** Integer ≥ test.

16   **IntegerEquality** Integer = test.

17   **IntegerNonEquality** Integer ~ = test.

18   **IntegerMultiplication** Return the integer product of the two arguments.

19   **IntegerSlash** Return the integer result of the // operation on the two arguments.

Bit manipulation and other integer-valued functions

In all cases there should be only two arguments, which must both be integers.

20   **GCD** Return the integer greatest common divisor of the two arguments.

21   **BitAt** Return the bit value (zero or one) of the first argument at the location specified by the second argument.

22   **BitOR** Return the bit-wise logical OR of the two arguments.

23   **BitAnd** Return the bit-wise logical AND of the two arguments.

24   **BitXOR** Return the bit-wise logical exclusive-or of the two arguments.

25   **BitShift** Return the first argument shifted by an amount given by the second argument. A positive second argument indicates left shifting; a negative value indicates right shifting.

26   **RadixPrint** Return a string representing the first argument printed in the base given by the second argument.

27   not used

28   **IntegerDivision** Return the quotient of the integer division of the two arguments.

29   **IntegerMod** Return the remainder of the integer division of the two arguments.

Other integer functions

In all cases except for primitive 30 there should be only one integer argument. For primitive 30 the first argument must be integer and the second argument an array.

30   **DoPrimitive** (two arguments) Return the result of executing the primitive given by the first argument using the values given in the array provided by the second argument as arguments for the primitive.

31   not used

32   **RandomFloat** Converts an integer value into a number in the range 0.0 to 1.0. Used to convert a random integer into a random floating point value.

33   **BitInverse** Return the logical bit-wise inverse of the argument.

34   **HighBit** Return the position of the first one bit in the argument. Returns **nil** if no bit is one in the argument.

35   **Random** Using the argument value as a seed, return a random integer.

36   **IntegerToCharacter** Return the argument converted into a character value.

37   **IntegerToString** Return the argument converted into a string value.

38   **Factorial** Return the factorial of the argument. May return as float if the argument is too large. See also primitive number 77.

39   **IntegerToFloat** Return the argument converted into a floating point value.

Character manipulation

In all cases there must be two-character arguments.

40   not used

41   not used

42   **CharacterLessThan** Return **true** if the first argument is less than the second; **false** otherwise.

43   **CharacterGreaterThan** Character > test.

44   **CharacterLessThanOrEqual** Character ≤ test.

45   **CharacterGreaterThanOrEqual** Character ≥ test.

46   **CharacterEquality** Character = test.

47   **CharacterNonEquality** Character ~ = test.

48   not used

49   not used

Character unary functions

In all cases there must be only one argument which must be a character.

50   **DigitValue** Return the integer value representing the position of the character in the collating sequence.

51   **IsVowel** Return **true** if the argument is a vowel.

52   **IsAlpha** Return **true** if the argument is a letter.

53   **IsLower** Return **true** if the argument is a lowercase letter.

54   **IsUpper** Return **true** if the argument is an uppercase letter.

55   **IsSpace** Return **true** if the argument is a white space character (space, tab, or newline).

56   **IsAlnum** Return **true** if the argument is a letter or a digit.

57   **ChangeCase** Return the argument with case shifted either from upper- to lowercase or vice versa.

58   **CharacterToString** Return the argument converted into a string.

59   **CharacterToInteger** Return the argument converted into an integer.

Floating point manipulation

In all cases there must be two arguments, both instances of class **Float.**

60   **FloatAddition** Return the floating point sum of the two arguments.

61   **FloatSubtraction** Return the floating point difference of the two arguments.

62   **FloatLessThan** Floating point $<$ test.

63   **FloatGreaterThan** Floating point $>$ test.

64   **FloatLessThanOrEqual** Floating point $\leq$ test.

65   **FloatGreaterThanOrEqual** Floating point $\geq$ test.

66   **FloatEquality** Floating point $=$ test.

67   **FloatNonEquality** Floating point $\sim=$ test.

68   **FloatMultiplication** Return the floating point product of the two arguments.

69   **FloatDivision** Floating point division.

Other floating point operations

In all cases there should be one floating point argument.

70   **Log** Return the natural log of the argument.

71   **SquareRoot** Return the square root of the argument.

72   **Floor** Return the integer floor of the argument.

73   **Ceiling** Return the integer ceiling of the argument.

74   not used

75   **IntegerPart** Return the integer portion of the argument.

76   **FractionalPart** Return the fractional portion of the argument.

77   **Gamma** Return the value of the gamma function at the argument.

78   **FloatToString** Return the argument converted into a string.

79   **Exponent** Return the value *e* raised to the argument.

Other numerical functions

With the exception of primitives 88 and 89, there should be only one floating point argument given to the following primitives.

80   **NormalizeRadian** Return the argument normalized to between 0 and 2π. Normalization is performed by adding or subtracting multiples of 2π.

81   **Sin** Return the value of the sine function on the argument.

82   **Cos** Return the value of the cosine function on the argument.

83   not used

84   **ArcSin** Return the value of the arc-sine function on the argument.

85   **ArcCos** Return the value of the arc-cosine function on the argument.

86   **ArcTan** Return the value of the arc-tangent function on the argument.

87   not used

88   **Power** (two arguments) Return the first value raised to the power indicated by the second argument. Both arguments must be floating point values.

89   **FloatRadixPrint** (two arguments) Return a string representation of the first argument in the base given by the second argument. The first argument must be float; the second, an integer between 2 and 36.

Symbol Commands

90   not used

91   **SymbolCompare** (two arguments) Returns **true** if the arguments represent the same symbol; **false** otherwise.

92   **SymbolPrintString** (one argument) Returns the argument converted into a string.

93   **SymbolAsString** (one argument) Returns the argument converted into a string without the leading sharp sign.

94   **SymbolPrint** (one or two arguments) Print the symbol after first indenting an amount specified by the second argument. Second argument, if given, must be an integer.

95   not used

96   not used

97   **NewClass** (eight arguments) Return a new object of class **Class** initialized with the argument values. Arguments are class name, superclass name, instance variables, messages, methods, context size.

98   **InstallClass** (two arguments) Insert an object into the internal class dictionary. First argument must be a symbol (name of class); second argument is class definition.

99   **FindClass** (one argument) Search for an object in the internal class dictionary. Argument is a symbol representing the class name.

String operations

100   **String Length** (one argument) Return an integer representing the length of the argument string.

101   **StringCompare** (two arguments) String comparison with case distinction. Returns either − 1, 0, or 1 depending upon whether the first argument is less than, equal to, or greater than the second.

102   **StringCompareWithoutCase** (two arguments) String comparison without case distinction. Returns either **true** or **false** depending upon whether the two arguments are equal.

103   **StringCatenation** (any number of arguments) Return a new string formed by catenating the argument strings together.

104   **StringAt** (2 arguments) Return the character found at the position in the string indicated by the second argument.

105   **StringAtPut** (three arguments) At the position given by the second argument in the string, insert the character given by the third argument.

106   **CopyFromLength** (three arguments) Starting at the position given by the second argument in the string, return the substring of length given by the third argument.

107   **StringCopy** (one argument) Return a new string identical to the argument string.

108   **StringAsSymbol** (one argument) Return the argument converted into a symbol.

109   **StringPrintString** Return the argument string with quote marks appending to the edges.

Array manipulation

110   **NewObject** (one argument) Return an untyped object of the given size. Argument must be a positive integer. Untyped objects are used during system bootstrapping.

111   **At** (two arguments) Return the value found at the given location in the argument. Second argument must be a positive integer.

112   **AtPut** (three arguments) At the location given by the second argument, place the value given by the third argument.

113   **Grow** (two arguments) Return a new object with the same instance variables as the first argument but with the second argument added to the end. The argument is usually an array.

114   **NewArray** (one argument) Return a new instance of **Array** of the given size. Differs from primitive 110 in that the object is given class **Array.**

115   **NewString** (one argument) Return a new string of given size. Values are all blank.

116   **NewByteArray** (one argument) Return a new ByteArray of the given size. Values are random.

117   **ByteArraySize** (one argument) Return an integer representing the size of the ByteArray argument.

118   **ByteArrayAt** (two arguments) Return the integer value of the ByteArray at the given location. Second argument must be a valid index for the ByteArray given by the first argument.

119   **ByteArrayAtPut** (three arguments) At the location given by the second argument, place the value given by the third argument. First argument must be a ByteArray. Second and third arguments must be integer.

Output and error messages

120   **PrintNoReturn** (one argument) Display the argument, which must be a string, on the output with no return.

121   **PrintWithReturn** (one argument) Display the argument, which must be a string, on the output followed by a return.

122   **Error** (two arguments) Display a message on the error output. First argument is the receiver; second is a string. The class of the receiver will be printed, followed by the string.

123   **ErrorPrint** (one argument) Display a string on the error output.

124   not used

125   **System** (one argument) Execute the Unix system( ) call using the argument as value.

126   **PrintAt** (three arguments) Print a string at a specific point on the terminal. Second and third arguments are integer coordinates.

127   **BlockReturn** (one argument) Issue an error message that a block return was attempted without the creating context being active.

128   **ReferenceError** (one argument) A reference count was detected that was less than zero. A system error.

129   **DoesNotRespond** (two arguments) Print a message indicating that an attempt was made to send a message to an object that did not know how to respond to it. First argument is object to which message was sent; second argument is message.

File operations

In all cases the first argument must be an instance of class **File.**

130   **FileOpen** (three arguments) Open the named file. Second argument is file name, as a symbol. Third argument is mode, as a string.

131   **FileRead** (one argument) Return the next object from the file.

132   **FileWrite** (two arguments) Write the object given by the second argument onto the file. Argument must be appropriate for mode of file.

133   **FileSetMode** (two arguments) Set the file mode. Second argument is mode indicated, an integer.

134   **FileSize** (one argument) Compute the size of the file in bytes.

135   **FileSetPosition** (two arguments) Set the address of the file to the position given by the second argument, a positive integer.

136   **FileFindPosition** (one argument) Return an integer representing the current position in the file.

137   not used

138   not used

139   not used

Process management

140   **BlockExecute** (one argument) The argument, which must be a block, is started executing. This primitive cannot be executed via a *doPrimitive:* command.

141   **NewProcess** (one or two arguments) The first argument must be a block. If the second argument is given, it must be an array of arguments to be used as parameters to the block. A new process is created that will execute the block.

142   **Terminate** (one argument) The argument must be a process. It is terminated.

143   **Perform** (two arguments) The first argument is a symbol representing the message to be sent. The second argument is an array of values to be used in performing the message. The first element of this array is the receiver of the message. This primitive cannot be executed via a *doPrimitive:* command.

144   not used

145   **SetProcessState** (two arguments) The first argument must be a process. The state of the process is set to that given by the second argument, an integer.

146   **ReturnProcessState** (one argument) The argument must be a process. An integer is returned indicating the current state of the process.

148   **StartAtomic** (no arguments) Begin executing atomic actions. While executing in this mode, no new processes will be started. Thus the current process can execute uninterruptedly.

149   **EndAtomic** (no arguments) End executing atomic actions.

Operations on classes

In all cases the first argument must be an instance of class **Class.**

150   **ClassEdit** (one argument) Place the user in an editor, editing the description of the given class. When the user exits the editor, the class description will automatically be reparsed and included.

151   **SuperClass** (one argument) Return the superclass of the argument class.

152   **ClassName** (one argument) Return a symbol representing the name of the argument class.

153   **ClassNew** (one argument) Return a new instance of the given class.

154   **PrintMessages** (one argument) List all the commands to which the class responds.

155   **RespondsTo** (two arguments) Second argument must be a symbol. Return **true** if the class responds to the message represented by the second argument.

156   **ClassView** (one argument) Place the user in an editor, editing the description of the given class. Changed class is not included when the user exits.

157   **ClassList** (one argument) List all subclasses of the given class.

158   **Variables** (one argument) Return an array of symbols representing the names of instance variables for the given class.

159   not used

Date and Time, Terminal Manipulation

160   **CurrentTime** (no arguments) Return a string representing the current date and time.

161   **TimeCounter** (no arguments) return an integer that is counting as a seconds time clock.

162   **Clear** (no arguments) Clear the user's screen.

163   **GetString** (no arguments) Return text typed at the terminal as a **String.**

164   **StringAsInteger** (one argument) Return an integer taken from the argument string.

165   **StringAsFloat** (one argument) Return a floating point value from the argument string.

Plot(3) Interface

These primitives are effective only if the Little Smalltalk system was configured using the plot(3) interface and if the user is working on a terminal that accepts the plot commands. Only the long form of the primitive command using numbers is recognized. The Unix manual should be consulted for more information on the plot(3) interface.

170   (no arguments) Clear the screen. Although functionally this duplicates primitive 162, it uses the plot interface rather than the curses interface.

171   (two arguments) Move the cursor to the location given by the two integer arguments. (Interface to move(x, y).)

172   (two arguments) Draw a line from the current position to the position given by the two integer arguments. (Interface to cont(x, y).)

173   (two arguments) Draw a point at the location given by the two integer arguments. (Interface to point(x, y).)

174   (three arguments) The first two arguments give the center of the circle; the third argument, the radius. Draw a circle. (Interface to circle(x, y, r).)

175   (five arguments) Draw an arc. (Interface to arc(x,y,x0,y0,x1,y1).)

176   (four arguments) Establish the coordinate space for plotting. (Interface to space (a,b,c,d).)

177   (four arguments) Draw a line from one point to another. (Interface to line (a,b,c,d).)

178 (one argument) Print a label at the current location. Argument is a string. (Interface to label(s).)

179 Establish a line printing type. Argument is a string. (Interface to linemod(s).)

Appendix 5

Differences Between Little Smalltalk and the Smalltalk-80 Programming System

This appendix describes the differences between the language accepted by the Little Smalltalk system and the language described in (Goldberg 83). The principal reasons for these changes are as follows:

size
: Classes which are largely unnecessary or which could be easily simulated by other classes (e.g., **Association, SortedCollection**) have been eliminated in the interest of keeping the size of the standard library as small as possible. Similarly, indexed instance variables are not supported, since to support them would increase the size of every object in the system, and they can be easily simulated in those classes in which they are important (see below).

portability
: Classes which depend upon particular hardware (e.g., **Form, BitBlt**) are not included as part of the Little Smalltalk system. The basic system assumes nothing more than ASCII terminals.

representation
: The need for a textual representation for class descriptions required some modifications to the syntax for class methods. (See Appendix 2.) Similarly, the fact that classes and subclasses can be separately parsed, in either order, forced changes in the scoping rules for instance variables.

The following sections describe these changes in more detail.

1. No Browser

The Smalltalk-80 Programming Environment described in (Goldberg 83) is not included as part of the Little Smalltalk system. The Little Smalltalk system is designed to be little, easily portable, and to rely on nothing more than basic terminal capabilities.

2. Internal Representation Different

The internal representations of objects, including processes, interpreters, and bytecodes in the Little Smalltalk system is entirely different from the Smalltalk-80 system described in (Goldberg 83).

3. Fewer Classes

Many of the classes described in (Goldberg 83) are not included as part of the Little Smalltalk basic system. Some of these are not necessary because of the decision not to include the editor, browser, and so on, as part of the basic system. Others are omitted in the interest of keeping the standard library of classes small. A complete list of included classes for the Little Smalltalk system is given in Appendix 3.

4. No Class Protocol

Protocol for all classes is defined as part of class **Class.** The notion of metaclasses is not supported. It is not possible to redefine class protocol as part of a class description; only instance protocol can be.

5. Some Messages Different

Because Little Smalltalk does not support class messages (the redefinition of class protocol to provide messages specific to certain class descriptions), some actions, such as those dealing with processes, must be performed differently in Little Smalltalk. Thus the semantics of a few messages have been changed from those described in the Smalltalk-80 reference book. These messages have been marked in Appendix 3. The Smalltalk-80 user should refer to the reference manual for that system for information concerning the way these messages are interpreted.

6. Cascades Different

The semantics of cascades has been simplified and generalized. The result of a cascaded expression is always the result of the expression to the left of the first semicolon, which is also the receiver for each subsequent continuation. Continuations can include multiple messages. A rather nonsensical, but illustrative, example is the following:

```
2 + 3 ; − 7 + 3 ; * 4
```

The result of this expression is 5 (the value yielded by 2 + 3); 5 is also the receiver for the message − 7, and that result (− 2) is, in turn, the receiver for the message + 3. This last result is thrown away. The value 5 is then used again as the receiver for the message * 4, the result of which is also thrown away.

In the Smalltalk-80 system a cascaded message expression is *not* an expression; rather it can be used only as a statement. Also, the receiver for the continuation portions is not the expression to the left of the first semicolon; it is the receiver of the last message in that expression. Continuations can have only one message. Finally, since the cascaded message expression is not an expression, it is meaningless to ask what the result should be.

The nonsensical expression presented above would not be legal in the Smalltalk-80 language; however, the following (equally nonsensical) would:

```
2 + 3; − 7 ; * 4
```

The message 2 + 3 would be evaluated and the result thrown away. The receiver for that message, namely the 2, would be used as the receiver for the continuation − 7. The result of that expression would also be thrown away. Finally the same receiver, 2, would be used for the continuation *4.

In either form, a cascade tends to be used only to combine creation and initialization messages. The Little Smalltalk version has the advantage that it can also be used as an expression.

7. Instance Variable Name Scope

In the language described in (Goldberg 83), an instance variable is known not only to the class protocol in which it is declared but is also valid in methods defined for any subclasses of that class. In the Little Smalltalk system an instance variable can be referenced only within the protocol for the class in which it is declared.

8. Indexed Instance Variables

Implicitly defined indexed instance variables are not supported. In any class for which these variables are desired, they can be easily simulated by including an additional instance variable containing an array and including the following methods;

```
Class Whatever
| index Vars |
[
    new: size
        indexVars <− Array new: size

|   at: location
        ↑ indexVars at: location
```

```
|    at: location put: value
         indexVars at: location put: value
    ...
```

The message *new:* can be used with any class with an effect similar to *new*. That is, if a new instance of the class is created by sending the message *new:* to the class variable, the message is immediately passed on to the new instance, and the result returned is used as the result of the creation message.

9. No Pool Variables / Global Variables

The concepts of pool variables, global variables, or class variables are not supported. In their place there is a new pseudo-variable, **smalltalk,** which responds to the messages *at:* and *at:put:*. The keys for this collection can be arbitrary. Although this facility is available, its use is often a sign of poor program design and should be avoided.

In the Smalltalk-80 system, an undeclared identifier in a class description is treated as a global variable. In Little Smalltalk, it is an error.

10. No Associations

The class **Dictionary** stores keys and values separately rather than as instances of **Association.** The class **Association** and all messages referring to instances of this class have been removed.

11. Generators in place of Streams

The notion of *stream* has been replaced by the slightly different notion of *generators*, in particular the use of the messages *first* and *next* in subclasses of **Collection.** External files are supported by an explicit class **File.**

12. Primitives Different

Both the syntax and the use of primitives has been changed. Primitives provide an interface between the Little Smalltalk world and the underlying system, permitting the execution of operations that cannot be specified in Smalltalk. In Little Smalltalk, primitives cannot fail and must return a value (although they may, in error situations, print an error message and return **nil**). The syntax for primitives has been altered to permit the specifications of primitives with an arbitrary number of arguments. There are two forms of primitive call. In a class description certain names are recognized for primitives. Thus a primitive can be written by giving the primitive name followed by the list of arguments, surrounded by angle brackets, as in:

<IntegerAddition i j >

The second form of primitives works both at the command level and in class descriptions. Using this form, the primitive is specified using a number, as in:

<primitive number *argumentlist*>

Where **number** is the number of the primitive to be executed (which must be a value between 1 and 255), and *argumentlist* is a list of Smalltalk primary expressions. (See Appendix 2.) Appendix 4 lists the meanings of each of the currently recognized primitive numbers.

13. Byte Arrays

A new syntax has been created for defining an array composed entirely of unsigned integers in the range 0 to 255. These arrays, instances of class **ByteArray,** are given a very concise encoding. The syntax is a pound sign, followed by a left square brace, followed by a sequence of numbers in the range 0 to 255, followed by a right square brace.

#[*numbers*]

Byte arrays are used extensively internally.

14. New Pseudo Variables

In addition to the pseudo variable **smalltalk** already mentioned, another pseduo variable, **selfProcess,** has been added to the Little Smalltalk system. The variable **selfProcess** returns the currently executing process, which can then be passed as an argument to a semaphore or be used as a receiver for a message valid for class **Process.** Like **self** and **super,** **selfProcess** cannot be used at the command level.

The global variable **Processor** and the class **ProcessorScheduler** are not included in the Little Smalltalk system.

15. No Dependency

The notions of dependency and automatic dependency updating are not included in the Little Smalltalk standard library.

Index